World Religions

Major and Minor World Religions

R. L. Cohen

Humanities
ACADEMIC PUBLISHERS

Humanities
ACADEMIC PUBLISHERS

ISBN: 978-1-988557-8-54 (Hardcover)
ISBN: 978-1-988557-8-61 (Softcover)
ISBN: 978-1-988557-8-78 (Ebook)

Published in New Zealand and the United States of America

Humanities Academic Publishers

A catalogue record for this book is available from the National Library of New Zealand.

Kei te pātengi raraunga o Te Puna Mātauranga o Aotearoa te whakarārangi o tēnei pukapuka.

Contents

CHAPTER 1

Zoroastrianism

Founded some three millennia ago by Zarathushtra (in Greek, Zoroaster; in Persian, Zartosht), the long history of Zoroastrianism (also known as Mazdeism, coming from the Zoroastrian name for their religion, Mazdayasna or worship of Mazda) has given rise to much diversity. This chapter presents the religion mainly as it is practiced today by the majority of its followers. Historically speaking, Zoroastrianism may be one of the most important religions that ever existed, as it might be one of the oldest monotheistic religions in the world. It originates from what is today Iran, with the appearance of the prophet and religion's founder Zarathustra. However, it is a very important fact that there is not a single new religion that does not have a rich background and source. In many ways, new religions are just a "perfection" of the old faith and are translated into new forms of belief and religious rituals, codified in the holy texts. Its prophets too do not come from an ideological vacuum; their capability to preach salvation rests upon a good knowledge of tradition and talent to interpret it. The ancient Iranian religion, from which Zoroastrianism came from, dates to the second millennia BCE when Indo-Arians and Iranians made one group of people. Indo-Iranian religion is a reconstruction based on both Iranian Avesta and Indian Rig-Veda. With time, this group of people split and Indo-Arians settled contemporary India, while Iranians inhabited parts of the Middle East and, primarily, the Iranian plateau.

The Teachings of Zoroastrianism

The most significant of all Zoroastrian teachings are monotheism and dualism—the ongoing opposition between the forces of order and chaos, of good and evil.

Zoroastrianism teaches that reality is divisible into two realms: that of spirit and thought and that of matter and physicality. Human beings must orient themselves toward the spiritual realm to live righteously and ultimately to achieve salvation. Dualism involves two key concepts. *Asha*, "order," pervades both the natural and social spheres of reality, including righteousness and justice. *Asha* is opposed by *druj*, the "Lie." Whereas *asha* gives rise to good thoughts, words, and deeds, *druj* gives rise to evil thoughts, falsehood, violence, words, and deeds. The two are fundamentally incompatible and locked in a cosmic struggle.

Zoroastrian teachings the existence of a pantheon of divine beings. Zarathushtra, whose own culture was polytheistic, seems to have been responsible for declaring that one god—Ahura Mazda, the "Wise Lord"—is the only eternal deity and is qualitatively above all others. Ahura Mazda was nothing new to the Persians. He was a god praised by the people well before Zarathushtra as one of the more exalted gods in the pantheon, belonging to the class of gods called Ahuras (in India, Ashuras). Zarathushtra's life changed dramatically one day when he was celebrating the spring festival (Nowruz). The basic point of departure of Zarathushtra's prophecy rests upon the aforementioned revelation of all-powerful, holy and good Ahura Mazda. He fetched some water for the festival from a nearby river. While standing in the water, and thus being ritually purified, he suddenly had an intense vision of light. In this light, he experienced the presence of Ahura Mazda and six other radiant beings from whom he received his first revelation. These were Asha (Justice); Vohoo Manah (Good thought); Armaiti (Piety); Shathra (Kingdom or Power); Haurvatat (Integrity or Health) and Ameratat (Immortality). The message was clear: Ahura Mazda is not some god, but one uncreated and eternal god who created the world and everything good. He is the creator of Asha.

Ultimately, Ahura Mazda will overcome evil, which also has existed since the beginning of time and was not created by him. Ahura Mazda is assisted in his governing of creation by seven Amesha Spentas, the "Beneficial/Holy Immortals," chief among them Spenta Mainyu, Ahura Mazda's Holy Spirit. The seven in turn are assisted by a large number of deities called yazatas, "ones worthy of worship." They may sometimes be understood as gods, but not in a manner like Ahura Mazda's divinity. Many scholars, thus, point to the idea that these beings are lesser in divine meaning and aspects and attributes of Ahura Mazda, like righteousness, devotion, health, etc. They are part of his creation and not equal to the highest being. The worship of old gods continued and especially the highest six divinities.

As the highest divine being, Ahura Mazda is the Father of other deities and particularly of two twin spirits, Spenta Mainyu and Angra Mainyu. From the beginning of time, Spenta Mainyu (Spirit of Good Deeds) has battled against his adversary Angra Mainyu, (the "Foul Spirit"). Their characteristics were chosen by themselves: one of them chose the Good and the Life, while the other chose the Evil and the Death. Also on the side of evil and disorder are the daevas, various demonic powers. These hostile spirits created the Druj. These gods represent violence and war and serve the hostile spirit. Zarathushtra very strongly objected to the worship of daevas, which are found also in Hinduism but as good deities.

Zoroastrian cosmology posits three progressive and cyclical phases: (1) the creation of the physical world, when Ahura Mazda created the world in a perfect state, free of all evil and darkness; (2) the mixing in the physical world of the embodied spirits of evil forces with those of good forces, when both poles are present and are in a constant battle between themselves and this is the time where we live now; (3) and the final transformation, in which the world will be cleansed of all evil. Ahura Mazda is said to have created the universe and life forms, including human beings. The world of creation is a constant battlefield between the forces of Asha and Druj, Good and Evil, Light and Darkness. Human beings are also an important part of this battle, just as the good deities have an obligation to pursue good deeds and fight against evil. This is done in a number of ways, but basically through moral principles laid down by Zarathushtra: good thoughts (humata), good words (hukhta), and good deeds (hvarshta). Good words and good deeds come from good thoughts which are inspired by Vohu Mano, one of the first creations of Ahura Mazda. Human forms own thoughts and thoughts make a human being. Kind of thoughts makes kind of being: one may be a human, a saint or an angel, but also one may become an animal, a sinner or a demon. A being is a taught manifested in words and deeds. Thus, humans have a clear purpose in the Zoroastrian worldview, as they would gradually expel the evil forces of Angra Mainyu and welcome the third phase of existence. Zarathushtra taught that a man himself should learn to discern between Good and Evil because it is not directly visible. One should be drawn to the good and just, and for that one should make efforts. Zarathushtra's teaching had a goal to reform the world spiritually and ethically.

Dualism is, thus, the very nature of Zoroastrian theology. It is also a point of disagreement among the scholars of religion: how to determine and categorize Zoroastrianism, as a monotheistic or dualistic religion? Both scholars and Zoroastrians themselves never really agreed on this question. If it is a monotheistic religion, it would most likely be the oldest such religion in known world history. Scholars like Mary Boyce argue that Zoroastrianism is a dualistic religion, where Ahura Mazda and Angra Mainyu as equal creators of the world, while scholar Farhang Mehr offers an understanding that Zarathushtra received a message that Ahura Mazda is the only god and that forces of Good and Evil is created by him. Because of the religious teachings of the free choice of the Twin Spirits, many argue Zoroastrianism cannot be dualistic as Ahura Mazda himself is not challenged by another anti-god, but is the creator of two spirits. James W Boyd and Donald A Crosby see an alternative that objects to a rigid dichotomy between monotheism and dualism. They offer an explanation that defines Zoroastrianism as a unique system of belief, not to be found anywhere else in the world. it combines cosmogonic dualism and eschatological monotheism and because of that cannot be termed straightforwardly as either monotheistic or dualistic. In fact, later interpretations of old Persian religion suggests that the earlier pantheon of gods and deities remained in the Zoroastrian belief system, as explained above.

The meaning of human life rests in ethical choice: whether to live in accordance with asha or to succumb to the evil ways of druj. This choice determines how the soul will fare when judged after death. It was a revolutionary thought for that time, as the judgment will arrive according to their deeds in this life and not on their status or wealth, which has been a case in earlier religions. The rewards and the punishments were open to everyone, regardless of their social position. Those who are good will be able to cross the bridge to the paradise of lights, but those who behaved badly, would find this bridge to contract to a blade's edge and they would most likely fell into hell, a place of torments and tortures. At some point in the development of Zoroastrianism (the date is uncertain), new teachings arose that asserted that a messianic savior figure named Saoshyant will appear to usher in the events that will transform the wicked world into the eternal kingdom of Ahura Mazda. The dead will be resurrected, and all souls will be judged by Ahura Mazda.

The History of Zoroastrianism

The roots of Zoroastrianism reach back nearly 3,000 years to ancient Iran and its Indo-Iranian tribes and is arguably the oldest surviving religion in the world. The religion of these early Iranians focused on the daevas, gods or spirits who personified the sky, sun, earth, and other aspects of nature, and the ahuras, a higher order of deities responsible for maintaining order in the universe. It was a polytheistic religion, with probably a common source in Vedic religion which was the basic set of beliefs from which Hinduism, Jainism, and Buddhism later developed. Many gods and deities are shared by two traditions (Indian and Iranian), with slightly different names. Early Iranian religion assumed an ongoing universal struggle between order and chaos. Their deities were connected to water and fire, as well as natural phenomena or abstract concepts like love and wisdom. Its major institution was a class of priests, very similar to the Brahman class in India, who presided over sacrificial rituals and whose influence could sometimes be oppressive.

Scholars are uncertain about the life of Zarathushtra, as it is also the case with the founders of many other religions in the world. Most place him between 1300 and 800 b.c.e. According to tradition, Zarathushtra was a priest (zatoar) who became a reformer after a powerful revelatory experience in which the supreme god, Ahura Mazda, called him to reveal to the world the danger posed by Angra Mainyu and to urge human beings to take the side of Ahura Mazda in this struggle by resolving to live lives of exemplary virtue. According to the Gathas (see below), Zarathushtra was part of the Spitama clan, famous for the horse herders. His father Purushaspa was also a priest, married with two kids. Zarathushtra framed his message to his community, consisting of non-nomadic shepherds with chieftains (Kavi) and priests (Karapan). The priests were the keepers of the traditional Arian religion and Zarathushtra attacked them. Because of this "sacrilegious" act, he had to leave his community. He found a refuge with king Vishtasp who was among his first converts and protectors. Zarathushtra names his enemies; these were Bandva and prince Vaepia who did not offer hospitality to Zarathushtra. It is said he was travelling all around Persia in pursuit of truth. On these voyages, he saw a lot of injustice and violence. This will influence a very ethical message he will offer later. According to the holy texts, Zarathushtra was killed in his 77th year of life by a tyrant Bratvarhsh in a fire temple. Some sources claim the killers were dressed as wolves. Such a legend symbolically expresses the fate of the prophet himself as the "wolves" were the members of the Arian male societies which Zarathushtra vehemently criticized.

As with Zarathushtra himself, the early history of Zoroastrianism is uncertain. The historical record becomes clear only with the rise of the Persian Achaemenid Empire (550–330 b.c.e.), whose kings promoted the new religion, as is demonstrated by surviving monuments and inscriptions. There is also evidence from this time for the rise of a class of Zoroastrian priests known as the Magi. No proof tells us that Zoroastrianism was indeed also the official religion of the Achaemenid state. However, Vishtaspa, the father of Darius I, was also the protector of Zarathushtra, which means the Achaemenids are indeed the true Zoroastrians. At the same time, this religion was almost identical to the Aryan/Vedic religion. Most authors argue that the official religion of the Achaemenid court went through two phases. First was during the reign of Darius I (522-486 BCE), when the state accepted the Zoroastrianism as the valid teachings, and the second began with Artaxerxes I (465-424 BCE) when the state accepted Zoroastrianism as a religion with the mixed components. Dairus I, Xerxes (486-465 BCE) and Artaxerxes II (404-359 BCE) stated their belief in Ahura Mazda as the supreme Lord, the creator of everything and protector of all living beings. They all considered their victories in war and peace as the protection of Ahura Mazda. Some of them respect other gods as well, but well beneath the level of Ahura Mazda. This still testifies there were other gods in the Achaemenid Empire and that Zoroastrianism in its purest form was not implemented as the state religion.

With the demise of Achaemenids, priests lost their privileged positions and gradually lost their oral knowledge. Zoroastrianism continued to thrive during the Parthian Empire (247 b.c.e.–224 c.e.) and the Sassanid Empire (224–651). The Parthians accepted Zoroastrianism very soon after they took the reins of power. This religion, however, was not so monotheistic as before. Some later sources mention Ahura Mazda as the supreme deity, but also Anahita as a beloved goddess, Vahang as the national god of war and many other deities personifying gods of sun, moon, etc. The spring holiday, Nowruz, was celebrated in Ahura Mazda's name, who was still considered to be the only creator of everything. Great Parthian kings like Mithridates I (171-132 BCE), Mithridates II (124-88 BCE), and Mithridates III ((7-80 BCE) revived old Zoroastrian beliefs as much as possible and renovated the old religion to new glory.

Persia's Sassanid rulers were the only ones to make Zoroastrianism an official state religion, but this was a heterodox form of the religion that introduced Zurvan and made Ahura Mazda and Angra Mainyu his twin sons. Under Sassanids, Persia lived through a huge cultural development. The rulers kept consciously the Achaemenid traditions and Zoroastrian religion played an important role in the national revival. The first two Sassanid rulers, Ardashir I (224-240) and Shahpur I (240-271) are traditionally considered to be the founders of Mazdeism. They had help in the priest Tosar who was one of the reformist priests and chief supporters of the Mazdeism as the state religion. Another priest, Karter, destroyed a rising hierarchy of his challenger Mani, after which Mazdeism became indeed the main religious thought. The Sassanid rulers were trying to suppress other religions that existed in Iran at that time: Judaism, Christianity, Mazdakism, Manichaeism, Hinduism and Buddhism. The population was prone to syncretism, accepting Manichaeism, Mithraism, and local venerations together with the official Mazdeism. Sassanids had to confront also with the gnostic teachings that spread rapidly in all religions but had a strong influence on Manichaeism.

After few generations, the collective memory cannot keep a truthful and authentic biography of a person and becomes an archetype, ie only certain positive features are kept through paradigmatic events, akin to the model this person embodies. This is true for the founders of religions as well as for the national heroes. Zarathushtra himself left a collection of hymns known as the Gathas, first orally transmitted and then written down in times of the Sassanid Empire. The Gathas are the most sacred collection of holy scripts for the Zoroastrians. They contain autobiographic elements which confirm (to a certain level) the historicity of its author. The myth of Zarathushtra survived because of the Gathas, and mostly because Zarathushtra was smart enough to write it down. The Gathas are a typical Indo-Iranian genre of sacred poetry. It is part of a larger set of texts called Avesta, passed down after Zarathushtra's life and compiled by the priests. Current Avesta got its final form in the 3rd century, in the time of the Sassanids. It contains manuscripts not destroyed by Alexander the Great. Avesta is a compilation of hymns, liturgy texts, prayers and laws. The oldest and most cherished part is seventeen hymns called Yasna Haptanghaiti (Worship in seven parts) and two prayers. It contains seventy-two chapters where seventeen hymns from the Gathas. An addition to Yasna is Visperad, consisting of twenty-four parts that praise the spiritual teacher. The third book is Yasht, where twenty-one mythical hymns describe the ancient heroes and angels (yazat) like Mithra, Verethrang, Aredule, Sur Anahita, etc. The fourth book of Avesta is Videvadat with twenty-one chapters, the main source of Zoroastrian rituals and laws. Bundahishna narrates about creation, history and making of the world, nature of the universe, and first man Yima. There is also "small Avesta" (Khurda Avesta), with shorter texts, hymns, and prayers used on special occasions. It contains five introductory citations from Yasna, continues with five prayers or Gahas for five times in a day; Niyayash (five prayers to the Sun, Mithra, Moon, Water, and Fire); hymns to Ahura Mazda; Siroza or memories of protectors through thirty days in a month; and Afrinagan, the rituals and blessings, as well as the prayers for deceased before the ritual meals in their honor. Avesta was mostly transmitted orally and in the written form are kept only texts recited during the Zoroastrian rituals.

Zoroastrianism spread to the West, where it met other types of religions and mutual exchanged influences. The original faith was not constant. Darius' son Xerxes forbid in his whole empire the cult of daevas, thus purifying the Zoroastrian religion. After that, however, novel ideas sprung. Artaxerxes II mentions not only Ahura Mazda but also Mitra and Anahita as high gods. New Avesta mentions them along with Ahura Mazda. The Arab conquest of Persia in the seventh century meant that Zoroastrianism would thereafter exist as a minority religion in its own, now Islamic, homeland. When Sassanid ruler Yazdegerd III was dethroned in 651, anarchy swept the old order and the Arabs very quickly conquered Iran. The haste of the Arab conquests and destruction was so catastrophic for the Iranian people that even today Zoroastrians (and some Muslim Persians) keep tales of their viciousness. The fate of Zoroastrians was the same as many other peoples and religious communities in the Middle East. There was, still, some groups that survived. One of them is Manai, who organized sporadic uprisings against Arab rule. This only exacerbated the fight against Zoroastrianism. While Zoroastrians were deemed "protected" by the Muslim rulers, this did not mean there was no persecution, forced conversion to Islam, and destruction of temples. At the end of the 8th and beginning of the 9th century, two distinctive Zoroastrian groups formed, one in India and one in Iran.

Muslim persecution encouraged some Zoroastrians to flee to India, where religious toleration was the norm. Known as Parsis ("Persians"), they make up what is the largest population of Zoroastrians in the world today, from where famously Freddie Mercury comes from. The Persian refugees from the 9th century were not the first ones who came to India. Even before the Arab conquests, Persians were drawn to the Indian subcontinent with trade and in warfare, when the Sassanid emperors attacked Punjab and Sindh. Parsis never really integrated into the Indian society and their distinctiveness and certain purity of the old Zoroastrian beliefs persists. Still, the Parsis tried to adjust to the new environment. Gujarati became the primary language of the Zoroastrian community, and women started to wear sari as their traditional clothing. They respected the Indian authorities but remained seclusive until the arrival of the British colonialists in the 17th century. They were seen as mediators between the British and Indians, as they were considered to be entirely independent. First Indian to be a British MP was a Parsi Zoroastrian named Sir Dadabhai Naoroji, while the Parsis also took a large part in the independence movement of India.

The second largest is found in Iran, where Zoroastrians now have one guaranteed representative in the Islamic Consultative Assembly (Majles) or Iranian parliament, but the hidden persecution is continuing. Zoroastrians have official interreligious dialogue with the Iranian Shi'a Muslims, and a sort of legal protection by the government, although the discrimination occurs all the time. Iranian Zoroastrians were again revived after the great Persian poet Ferdowsi wrote his epic Shahnameh (the Book of Kings) where he reminds heavily of the Persian Zoroastrian heritage and myths, particularly of the hero Jamshid and pantheon of spirits and deities. It is a book held dear by both Zoroastrian and Shi'a Iranians, as it is a source of national pride. Today, most Zoroastrians live in the Yazd and Kerman areas, where the main fire temples still survive, together with numerous smaller temples and religious sites. They also form larger communities in Tehran and other bigger Iranian cities and number between 10 and 30 thousand people. Interestingly, the Iranian solar calendar kept the names of the Zoroastrian saints and angels and is even today the official calendar of the Islamic Republic.

Zoroastrians do not accept any converts and are thus sometimes called "a dying religion" as their number constantly drop. Apart from Iran and India, most Zoroastrians nowadays live in Singapore, Hong Kong, Zanzibar, Great Britain, Australia, Canada, and the United States. Estimates show there are between 111 and 113 thousand Zoroastrians worldwide, mostly gathered around fire temples and yearly holidays. Without living communities and resistance to demographics, Zoroastrianism is in a danger to completely vanish as a living religion.

Zoroastrianism as a Way of Life

Zoroastrianism has gone through a number of changes and developments in ritual practice. Social and ethical responsibilities and ideals are summarized in the popular contemporary motto, "good thoughts, good words, good deeds." With regard to the once prevalent purification rituals, a newfound emphasis on personal hygiene has become the equivalent of the older insistence on "purity." Zoroastrians have been often regarded as "fire-worshippers" by the Muslim conquerors, but it is a misleading term. Fire indeed plays an important part in the Zoroastrian ritual, as a symbol of purity, God's wisdom and light. Fire (and also water) have been a very important aspect of Zoroastrianism since its very beginning. However, fire temples and fire altars appear to be a much later addition to this religion, probably during the Achaemenid Empire. Fire and temples remained very important aspects of this faith and its practice. They were not "temples" in the ancient meaning, ie places where gods resided or where their statues were venerated. In the early times of the Achaemenid state, the altars were probably situated outdoors as only a few fire temples are recorded, primarily the one at Pasargadae. Zoroastrians did, however, venerate images. Classic Zoroastrian imagery features Faravahar, a winged disk with a human character. It is a false idea that it represents Ahura Mazda, as the Zoroastrians never tried to depict a formless god. There are two main understandings of Faravahar. One is that it represents divine glory, depicting primarily the sun. The second is that it represents Fravashi or Frawahr, part of the human soul that acts as a protector and as a blessing from Ahura Mazda. The symbol is used today as the official semiotics of Zoroastrianism, and every detail of it is understood through some of the main Zoroastrian concepts. The temples additionally have an element of fire inside and an element of water outside. Many temples also feature cypress trees, a symbol of eternity. Even today, many (Christian) graveyards have cypress trees present with the same symbolics.

Connected to fire is the idea of ritual purity, one of the most important aspects of Zoroastrianism as it commands cleanliness for every person. Dirtiness or uncleanliness is a manifestation of evil and darkness. This led to certain laws regarding ritual purity. For instance, these laws limited the movement of women during their menstruation period. This may also apply to famous funeral rituals. The most elaborate religious activities marking a rite of passage occur at death. Traditionally, in an attempt to dispose of the dead in a manner that maintains purity as best as possible, the corpse is exposed on dakhmas, or "Towers of Silence," to be devoured by vultures and other scavengers. As the bodies were considered unclean, once the soul departed from it, priests would take the body to an open space where it would be eaten by animals and vultures. The bones would be later collected to await the date of resurrection. All of these laws are tightly connected to the battle between Asha and Druj, and thus necessary and logical measures. It was so important for the Zoroastrian rulers to follow these laws that even other religious communities could not keep their funeral traditions. For instance, many Christians buried their deceased secretly and when the Sassanid rulers found out about that, they excavated the bodies and left them to rot in the sun. Such a rigid following of the law left some parts of the Zoroastrian lands angry. Armenia, for instance, was a Zoroastrian land until the first Christian missionaries in the fourth century. Since then, it became the first Christian country in the world.

More so than most other religions, perhaps because of its status as a minority religion, the Zoroastrian way of life is based on a tightly knit sense of community and the routine practice of well-established customs. Prayer, the most commonly practiced ritual activity, is performed five times daily. The kusti ritual, involving the untying and tying off the kusti cord, also should be done several times daily. In addition, Zoroastrians are expected to undergo rituals of purification on a daily basis. This strong emphasis on purity is evident in the designation of certain spaces as appropriate for worship. Temples and other sacred precincts are set apart from the impurities of the world outside, and spaces in private houses must be pure in a religious sense to be used for rituals. Temples are equipped with special ceremonial rooms and fire chambers. Fire is of supreme significance for Zoroastrianism. There are three main categories of sacred fires; in India, only eight fires of the highest category (Atash Bahram) currently exist. The Yasna liturgy, one of the most important ritual activities, involves the sacrifice of the sacred drink haoma before a fire. Although there is a codified liturgy, ways of practicing them are very liberal. There is no prescribed way how to perform prayer (such as, for instance, in Islam). All radical notions of religious life are discouraged. That is why Zoroastrianism has no ascetic or monastic tradition.

Many rituals are orchestrated by priests, who have throughout the history of Zoroastrianism occupied an important place in religious society. They were called the Magi by the Greeks. According to the Christian New Testament, three Magi visited small Jesus in Bethlehem, bringing gifts. They are also known as the Three Wise Men. However, the Magi are considered to be a tribe of sorcerers guilty for the distortion of Zoroastrianism, while other authors claim they were real followers of Zarathushtra and his missionaries in Western Iran. Only in the Median Empire were they a priestly caste very much like Levites and Brahmans. During the Achaemenid Empire, the Magi represented first-class priests, explaining dreams, foretelling through the sacrifices, and keeping the religious poetry. Even Zarathushtra himself was considered a Magi by some Greek authors. As with most religions, the status of women in Zoroastrianism has recently evolved markedly. Today, in Iran but not in India, women are allowed to become priests. Most Zoroastrians today support a general attitude of egalitarianism, even if some limits are still imposed because of ritual regulations and other traditional aspects. For the most part, traditional teachings made clear that women were to be subordinate to men, although Zoroastrianism calls for and teaches about spiritual equality and duty for men and women alike.

Various days of the year and crucial points in a person's lifetime are marked by special rituals and ceremonies, especially the seven yearly festivals, all connected to the higher divinities. The Zoroastrian calendar, which honors Ahura Mazda and other divine beings on specific days and months of the year, sets forth seven obligatory holy days, Nowruz, the Zoroastrian New Year's Day, being the most important. It signifies the partial and temporal victory of light against the darkness. Nowruz is accepted by the Iranians (and other nations connected to the Persian culture and civilization) as the official start of the New Year in the Islamic Republic of Iran. Nowruz is celebrated in many ways, but the Zoroastrian heritage is particularly visible in the traditional Haft-Sin decoration. It is an arrangement of seven symbolic items that start with the Arabic letter "sin". These are Sabzeh (sprouting, the symbol of rebirth and growth); Samanu (sweet paste, symbol of power and strength); Senjed (wild olive, the symbol of love); Somaq (spice, the symbol of sunrise); Serkeh (vinegar, the symbol of patience); Seeb (apple, the symbol of beauty); Seer (garlic, the symbol of health and medicine). Sometimes, additional elements are to be found, like Sonbol (hyacinth, the symbol of spring's arrival); Sekkeh (coin, the symbol of wealth and prosperity), and Saat (clock, the symbol of time). The number seven is considered to be a holy number, as it evokes the seven holy immortals (Amesha Spentas). A "Book of Wisdom" is regularly added to this table. While it was originally Avesta, today Iranians usually put the Qur'an, the Divan of Hafez or Shahnameh as this venerable book. The celebration of Nowruz has many Zoroastrian elements, particularly Chaharshanbe Suri, the last Wednesday before Nowruz when people gather in an open space, make several small bonfires and jump over the flame, singing "Sorkhi-ye to az man, zardi-ye man az to", meaning "Let your redness be mine, my paleness yours". It is basically a remnant of the Zoroastrian purification rituals, with a focus on fire.

Connection to Vedic religions but also Christianity is what makes Zoroastrianism so special. Concepts introduced by Zoroastrians such as the Heaven and Hell, resurrection and the Day of Last Judgment, as well as dualistic cosmology with its good and evil counterparts, and even an idea of Savior, may have entered Judaism after the rule of Cyrus the Great, who liberated the Jews from the Babylonian slavery and returned them to Palestine. These ideas were later accepted by both Christianity and Islam; it is also the reason why Shi'a Islam in contemporary Iran almost exclusively puts Zoroastrians among the "People of the Book" (Ahl al-Kitab), together with Jews and Christians, as "protected" people. Many of the fundamental principles of the three Abrahamic religions (as well as the Baha'i faith) have their direct origin in Zoroastrianism, while Manicheanism influenced the Hellenic philosophy and created the early Christian Gnosticism, kept alive by some medieval movements such as the Bogomils. Today, a reformist and traditionalists are the main two branches of Zoroastrianism. The traditionalists are mostly Parsis in India, dedicated to preserving the old documents, while reformists are Zoroastrians in Iran, where many documents were destroyed and the Zoroastrian religion had to be rebuilt after centuries of Muslim rule.

SUGGESTED READINGS, WEBLINKS, AND OTHER MEDIA

Readings

- Boyce, Mary. *Textual Sources for the Study of Zoroastrianism.* Manchester, England: Manchester University Press, 1984.

- Boyce, Mary. *The Zoroastrians: Their Religious Beliefs and Practices.* 2d ed. New York: Routledge, 2001.

- Mehr, Farhang. *The Zoroastrian Tradition. An Introduction to the ancient wisdom of Zarathustra.* Rockport: Element, 1991

- Rose, Jenny. *Zoroastrianism: An Introduction*. London and New York: I. B. Tauris, 2011.

- Skjaervø, Prods Oktor. *The Spirit of Zoroastrianism*. New Haven, CT: Yale University Press, 2012.

- Stausberg, Michael. *Zarathustra and Zoroastrianism: A Short Introduction*. Translated by Margret Preisler-Weller. Postscript by Anders Hultgård. London, England: Equinox, 2008.

- Williams, A. *The Zoroastrian Myth of Migration from Iran and Settlement in Indian diaspora*. Leiden: Brill

Weblinks

- Zoroastrianism—http://www.fas.harvard.edu/~iranian/Zoroastrianism/—Created and maintained by Harvard University professor emeritus Prods Oktor Skjaervø, a leading authority on Zoroastrianism. Includes a large selection of annotated sacred texts.

- Religion Facts: Zoroastrianism—http://www.religionfacts.com/zoroastrianism/index.htm—A good resource for, as the site states, "just the facts."

- The Metropolitan Museum of Art Heilbrunn Timeline of History. The site offers three essays with links to illustrations that are pertinent for studying the historical context of Zoroastrianism:

  o The Achaemenid Persian Empire: http://www.metmuseum.org/toah/hd/acha/hd_acha.htm

  o The Parthian Empire: http://www.metmuseum.org/toah/hd/part/hd_part.htm

  1. The Sasanian Empire: http://www.metmuseum.org/toah/hd/sass/hd_sass.htm

  2. The World Zoroastrian Organisation—http://www.w-z-o.org/—Created and maintained by Zoroastrians, a dependable resource that provides an "insider's" perspective on the religion.

Other Media

1. Zoroastrianism: A Symposium. University of California, San Diego, 2014. https://www.youtube.com/watch?v=cCn1XJ3MIH8 (2 hours, 35 minutes).

2. Zoroastrianism: The Parsees of Bombay. https://www.youtube.com/watch?v=FTGhmWVTbo4 (51 minutes)

SACRED TEXTS

www.avesta.org

This site includes the Avesta and many other Zoroastrian scriptures.

KEY TERMS AND DEFINITIONS

Ahura Mazda (uh-hoo'rah moz'dah; "Wise Lord") The God of Zoroastrianism; also known as Ohrmazd.

Amesha Spentas (ah-mesh'-ah spent'ahs; "Beneficial Immortals") Seven angels—including Spenta Mainyu, the Holy Spirit of Ahura Mazda—who help Ahura Mazda govern creation.

Angra Mainyu (ang'grah mine'yoo; "Foul Spirit") Evil adversary of Ahura Mazda; also called Ahriman.

asha (ah'shah) The true, cosmic order that pervades both the natural and social spheres of reality, encompassing the moral and religious life of individuals; opposed to *druj*.

Avesta The oldest and most important of Zoroastrian scriptures, consisting of a collection of texts including the *Yasna* and *Gathas*.

Chinvat Bridge The bridge that needs to be crossed by the soul to reach the afterlife, wide and easy to cross for the good, razor-thin and impossible to cross for the evil.

Daena (die'nuh) The feminine being who embodies the individual's ethical quality and who appears to the soul after death.

daevas (die'vuhs) The various demonic powers aligned with Angra Mainyu.

druj (drooj; "lie") Cosmic principle of chaos and evil, opposed to *asha*.

dualism In Zoroastrianism, of two types: cosmic dualism of order and chaos (or good and evil); dualism of spirit and matter (or thought and body).

fravishis (frah-veesh'ees) Preexisting higher souls and guardian spirits of individual human beings.

haoma Sacred drink made in ancient times from the sour, milky juice of the soma plant; in modern times from water, pomegranate, ephedra, and goat's milk.

kusti (koo'stee) Sacred cord that is to be worn daily by Zoroastrians who have undergone the initiatory rite of the investiture ceremony.

Navjote (nav'-yoht) For Parsis, the name of the ceremony of initiation into the community of Zoroastrians. See also **Sedreh Pushi**.

Nowruz (now-rooz') Zoroastrian New Year's Day coinciding with the vernal equinox, the most popularly observed annual holy day; celebrated in varying ways throughout western Asia by people of all religious and ethnic backgrounds.

Sedreh (sed'reh) White cotton vest worn by Zoroastrians that symbolizes the path of righteousness.

Sedreh Pushi (sed'reh poo'shi) For Iranis, the name of the ceremony of initiation into the community of Zoroastrians. See also **Navjote**.

Spenta Mainyu (spen'tah mine'yoo) Ahura Mazda's Holy Spirit; one of the seven *Amesha Spentas.*

Yasna Seventy-two-chapter section of the Avesta containing material recited by priests in rituals; includes the *Gathas.* The Yasna liturgy, an important ritual, is the sacrifice of the sacred drink *haoma* before a fire.

yazatas (yah-zah'tahs; "ones worthy of worship") A large number, eventually fixed at thirty, of deities on the side of Ahura Mazda and order/good.

Zarathushtra (zare'ah-thoos'trah) Called Zoroaster by the ancient Greeks; ancient Iranian prophet and poet, founder of the Zoroastrian religion; dates uncertain (between 1300 and 550 b.c.e.).

CHAPTER 2

Native American Religions

The religious and spiritual practices of North and South America cannot be perceived as a single religious practice. The native Americans were an incredibly diverse group of peoples and cultures that differed in every conceivable way from one another in terms of art and architecture, technology, state formations, etc. If they were so diverse, of course, they would be incredibly diverse when it comes to beliefs and practices. Furthermore, the word religion has no equivalency in most native American languages. Belief in a European/Western sense of the word was not the most important part of the Native American religions. The most important aspect of the native American spiritual worldview was a realization their idea of the cosmos makes real the universe that they live in. It is the frameworks, deeds, and institutions that help them to concretize and make true what is before that only an idea. Such a framework helps in general to situate oneself relative to everything that exists.

This idea of relationality reveals arguably the central theme in the native American religions and that is kinship. For native American cultures, this world is defined by an interconnected web of familial relationships. One can understand how to interact with anyone, any person or any thing, by understanding how one is related to them. The kinship itself is more than a blood relation to a group of people. It includes also the friends, people one cares about, people one loves, people who have an active role in one's life. Most native American religions have rituals and lifeways that allow making kin of a group of people or individuals that previously one had no connection to. They are suddenly referred to as a sister, a brother, or any other kind of kin. The kin is not only reserved for humans. In many Native American cultures, one is bound and related to all of the other things in one's surroundings. These are animals, plants, but also spirits, gods, goddesses. When one understands how one is related to them, the relationship is based on reciprocity. If one behaves in a proper manner to others, one may expect others to behave in the proper way to oneself too.

Nature plays an extremely powerful role. All of nature and all of the universe we found ourselves in is just one big interconnected web of family relations. Human beings, animals, plants, sun, moon, spirits, all of them are part of interrelated, interdependent and reciprocal relationships. There is no concept of the term of supernatural things in the native American religions. This term denotes something different from nature or something higher than nature. The native Americans did not perceive the world in that way. They considered physical and spiritual reality as one whole. The practitioners of native American religions would relate to the snake as much as to the Moon spirits as something unquestionably real. When one dies and leaves for an afterlife, to the world of the spirits, one is still a part of this natural world as one unified reality. Connection to the land and all elements of the land is of paramount importance. This deep reverence for the natural world and all of earth's creatures means that great care must be taken when interacting with them. It is commonly believed that showing respect for plan and animal life will ensure they continue to flourish and this, harvest and seasonal hunting will be bountiful. This reciprocal, care-taking relationship between humans and the environment has historically been essential for survival and is considered part of a moral code that forms the backbone of the spiritual beliefs and worldviews of native Americans. Consciousness permeates all parts of the living environment, including the plants and animals, so great care must be taken to not offend or displease the spirits of these elements or they may bring hardship for people. The spiritual realm is dominant, permeates all things and is intricately connected with the earthly experiences of humans. Native American religions also structured authority and power.

There are hundreds of tribes in North America whose religious beliefs and practices are as different as they are. Tribes in the southern mountainous region have significantly different elements of faith than tribes from great plains. The surrounding, geography, climate and features of the natural world had big effects on the development of their beliefs. We may roughly divide the native American religions into clusters akin to geographical and historical reasoning. That is why we have here short introductions to the belief systems of tribes of Northern America, Central America, and the Andes in South America.

Northern American religions

In the United States, there are 574 federally recognized tribes (with their tribal governments) of Native Americans, American Indians, First Americans, or Indigenous Americans, as they are all known in various terminologies. This includes predominantly continental American Indians and Alaska Natives but does not include native Hawaiians, Samoans and Chamorros, who are Pacific Islanders. The United States has also 326 Indian reservations. There are some 2,9 million people in the United States who identify themselves as Native Americans (0,9 percent of the total population), while another 2,3 million people are Native Americans mixed with one or more other races, totaling together 5,2 million people. Contrary to a widely believed idea, 78 percent of them do not live in a reservation area. They live mostly in California, Arizona, and Oklahoma. Following the arrival of the Europeans to the New World and the fall of the Aztec Empire, the Native Americans realize the danger they are in and they agreed to set their differences aside and unite into separate nations, divided by ethnic and religious boundaries, in order to better counter this new threat. By the year 1570, all the peoples of North America have formed their own countries and governments. The most famous ones were: (1) Apache Union, formed by a group of culturally similar tribes, together with their Navajo cousins they dominated the south; (2) Calusa Chiefdom in Florida, a small but culturally advanced tribe, specialized in fishing and trading with the Spanish colonies of the Caribbean; (3) Catawba Confederacy, a group of isolated Siouan tribes on the East Coast surrounded by Iroquois enemies; (4) Cherokee Nation, an agrarian society with permanent villages; (5) Cheyenne Confederacy, who, like their Arapaho cousins, are great mounted warriors and were the main enemies to the Sioux; (6) Chickasaw Nation, considered by the Europeans to be one of the five civilized tribes; (7) Choctaw Nation, descendants of the great Mississippian culture which dominated the southeast; (8) Chiefdom of Chumash that occupied a small territory in California with abundant resources; (9) Coahuiltecan Confederacy, a loose alliance of culturally similar tribes, formed to stop the Europeans from further expansion and backed by the Apache and Comanche; (10) Comanche Nation, who made their living off bison, horses, raiding and trading; (11) Confederacy of the Crow, professional bison hunters; (12) Dakota Confederacy, the most prominent state of the Sioux people; (13) East Algonquian Nation, which dominated the East Coast trade and grew very rich; (14) Eastern Cree Confederacy in vast territories of the Canadian Labrador Peninsula that gathered in certain seasons for politics, yet remain firmly united due to their strong kinship bonds; (15) Chiefdom of Haida in western Canadian coast, people who inhabited their archipelago for almost 20,000 years, kept to themselves and have no known related kin in the world; (16) Illinois Confederacy, who lived in seasonal cycles, switching between an agricultural lifestyle and hunting; (17) Inuktitut Confederacy, a loose collection of Inuit hunter-gatherers living north of the tree line, they gathered on rare occasions to determine foreign policies; (18) Inupiat Confederacy, collection of Inuit bands in high north of Alaska; (19) Iroquois Empire that adopted a warlike and expansionist lifestyle, allowing the Iroquoian to form a powerful empire; (20) Kalaallit Nunaat Confederacy, a loose alliance of people living in the Greenland; (21) Kansa-Osage Confederacy, a union between the Siouan Kansa and Osage, formed to counter the hostile neighboring tribes; (22) Karankawa Chiefdom, with skilled archers that communicated over long distances through smoke signals and worshiped the sun and the moon; (23) Republic of Keres-Tanoa with superior technology and geography that allowed this union of two peoples to become a local great power; (24) Kiowa Nation, with a long history of peaceful relations with unrelated tribes; (25) Kutenai Nation, with a strong connection wit nature and highly skilled hunters; (26) Lakota Confederacy, a collection of Sioan bands highly specialized in bison hunting and mounter warfare; (27) Mi'kmaq Nation who became great trading partners with Europeans, specialized in fishing; (28) Muskogee Nation who quickly incorporated many aspects of European modernity, such as written language and farming methods; (29) Navajo Nation, with spectacular agriculture and construction; (30) North Athabaskan Confederacy, a collection of tribes in vast territories of Alaska and Northeast Territories; (31) North Penutian Union, a collection of small and diverse tribes, joined in an economic alliance; (32) NunatuKavut Confederacy, with independent tribes and bands skilled in fishing and hunting; (33) Ojibwe Confederacy, a fierce Canadian opponent to the Sioux and Iroquois; (34) Republic of Pacific Athabasca, located in the most ethnically diverse region in America, this small union of tribes lived among the giant red wood trees and made their living off trade; (35) Pawnee Confederacy, warred with almost all of their neighbors for decades; (36) Pima Nation, who have been able to avoid contact with the Spanish because they lived in an area with scarce resources; (37) Kingdom of Pomo, small kingdom in California; (38) Potawatomi Nation, famous fierce warriors; (39) Kingdom od Salishia, known for their totem poles on which they recorded their cultural history and trade much along the Northwestern coast; (40) Shawnee Nation, great barrier to the Iroquois expansion; (41) Shoshoni Confederacy, originating from the Great Basin but moved to the Rocky Mountains; (42) Republic of South Penutia, a collection of related tribes in southern California; (43) Unified Chiefdoms of Timucua in Florida who, following contact with the Spanish, formed a union to act as one against the technologically superior threat; (44) Tlingit Confederacy that have developed a complex fishing culture along the western coast of Canada and Alaska; (45) Wakasha Confederacy made up of culturally similar tribes worshipping animal spirits; (46) Western Cree Confederacy, diverging from their eastern brethren by their way of life and varying climate in central Canada; (47) Yop'ik Confederacy, whose people spend the summers with their families at fishing camps and gather into larger villages when winter comes in western Alaska.

In Canada, the First Nations, Inuit and Metis peoples have also lived in harmony with the natural environment and practiced their traditional lifeways. Just as in the United States, Canada too is defined religiously by its various geographical and natural settings (Eastern Woodlands, Great Plains, Northwest Coast, Subarctic plateau, and the Arctic) where some 50 distinct indigenous nations lived. Today, there are about 1,7 million indigenous Canadians, 65,000 of which identity as Inuit and 250,000 as Metis. There is no overarching native religion among them. Beliefs, values, and practices vary widely across Canada and over thousands of years. Some have combined with Christianity or were left behind as other religions or secular ways replaced them. However, there are common links between all of these peoples as well, mostly through creation stories, the role of supernatural beings in folklore and the importance of sacred organizations, objects, and places. The spiritual beliefs in Canada and elsewhere in Northern America have traditionally been shared orally and these narratives have been passed on from generation to generation. These narratives are similar across the Northern American continent which was known as Turtle Island. In this story, the earth and the life it supports are symbolized by a giant turtle. In the Ojibwe version of this tale, the creator had flooded the earth to clear away the people that had been fighting among each other. To create a new earth, the Great Spirit asked some of the surviving animals to dive down into the ocean and bring him back some soil. All but one failed, the muskrat. Muskrat succeeded but sadly lost his life in the process. The creator took the soil that Muskrat brought back and placed it on the back of a turtle, which became known as Turtle Island. An additional element of this story, as told by the Haudenosaunee peoples, is that a pregnant Sky-Woman fell from the spirit realm onto the turtle's back, guided safely by the birds. Her appreciation for the animals was so great that the earth formed around her and became the land on Turtle Island. This story speaks of resilience in the face of challenges as symbolized by the role of Muskrat as well as conveying the importance of appreciating the earth and the animals.

The Northern American native tribes lived in significantly diverse geographical areas and this was paramount in defining the mode of their kinship to nature.

However, there are some major features shared by everyone. All of them have creation stories. This is not only about the creation of mankind, but more importantly a direct story of how a particular tribe was made and how they should behave in relation to their tribesmen, world and universe in its totality. For instance, Iroquois share a story about Tepe and Gucumatz who sat and thought about earth, stars, oceans. In the end, they got the help of a coyote, a crow, and several other animals and created four beings with two legs, the ancestors of all Iroquois people. The Sioux people tell a story about a creator who was not satisfied with the original people, so he decided to make a new world. He sang many songs and created new species, including a turtle he brought in mud from the sea to create the earth. The creator reached deep into his sack and brought many animals. Then, he created men and women from mud. The remembrance of the origins is ritually celebrated, shared and commonly remembered. In Pueblo people, a subterranean circular sacred space called Kiva is used to constantly remind them of their creation story. Altars, fire pits, and vents support and benches the Sipapu, a symbolic emergence hole from the creation story.

In the Southeastern parts of the contemporary United States, the geography of plains, great rivers and swamps influenced the cosmology. In the Mississippian native religion (which covered a huge area that stretched to Florida and East Coast), our world floats and is guarded by the Sun God (who is a half-human and half-bird) who gives authority to the worldly leader. On the other side is the underworld Panther that guards the portal between earth and below the world. A turtle has a prominent role in the underworld and is associated with fertility as well. All of these levels are connected through the Axis Mundi that allows communication and travel.

While we may say that Northern American native religions are polytheistic, they seem to be more pantheistic and without a clear understanding of who is a god and who is a spirit. There is certainly a big group of deities. Some of them are creators, others are spirits and healing forces. The Great Spirit is often used in the American belief systems and is considered to embody the concept of total power. Many tribes have their own names for this creator spirit, who is above all a great mystery, but who permeates everything and everyone. According to various traditions, strong spiritual power also resides within living beings, the natural environment, weather events and ritual objects. This great power also belongs to spiritual beings such as tricksters and shapeshifters as well as to those that perform ceremonies and rituals. Dwellings such as ritual sanctuaries and sweat lodges have powerful spiritual components, such as the central pole or column, where the connection to spirit is especially strong. The creator or Great Spirit is an all-powerful supernatural being that may have different names, origins and even genders depending on that culture's beliefs.

Many spirits take their place in everyday interaction with humans. For instance, animals have spirits or souls that are communicating with people, and they may often guide people, offer their wisdom or any other kind of help or gift. Other spirits may turn to be more challenging. The tricksters can take on various forms such as human, half-human, animal or spirit, while shapeshifters or transformers are beings that can change their shape, to or from animal to human and even inanimate objects. Guardians are beings that represent attributes such as courage and strength and may control aspects of daily life such as hunting and fishing stocks. These powerful beings, much like shamans, may act as spiritual mediators responsible for communication between the Great Spirit and human beings. Contact with a guardian spirit is extremely beneficial and especially important during a vision quest, as a right of passage at puberty or at other significant times of life. A person on a vision quest journeys into the woods to seek knowledge, spiritual communion, and purification, through fasting and prayer. To encounter a Guardian spirit on a vision quest is said to bring prosperity, success and good health.

To reach one's internal understanding, one has to communicate with nature. It is a common vision of a tribe that affects a profound change in one's life and worldview. At the same time, it is an individual spiritual journey and communal rituals such as the sun dances or natural saunas. All of it is under the guidance of a spiritual leader. It is a shaman or a medicine man. The latter term is more correct, as a shaman is not used in the native American dictionary and is academically connected to the Indo-European peoples to denote a person who deals with prophecies, spiritual communication and magic. The Native American medicine man may use the same practices, but he is more than that. They were seen as specialists for wellbeing in both spiritual and physical manner, as the native Americans never distinguished the two as something separate. They hold prominent positions, acting as intermediaries between the spirit and human world as well as healers, prophets and storytellers. Shamans may preside over and perform rituals and ceremonies and use forms of divination to make predictions and determine the cause of problems in the community. They are also custodians of ritual objects used in ceremonies and have special knowledge of natural medicines for healing. In some cultures, a single medicine man performs all duties and in others, there are individual specialists to fulfill different needs.

Fertility, birth, initiation, and death rites are often clearly stipulated in ceremonies, rituals and practices. Medicine men performances may be involved as well as sacred items such as drums, rattles, and medicine bundles. Some ceremonies are preceded by stringent purification rites, such as sweat lodges or baths, fasting and sexual abstinence. Feasting is also a common feature of ceremonies along with music and dance. Intrinsic to most native American cultures is the core ideology of the cyclical nature of life, death, the seasons, weather and the movement of the cosmological elements of the universe. Death is a part of these cycles and ancestors play a big part in the daily lives of living people. The spirit realm exists in the sky world with the sun, moon, stars, and planets. This divine power has the ability to affect these cycles so humans must maintain a good relationship with the spirit world to ensure that these cycles stay in balance. Different colors of face paint symbolize the purpose of the event as well as the expression of emotions. For example, red signifies life, black means death or grief and purple denotes special occasions. Feasting ceremonies with traditional foods, naming ceremonies where the spirit or traditional clan names are given and sweat lodge ceremonies for healing and purification are but a few of many types of special occasion ceremonies that take place throughout the year. Ceremonial instruments and items such as rattles, drums, masks, charms, medicine bundles, may be used in ceremonies and rites.

Native Americans have had deep importance with the lands that they have inhabited for countless generations, but certain sites have sacred significance. Sacred sites may be the birth or death sites of ancestors, places of prayer for spiritual leaders, geographically unique or part of the historical narrative of a clan or nation. Sacred sites must remain undistributed so as not to drive the spirits away. Many sacred sites have been altered, polluted, removed, or forgotten due to the effects of colonialization, tourism and the increasing industrialization in the remote areas of North America. Some sacred sites have been designated as protected sites and provided with Federal governments protection but perhaps at the cost of disrupting the right of access of native Americans to these sites.

In both the United States and Canada, the introduction of Christianity by colonial settlers caused irreparable damage to the native Americans and their traditional ways of life and spiritual practices. Early interference of missionaries encouraging the native people to convert to Christianity, church and government-sponsored residential schools causing native American children to be stripped of their culture, and the outlawing of native American ceremonies and spiritual practices all contributed to a traumatic loss of cultural identity for Native Americans. While the conversion to and adoption of Christianity by many native Americans has led to the syncretization of colonial and indigenous religions in many parts of North America. This fusion has come at a cost for some, with the loss of traditional languages and customs.

The Aztecs

The Aztec Empire in Central America was an alliance of three indigenous people groups, the Acolhua, the Tepanec, and the Mexica, the last one being also the dominant group living in the capital Tenochtitlan, a huge city on an island in the middle of the Lake Texcoco. Their descendants occupy now Mexico City and some still practice the old religious traditions coupled with Roman Catholicism. Much of what we know about the Aztec religion comes from the 16th-century Spanish sources, like those composed by the Franciscan Bernardino de Sahagun. His compilations give a tremendous number of information coupled with illustrations made by indigenous artists. However, one has to be aware this information are filtered through the European and Christian lens. We know much about the state religion of the Aztec Empire but very little about the folk religion. The historians of religion call this state religious framework the mystical-military religion of the Aztec warrior class. This includes the infamous human sacrifices and mythology recorded by the Aztec nobility.

The Aztec religion was polytheistic that included more than 200 gods. They may be categorized into three loose clusters. First is the celestial creativity or divine paternalism gods. This would include the divine couple of Ometecuhtli and Omecihuatl that created the universe. Sometimes they are conceptualized as Ometeotl or dual supreme god. The second cluster is rain and agricultural fertility which includes the rain god Tlaloc. The third cluster is war-sacrifice, nourishment of the Sun and the Earth which includes the feathered serpent Quetzalcoatl (also revered in Mayan culture), underworld god Mictlantecuhtli, and the Aztec patron god Huitzilopochtli who led Aztecs from their ancestral homeland to Tenochtitlan. However, the identities, attributes and functions of Aztec gods were fluid. Some scholars argue one should not categorize Aztec gods as personifications but more as pantheistic ideas of sacred powers or forces that move through the cosmos. Many gods simply blend in with one another since they had multiple aspects. Whenever Mexica people conquered another nation, they would take statutes of their gods and put them into their temples, thus constantly enlarging their own pantheon. The same happened when Catholicism came to the Americas. Saint Mary and Saint Anne were renamed Teteoinnan and Toci, blending them with previous Aztec goddesses. Some gods became less relevant with the political changes.

In the very center of Tenochtitlan was the great Aztec temple (Templo Mayor), whose foundations are still preserved after its destruction by the Spanish forces. The archaeologists have found similar dual-staircase temples in other major Aztec settlements. The Templo Mayor is associated with a legend of Huitzilopochtli who protected his mother from certain death. The temple was regarded as the center of the world and mythology.

Aztecs used the 365-days solar calendar and 260-days ritual calendar that align every 52 years when the New Fire ceremony took place as a big renewal. Aztecs believed the universe has gone through four stages, each ending with a disastrous collapse. The sun god Tonatiuh presides over the fifth age in which we live now. People have to sustain the fifth age through nourishing the sun, earth and rain through rituals like processions, fasting, purification, deity impersonation, and ritual killing. Deity impersonation was an event when the person genuinely believed he or she became a god. On the other hand, one of the most pervasive notions of the Aztec religion is the sacrality of the human body and its potential to return its energy to the cosmos. Aztecs believed the human body was a sacred reservoir of divine forces called tonalli and teyolia. Tonalli was a gaseous substance that the Aztecs believed resided in the head and the hair. Ometeotl sends it to the head of every fetus. The word means "to make warm with the sun" or to irradiate, as tonally is associated with solar heat. It is also associated with the body's strength and health which is why Aztec warriors are depicted as grasping their enemies by their hair. Teyolia resided in the human's heart and was associated with human reasoning, perception, and understanding. It may be understood as the divine fire, the divine spark, or the light matter. It was particularly strong among the priests and people close to the gods. Both elements permeated reality, not only in the human body but in nature, temples, animals, plants.

Human sacrifices were understood as a form of energy recycling for gods. Such sacrifices were widely practised in Central America but gained prominence among the Aztecs in the zenith of the Empire. Human sacrifice was not a random or occasional ritual practice. It was practiced every single month. Some 20,000 people were sacrificed per year. The rituals were not the same. There were up to 18 different ceremonies involving human sacrifices, sometimes involving the elite and nobles eating the flesh of sacrificed victims. The most famous sacrifice was done at the yearly festival of Toxcatl which celebrated one of the creator gods, Tezcatlipoca or the Lord of the Smoking Mirror. The priest would choose a young captured warrior who needed to be in perfect physical condition. They dressed him to impersonalize a god and made him live among the people for a year. After one year, the god would be sacrificed at the Templo Mayor. The priest would cut out his heart and display his skull. This resonates with the importance of both the head and the heart as tonalli and teyolia. The sacrifice would then replenish the Sun.

Inka

Many Native American religious traditions depend on geography where a particular ethnic community lives. Inca is certainly one such example. The Andes, home of the Inca, provide a challenging environment, which frames Andean worldviews and connects everyone very strongly with the natural world and with each other. Three geographical zones – jungle, mountains and desert coast – promote verticality, vertical economy, recognizes interdependence due to the straightforward fact that a single zone cannot produce enough for all needs. Such a geographical position promotes a sense of reciprocity and increased awareness of dualities, which is particularly echoed in religion.

Human rituals are connected with the nature and cosmos. Gods are often drawn from natural forces needed for survival and are celebrated through festivals in agricultural and astronomical cycles. The mightiest of all gods is the Great Creator God Viracocha, to whom the Golden Temple of Corichancha in Cuzco was dedicated. The temple earned his name because at one point it was literally covered in gold. Very much like the Aztec rulers, the Inca link their legitimate rule to the Sun. Son of Viracocha and Mama Cocha (Goddess of the Sea), Inti is the Sun God. Inti provides light, warmth, and is important for agriculture and farming. It is through Inti that the Sapa Inka (the ruling Inka) claims the right to rule as Sapa Inkas are considered to descend from the Sun God. In fact, the name Inca means the royals, the nobility or the ruling class. The Moon Goddess Mama Quilla is the sister of Inti, the brother and sister often described as "the sweat of the Sun, the Tears of the Moon". Namely, Inka believe that gold was the sweat of the Sun and thus gold became an important religious material. Silver is the religious material of the Moon. This is a strong duality between brother and sister, sun and moon, gold and silver.

One of the most important deities that are still worshiped in the Andes is the Pachamama or Mother Earth. Her importance is vividly seen in the ritual item for sacrifice to Pachamama called the Paccha. It combines the Andean foot plough, storage vessel for the corn beer (Chincha) and a cob of corn. The plough was stuck into the Earth and an offering was made to Pachamama while expecting in return a good corn season. Maize or corn was the food staple for the Andes and also the sacred plant used in many rituals. Mother Earth remains incredibly important in the Andes and offerings are still given to her. One may still find buried in the fields small Canopas, carved alpacas or llamas filled with offerings. Again, in return, one expects abundance in this field.

Inka found all around them Huacas (or Wakas), sacred objects, special or unique things allowing for connection between this world and the spirit world. It was used as a kind of portal or interconnection. Although Inka, like other Native Americans, did not distinguish between physical and spiritual reality, they did find places where the duality of physical and spiritual reside. These places or things could be stones, waterfalls, mountains, mummies, virtually any place where spiritual energy might be transferred or contacted. Priests often spoke for Huacas and translate their intentions. Mountains are generally considered to be the home of the gods, from where deities provide water through melting snow. A particular Huaca is the Sacred Rock at Machu Picchu.

One of the most important Huacas of the Inka would be the ancestral royal mummies. In South America, there was a belief in continuation after death and the ability of the death to communicate with the living. Dead were often well preserved and would communicate through dreams, signs and interpreters. The noble Inka's mummies were kept in the Coricancham but brought out for festivals and important events. They were clothed and fed and had interpreters by their side. Such an adoration of mummies had its weird twists. Some mummies were sent even to diplomatic missions, while one record testifies that one mummy was married to the mother of a Sapa Inka to justify his right to rule. They also attended all the other important events, such as weddings, ritualistic holidays, and would have been asked for an opinion on important matters. Most mummies were destroyed by the Spanish conquistadors. The mummies were perfectly preserved by various manners of expertise, but there were also naturally preserved mummies in the high Andes. These are the bodies that are preserved by freezing. Some of them were also ritually left to freeze to death.

After the Spanish conquests, there was a strong blending between indigenous and Christian theology. For instance, the Virgin Mary is blended with Pachamama, while the display of the Eucharist used gold and the sun rays similar to the Inti images.

Further reading

Brown, Brian Edward. *Religion, Law, and the Land: Native Americans and the Judicial Interpretations of Sacred Land.* Greenwood Press, 1999

Deloria, Vine Jr. *God is Red: A native view of religion.* Fulctrum Publishing and North American Press, 1994

Martin, Jowl W. *Native American Religion.* Oxford University Press, 1999

McGaa, Ed and Buchfink, Marie N. Mother Earth Spirituality: Native American Path to Healing Ourselves and Our World. Harper, 1990

Read, Kay Almere. *Time and Sacrifice in the Aztec Cosmos.* Indiana University Press, 1998

CHAPTER 3

Chinese Religions: Confucianism and Daoism

This chapter focuses on the two indigenous Chinese religious traditions of Confucianism and Daoism. Both share a common source spring—an ancient Chinese religion that dates back at least to the middle of the second millennium BCE. The texts that articulate this religious mentality are later revered as the Five Classics by the Confucians, although Daoists also acknowledge the authority of some of the texts, especially the Book of Changes (*Yijing*), and use some of the same terms (though giving them different content and meaning). Daoism is philosophical and religious teaching based on a metaphysical interpretation of the Chinese sign Dao - a sign that in different contexts can be a path, a way, a principle, a truth, a skill. The Dao is the Daoist term for the path of nature and the cosmos. Its founder according to tradition is Lao Tze or Laozi. His original name is Li Er, and his descendants named him Laozi out of respect. He was an archivist of ritual books and documents by profession. Some principles of Daoism are common to other religions: humility, generosity, nonviolence, simplicity. Other attributes are the beliefs of the Chinese shamanic religion (the theory of the five elements, alchemy, and the cult of ancestors) as well as the cultural ideas and practices of Buddhism. Confucianism was founded by Chiu Kong or K'ung-fu'-tse in the 6th century BCE. He emphasized the importance of three principles: proper behavior, compassion, and respect for ancestors. It is known as a religion that highly valued the responsibility of an individual towards the emperor, the state, and neighbors. Confucianism has been considered the state religion for many dynasties, and from the very beginning, it has been closely associated with Daoism.

History of Confucianism

Confucianism (used here somewhat reluctantly as Confucius, a Latinized name for Master Kong, was neither the founder of the tradition nor a divine being), properly understood as the teaching of the *"ru"*—scholars, ritualists, scribes—was the first to emerge from this ancient Chinese religious background as a distinct tradition. From a Western perspective, Confucianism is often considered to be more a philosophy than a religion. Gottfried Wilhelm Leibniz and Nicolas-Gabriel Clerc introduced Confucius to 18th-century Europe as the first and greatest Chinese philosopher, quite distant from images of idolatry as seen in Buddhism, Shamanism and Daoism. If one compares Confucianism with the Western religions or even some Eastern ones, it indeed lacks many of the traditional beliefs. Still, Confucianism has transcendental and metaphysical ideas, such as a very strong reference to heaven as a source of life. It is a strong belief in *Tian*, which has a pantheistic meaning of heaven or nature. *Tian* gives the power of virtue and it is the source of values Confucianism is known for. The whole cosmic order is based on the ethics and it controls all the events in heaven, on earth and in human society. Chinese believed that these levels are not separated; instead, Confucianism is very holistic in its approach to reality. Violating ethical norms and values is equivalent to sin because it brings disorder into the cosmos.

From the very beginning, Confucius was surrounded by other teachings. Born around 550 BCE, he was a contemporary of Buddha in India, while he had to confront the Daoist teachers in China and many various shamans that dwelled in China. According to the traditional records, Confucius was in the government service where he had many roles, including the minister of crime under Duke Ding in the state of Lu. The relationship between Confucius and Duke Ding fell apart when the duke received gifts from a neighboring country: 80 beautiful women and 124 horses. The duke spent his time riding these horses and being entertained by these women which Confucius found deeply improper for a ruler. That is why he left the court and wandered around China. When he was 34, Confucius visited the Zhou capital where his teacher for a year was Laozi, the founder of Daoism. What Confucius and his first few generations of followers did was to make the ancient Chinese religion they inherited far more personally relevant and religiously inspiring. They formed a movement (rivaled by Daoism and others) to deal with the moral, social, and political crises that afflicted China during a very chaotic period in her long history.

By the middle of the second century BCE, the Confucian tradition was elevated to be the state orthodoxy by the court. Imperial academies were established to study the classics of the School of Principle (*Lixue*). For the unified Chinese state under the Han dynasty Confucianism was used as a major political ideology. Han emperors equally introduced other ideas to this Imperial Confucianism, particularly legalism. While Confucianists stressed the importance of morality, the legalists accentuated the power. In their core thinking, legalists established a world where the only distinction is between those who have power and those who do not have it. Consequently, they established an authoritarian government that would be filled with Confucian values and institutions in an almost cynical manner. But this triumph of Confucianism was neither total nor lasting. Its initial impulse and vitality became obscured by empty formalism and hair-splitting scholasticism. In time, the new faith of Buddhism entered China from India by way of the Silk Road. At the same time, a popularized form of Daoism held sway over a substantial portion of the populace. The government collapsed, and for centuries thereafter Confucianism existed only as a superficial framework of the state.

It would be in the later Song dynasty (960–1279) that Confucianism would enjoy a revival in the form of Neo-Confucianism. Intensely bent on reviving what is idealized as the original and pure teaching of the early masters, various groups of Neo-Confucians would offer their own interpretations of the vision of Confucius and that of his immediate successors, with a metaphysical twist which is a step further from anything Confucius ever taught. Many scholars suggest this twist came under influence of very metaphysical Buddhism, developed by Zhu Xi. Confucian masters were also vigorously battled against the prevailing influence of Buddhism and Daoism, but with a need to answer those metaphysical questions which persisted in Buddhism. They started to make philosophical concepts in finding a role of *Li* (principal order or cosmic pattern) and *Chi* (material force or matter, even considered as pneumas) and their interaction in this world as dualism. Zhu Xi was questioning how to develop and maintain order (*Li*) starting from one's own heart and one's own mind, and how to transfer it to family, community, and polity. It was a substantially deeper addition to the already institutionalized social and political ideology that ruled China. In this effort Neo-Confucianism succeeded brilliantly, thereby establishing itself, once again, as the orthodox religious and intellectual tradition in China. Its view of the ideal human relationship, its standard of ethical values, and its concept of social and political order were accepted as normative by most of the Chinese populace through court sanctions and educational incentives. Despite the metaphysical twist, Confucianism of the Song dynasty was oriented mostly to very political things such as administration, economy, military. The traditional way of life of most Chinese was shaped by Confucian teachings and enacted in elaborate rituals at the state, community, and family levels. Between 1313 and 1905, the content of the civil service examination, which served almost exclusively as the recruitment tool of all government officials, was based on designated Confucian texts known as the Four Books, including the *Analects* (*Lunyu*), a collection of sayings of Confucius written down by his followers, and the *Mencius*. In this manner, the fate of Confucianism became intimately tied to that of the imperial government.

When, since the middle of the nineteenth century, the Chinese government proved unprepared and unable to withstand the challenge of an expansionist West, China was defeated militarily and disgraced culturally. Confucianism was seen by a new generation of Chinese intellectuals as a reactionary and oppressive ideology that was responsible for China's backwardness and humiliation. This antagonistic and dismissive attitude toward the Confucian heritage among China's elite lasted until the late 1970s. Since then, a reappraisal of Confucianism by the Chinese government and rejuvenation of interest in this indigenous tradition has taken place. The perennial value of Confucius's teaching and the quintessential Chineseness of its values are being recognized. Confucianism remains a vital religious tradition not only for China and East Asia but also for the entire world.

History of Daoism

Daoism, when it first appeared from the same ancient Chinese religion that gave rise to Confucianism, offered an alternative view of humanity, society, and the cosmos. Just like its descendent, Daoism is often interpreted in the West as both philosophy and religion, although the Chinese thought never distinguished between the two. Laozi and Zhuangzi, regarded as "proto-Daoists" in this chapter, articulated a worldview and a moral-political approach that were largely the polar opposite of those embraced by Confucius and his followers. While many of its early advocates were individualistic searchers of the Dao and were very much allergic to collective, mass actions, Daoism became a popular religious movement by the middle of the second century CE, with the deification of Laozi as the giver of a secret formula for achieving health and immortality, as well as a god who promises the creation of a perfect political order on earth. Inspired by Buddhism and often in direct competition with it, Daoism borrowed many of the organizational principles and terms of the discourse of the former to enhance its appeal. It was, in fact, this Daoism that perpetuated the Daoist tradition through Chinese history, producing schools and lineages of priests, compiling revealed texts that eventually became the Daoist Canon (*Daozang*), envisioning a pantheon of deities (many of them female), pursuing physical well-being and even longevity through herbs and other unique medical practices such as acupuncture, and devising elaborate rituals that allow the practitioners to communicate with the divine as well as to create cohesion in the community.

Daoism is inherently tied to the *Daode jing* or Book of the Way and Its Virtue, ascribed to Laozi himself, as a revelation of Laozi in both his human and his divine nature. Laozi (meaning the Old Master) is not considered by many Western scholars as a historical character, but as a collective entity of an old Chinese oral tradition. This tradition has roots in shamanism and exorcism practices done by the *Wu*, a medium, a healer or a shaman. They were capable of fighting or neutralizing demons and making amulets and talismans for protection. Some sources mentioned also possibilities of ecstatic journeys through space and time, which will be developed later into *yuanyou* or far roaming. More intellectually prone practitioners were known as the *fangshi* who would have solid knowledge about astrology, divination, esoteric, medicine, alchemy, etc. Other early source of Daoism are Inner Chapters, Outer Chapters and Miscellaneous Chapters, written by Zhuangzi (370-280 BCE). He acknowledges the validity of Dao as presented by Laozi, but Zhuangzi tries to make Dao more understandable to the people, through an interesting episteme: Dao cannot be known through the ordinary human mind, but through "the knowledge that does not know". Zhuangzi was very influential in many Daoist schools by giving concepts and ideas like the fasting of the mind (*xinzhai*) and sitting and forgetting (*zuowang*), two expressions of *wuwei* and self-cultivation.

In the early Han period, *Huang-Lao Dao* became a basic principle for governance. The legend has it that Laozi was a master who has these principles and Huangdi (the Yellow Emperor) applied them. The emperor received divine knowledge in medicine, alchemy, sex, etc. The Yellow Emperor promoted the teachings of *Daode jing* and ruled according to the cosmic cycles suggested in this basic work, but the Han dynasty soon turned to Confucianism as a more understandable and more applicable political doctrine. Finding a relevant political doctrine was important for Daoism to stay afloat. In the 1st or 2nd century CE Daoism finally came up with the *Taiping jing*, Book of the Great Peace, where the peace is promised only if the ruler returns to the principles of Dao. With these millenarian expectations, the deification of Laozi also took place. He became Lord Lao in the 2nd century CE and it is encoded in the Book of the Transformations of Laozi (*Laozi bianhua jing*). According to that belief, Laozi descended to earth to teach people and rulers of Dao.

Daoism developed into numerous schools. Due to many different interpretations of Daoism, a conservative movement emerged first, aimed at preserving what was thought of as the Daoist orthodoxy. This movement became *Tianshi Dao* or the Way of the Celestial Masters, first mentioned in 142 CE and led by healer Zhang

Daoling. This school would strive to make a comprehensive model of society and religion through household and individual registers (*lu*) and by providing healing services to the population through rituals to deities of the earth, water, and heaven. After the demise of the Han Dynasty in the 3rd century, they spread all over China, eventually forming one of the main contemporary branches of Daoism, the Way of the Correct Unity (*Zhengyi Dao*).

When Daoist influence reached the areas south of the Yangtse River, it connected with the shamanistic traditions of that region and made the Southern Tradition in the late 3rd century. Based on the scriptural remnants, the Southern Tradition used talismans to protect people from demons, external forces and even death. It used heavily meditation of Guarding the One (*shouyi*) where the god of unity would be visualized within the human being. The Southern Tradition also relied on alchemy where the production of various elixirs flourished. Reforms of this religious heritage led to the creation of new schools. One is *Shanqing*, the Highest Clarity, which occurred in the mid-4th century near Nanjing. It also incorporated earlier traditions but with a greater emphasis on meditation i.e., visualization of inner gods and a more esoteric understanding of alchemy, as explained in The Book of the Great Cavern (*Dadong zhenjing*). The *Lingbao* School, or the Numinous Treasure, put the priesthood in the central position. The *Lingbao* is a mix of all previous schools, but it also was influenced by some Buddhist elements, particularly by the universal salvation and cosmological understanding of the heavens. It also developed a communal ritual as a more institutionalist religious comunity. One may conclude that *Shangqing* was an individualist in nature, while *Lingbao* was communal. Together with *Sanhuang* teaching, they form the Three Caverns, a system that incorporates all the major religious traditions of the South, with coherence in priesthood, rituals, and doctrines. The three caverns represent the three heavens with the three most important Daoist gods: *Yuanshi tianzun*, *Lingbao tianzun* and *Daode tianzun*, the last being the Laozi himself.

During the Tang dynasty (618-907), Daoism would effectively become the state religion, where *Shangqing* school prevailed. In the middle of Tang rule, around 740, Daoist Canon (*Kaiyuan daozang*) will become the official canon of the Daoist texts, with imperial approval. While having an imperial status during the Tang dynasty, Daoism was confronted with two challenges in the Five Dynasties times (907-960) and beyond, as the various religions competed for the court's benevolence, but also because of the court's wish to combine Confucianism, Daoism and Buddhism and use it equally. During the Song Dynasty (960-1279), systematized ordination of priests was given to the Way of the Celestial Masters, but the development of Daoist theology created also lineages that would have their ritual masters (*fashi*), specialized in exorcism, shamanism, alchemy and meditation. There were five major lineages: *Qingwei* (Pure Tenuity), *Tianxin* (Celestial Heart), *Lingbao dafa* (Great Rites of the Numinous Treasure), *Yutang dafa* (Great Rites of the Jade Hall) and *Shenxiao* (Divine Empyrean). When the Song dynasty was banished to the south, the Jin dynasty of northern China established the *Quanzhen* School (Complete Reality/Perfection). Founded by Wang Zhe, this school will become the major Daoist teaching in the north, recognizable for its celibacy and monasticism.

It was also this Daoism that the Confucian elites would disdain, regarding it as uncouth and superstitious. Though generally not regarded as the true equal of Confucianism, Daoism has always been a "loyal opposition" along with Buddhism. The three traditions cater to the different religious needs of the Chinese people. When Confucianism was called into question in the modern era, Daoism, too came under severe attack. Along with the restoration of Confucianism to respectability since the 1970s, Daoism has also enjoyed a revival. Daoist priests can pursue their formal training and provide services for the community, while rituals are performed in front of appreciative crowds for communal solidarity and prosperity. More important, the Daoist teachings of harmony with nature, environmental concern, health and hygiene in food consumption, and medical procedures are all part of the perennial appeal of Daoism.

The teaching of Confucianism and Daoism

Principal among the ancient Chinese religious view is the belief in the reciprocal and complementary nature of the bipolar components of the cosmos, expressed as *yin* and *yang*. There is also the notion of the easy accessibility between the worlds of the spirits and humans and the continued relevance of the dead ancestors to the living descendants. Equally significant is the belief in the existence of a normative "Way" (*Dao*) that originates from an Ultimate Reality that governs both the natural and the human worlds. To the Confucians who inherited this religious outlook, the Dao assumed a new meaning of being a normative cosmic and moral order ordained by *Tian*, a moral will and source of being for the myriad things.

Confucian religion

The Confucians also subscribed to the centrality of humans in the process of overall moral transformation as well as material improvement of the entire world. As

articulated by Confucius and his students in the *Analects*, and the next few generations of Confucian followers such as Mencius and Xunzi, it is the ultimate religious
obligation of humans to heed the injunctions of *Tian*. This means to cultivate oneself
morally and to behave ethically in society so that the entire human world can enjoy
peace and prosperity while the whole universe can attain perfect order and equilib-
rium. Through the assumption of the fundamental perfectibility of humans and their
co-equal status with the supreme spiritual entities, this Confucian teaching insists on
personal moral cultivation and harmonious relationship with the human and natural
worlds as a religious imperative, thereby making what is secular also sacred. When
the Neo-Confucians reasserted their predominance in Chinese religious discourse
after being overshadowed by the Buddhists and the Daoists for a millennium, they
aimed at repossessing the Dao that Confucius and other early Confucians had articulated, but in more speculative and metaphysical terms.

Confucianism is formed around ethics of right action, right behavior, and right
lifestyle. It is a moral philosophy that determines all actions in life and offers basic
moral concepts that should rule society. Among these is benevolence as the main virtue of Confucian thinking. Another is social hierarchy. Various types of relationships
are the cornerstone of Confucian society. There are five relationships that Confucianism mentions as the most important ones: parent and child, minister and ruler,
husband and wife, older and younger brother, friend and friend. These relationship
networks were written down by the most famous student of Confucius, the Chinese
philosopher Mencius. The basic relationship is the one between the ruler and his subjects, and the moral relationships within a family, among spouses and between father
and son. It is a very hierarchical system of relationships, where patriarchy is based on
the primacy of the father's decision for his children and where precedence is given
to the older brother. From family members, filial piety is requested. In the public
sphere, powerful friendships form the basis of a hierarchal governance system where
personal political loyalty is the core of the political realm. There is no egalitarian idea
in Confucianism. In the *Analects*, Confucius is clear in determining roles one has:
"Let the ruler be a ruler, the subject a subject, a father a father and a son a son", as he
considered there are people worthy of our admiration and obedience. One has to be
modest enough to recognize the people whose experience and accomplishments out-
weigh one's own. Confucianism asks for duties to the state and to the family which
should be done in a disciplined and ethical way. Confucius reminds: "The relation
between superiors and inferiors is like that between wind and the grass: the grass
must bend when the wind blows across it". Here, bending is not a sign of weakness,
but respect and humility. Discipline is categorized as loyal but critical and thoughtful

behavior in service of family and emperor. If these men are loyal and virtuous, then a good government is guaranteed. In *Analects*, Confucius says: "If a ruler himself is upright, all will go well without orders. But if he himself is not upright, even though he gives orders, they will not be obeyed". In the latter case, people will always find a way to avoid the commands and break the law, without ever having a sense of shame. People should act based on personal morality and not upon coercion.

Confucianism rests upon three basic values: filial piety (*Xiao*), Humaneness (*Ren*) and Ritual (*Li*). The fundamental value is respecting parents through the concept of *Xiao*. All other values in life begin with filial piety. Confucius mentions in *Analects* that few people who are filial sons and respectful brothers would ever show disrespect to superiors and create disorder. He states, when the root is firmly established, the moral law will grow and that is why *Xiao* is the root of humanity. The parent-child relationship is the most fundamental one. Confucius had a very strict idea about how one should behave towards one's parents. He believed one should obey them when one is young, care for them when they are old, mourn them long after they die and make often demanding rituals in their memory thereafter. *Xiao* is a reciprocal system where an old man offers wisdom and guidance while a young man supports the old one. Just as the older generation takes care of its descendent, so the younger generation will support their elders when they reach old age. Another important aspect of filial piety is ancestor worship, seen as an obligation to respect the parents in life and keep the memory of them after they die. Confucianism reminds us that moral values begin in the family. One cannot be truly caring, wise, grateful and conscientious unless one is strongly connected to the family.

The second value is *Ren*, defined as humaneness or the care for other human beings. It may be translated also as benevolence or goodness. It is a positive relationship among human beings that form a solid society. Confucius mentions in the *Analects* mutual help in that relationship: if a human being desires to establish oneself or to succeed, he or she will seek to establish others and help others to succeed too. Everything one sees in the world comes from what one knows about himself and that is what Confucius calls a method of achieving humanity. It involves far more than just caring for others. It can involve being reticent in speaking to others or rejecting to use of clever speech, respecting the place where people live and always seek compromise. Mencius argues that benevolence comes from attention to compassion as the main virtue of men.

The third value is *Li*, which is translated as ritual, ritual consciousness or propriety, the proper way of doing things. Confucius stresses the importance of ritual as a way through which people could learn what are the right relationships and how to keep them. A ritual is a form, a framework, that makes the first two values possible to follow even for people who cannot understand Confucianism deeply. That is why *Li* is considered to be the most religious part of Confucianism.

These three values are also mentioned next to others in the *Analects* as the five behaviors of the gentleman (benevolence/*ren*; righteousness/*yi*, which is concerned with integrity and fairness and keeps a person away from corruption; ritual propriety/*li*; wisdom/*zhi*; and trustworthiness/*xin*). Confucius believed people are inherently good, but he also saw these five virtues to be in constant need of cultivation. He refused innovation as it is the work of a lifetime to care for these values.

While pursuing these values, a follower of Confucianism has to devote his life to continuous learning and self-improvement. That is why Confucianism put great emphasis on education. Without education, there are no order and no harmony, whether in personal or social life. Confucius himself was very much attached to the old compilation of literature and history records that he called the Classics. Together with Analects, the Classics were the foundation of Confucian education in China to the 19th century. Confucianism was embedded in all levels of education, from rural elementary schools all the way to the famous examination cycles. It consisted of the oldest five classics: (1) Book of History (*Shu Jing*) which are the historical records of the oldest Chinese dynasties; (2) Book of Songs (*Shi Jing*), a collection of lyric poems written between 1000 and 600 BCE; (3) Record of Ritual (*Li Ji*), as a guide to proper ritual consciousness; (4) Book of Changes (*Yi Jing*), which was used for prognostication and was full of diagrams recorded from the early Zhou dynasty onwards; and (5) Spring and Autumn Annals (*Chun Qiu*), a historical record of the state of Lu, written down every spring and autumn in the period between 722 and 476 BCE. During the Han dynasty, the Confucian curriculum was upgraded and another four books were added to the list of classics. These were: (1) Analects (*Lun Yu*) which are sayings and conversations of Confucius, the basic source about the historical man; (2) Great Learning (*Da Xue*) that gives the concept of virtuous government; (3) Doctrine of the Mean (*Zhong Yong*) a guide for reaching harmony, balance and moderation in all things; (4) Mencius (*Mengzi*) or conversations of Mencius, who was the most important and most known follower of Confucius.

Daoist religion

As explained by Laozi, Zhuangzi, and others who held the belief in the supremacy of the Dao, Daoism subscribes to a "naturalistic" view of all things in the universe—namely, that there is no explicit or hidden moral purpose imposed by a supreme deity. It also sees humans as merely one part of the cosmos, having no superiority over others. In fact, the human penchant for arbitrariness, contrived activity, and meddlesome intervention in the function of the universe is the source of the human malady. The Confucian insistence on moral behavior and social activism is particularly irksome to the Daoist masters, who perceive such undertakings as futile and harmful. The proper attitude is, therefore, to leave things alone and not to interfere with the natural flow of events, expressed by the teaching of *wuwei* (action without intention) and *ziran* (natural spontaneity). This recognition of the supremacy of what is natural and the attendant yearning for unity with it led to a somewhat unexpected twist in the Daoist outlook, already evident in the writings of the original masters such as the legendary Laozi and the more historically authentic Zhuangzi. It is the belief in the possibility of magical and physiological transformation of humans and other life forms to be coterminous with nature—that is, to be immortal and invulnerable to physical harm. Thanks to the Daoist understanding of the three basic components of the human body—*jing* (essence), *qi* (breath), and *shen* (spirit)—there emerged a Daoist alchemical theory of the proper nurturing and mingling of the three so that a magical transformation of the body can take place, resulting in immortality.

In *Daode jing*, Dao is described as the origin and source of existence. Its usual translation is "the Way", although the term itself is beyond translation as such. Dao is constant, invisible, inaudible, imperceptible, it contains an essence (*jing*), that is manifested without any particular intention. Instead, it can occur through *wuwei*. The only way for Dao to manifest itself is through *De*, which means virtue or power. Dao creates the world, a manifestation of its absoluteness, it is within the Dao that ten thousand things (*wanwu*, or all material things) emerge, but Dao is not the world or any other form. It is absolute (*wuji*) in a very similar sense to the Christian idea of god. However, Dao also makes the Unity in the sense that everything is One (*taiji*). As the One, it is represented on the sky as the Northern Dipper or *beidou* (Ursa Major) from where the vital energy of the cosmos emerges.

Furthermore, Dao is the source of all cosmology, particularly of three main components (three treasures): essence or *jing*; breath or *qi*; and spirit or *shen*. Each of them has an unmanifested and manifested appearance and they also compose the human being. The three treasures influence everything a human being can perceive. *Shen* is the immaterial principle and it presides over spirits or gods. *Jing* controls all the material entities, i.e., the ten thousand things, while *qi* maintains the whole cosmos. When these principles are applied to humans, then *shen* is the mind, *qi* is the breath *and* jing are liquid elements in the body – saliva, tears, semen and menstrual blood. Between the Dao, as the One, and the trinity of principles, there is the duality of *Yin* and *Yang*, effectively separating the whole creation into two basic types of existence. *Yin* and *Yang* are separated but also complementary. The cosmos functions through their alternation. All items in the manifested world belong to five different domains: wood/*mu*; fire/*huo*, soil/*tu*, metal/*jin*, and water/*shui*. The Daoist alchemists were particularly interested in the functioning of these domains and attributed colors, celestial bodies, foods, acoustics, organs etc. to them.

The celestial realm consists of the heavens. These systems diverge and may have thirty-two heavens in *Lingbao* and thirty-six in *Shangqing*. These are domains where deities reside, but it is also a gnostic system of priestly gradation and spiritual stages of humans. Every realm opens new and deeper teachings on a higher stage. In both traditions, the Grand Veil (*Daluo*) is the highest or center stage. Three greatest deities or the Three Clarities (*Sanqing*) live there, but with the development of the Daoist pantheon several other gods reached the level of ultimate greatness. This is particularly true for *Taiyi*, the Great One which represents cosmic unity, and *Yuhuang* or Jade Sovereign, an extremely popular and venerated deity among the medieval Chinese. All other principles from the Daoist cosmology are represented by different gods that sometimes have an external (Buddhist, Indian) influence.

A person who reaches high realization in Daoism is called *shengren*, translated as saint or sage. In comparison to Confucianism, *shengren* seems a very passive personality: the Daoist sage has no personal interest or desire, he does not lead others, but places himself in non-doing (*wuwei*). Daoists argue that Confucian virtues become part of men only when Dao is abandoned. This is also translated into politics, where the Daoist ruler should now issue many laws; instead, he should leave people to act by themselves. In Zhuangzi's works, *shengren* possesses inner freedom from social rules, essentialism and self-identity. In that sense, both *Daode jing* and Zhuangzi refute fabricated ethics and moral values, particularly in statecraft.

Daoist cherish long life. While there have been immortals, who have mastered the energy of *qi* and could indefinitely prologue their life, other people should have to satisfy themselves by release from the mortal body. Daoism recognizes a sort of reincarnation albeit the one where the physical body is used to form a new person that is immortal. That is why the human body is not seen as a physiological entity that can be influenced by traditional Chinese medicine. Daoists would condemn such practice as vulgar because the human body is seen more like a vessel that is tasked with a return to the celestial realm. After death, Daoists have a desire to reach the union with the Dao or to serve the deities in celestial realms, while the ascension to heaven (*shengtian*) or attaining celestial immortality (*tianxian*) is the ultimate form of returning to the One.

Ways of Life of Confucianism and Daoism

The rituals are an important part of Chinese religions but to whom these rituals are oriented is not so overly important. In comparison to some other great religious systems, the Chinese religions never made strong boundaries among themselves. From their very inception to the present day, Chinese may pray and make rituals according to Daoist, Confucian, Buddhist or shamanic principles. The clergy of these religions, of course, was not keen to support such syncretic tendencies. They used to demonize the gods of other religions or prohibit other cults, but they were not particularly successful in doing it. Another approach was to exploit and introduce a ritual from another religion and present it as one's own, which only led to a popular syncretistic innovation accepted by most Chinese.

Confucianism

As a religion that diffuses throughout society with little structure and organization, Confucianism focuses on personal and communal behavior as a way of practicing its faith. From individual conduct to family rituals and on through communal and state ceremonies honoring Confucius and *Tian*, Confucians enact their deep understanding of the religious significance of day-to-day living. In their ritual intercourse with others and with the spirits (ancestors and gods), they fulfill their religious obligations. However, Confucianism never developed a coherent religious institution with priests or prescribed rituals. Despite such a lack of a coherent religious structure, records show that Confucius was deeply involved in the proper performance of rituals and music as keys to developing moral dispositions. For Confucius, the ceremony is important. The *Analects* are full of conversations between Confucius and his disciples about premeditated, deliberate and precise gestures that should be done properly in relationships one has in a lifetime. Rituals make one's intentions clear and they help people to understand how to behave. In appeasing the ancestors, Confucians would have an ancestral altar in their homes where the ancestor worship should be exercised in form of asking the spirits of ancestors for help or protection. The right manner of performing the ritual is to avoid make offerings only to receive benefits, but foremost to gain an interior peace or a positive psychological state. The lineage of ancestors may be hundreds of years old, kept in very visible memory. Furthermore, Confucians were obligated to visit the graves of their ancestors at least once or twice a year. Sacred space for Confucians was the state itself and the fulfilment of sacred duty was seen through public service. To enter such a sacred position, a novice was tasked with the civil service examination. This examination was the institutional form of Confucianism as it asked from a future civil servant a total knowledge of the Confucian values and canon. After this entry into the realm of the state, the civil servant had to be a loyal administrator of his emperor, devoting his whole life to the imperial cause. The examination was not easy and only a handful of candidates mastered to enter the national level exams. They were men in their 40s and 50s, with a certain good standing in life. Wealthier candidates would try to bribe their way through, but most men had to be really knowledgeable in philosophy, politics, literature, history and Confucian values. In the end, they would form the ruling elite that would constitute China's heritage of ethics, poetry and politics. This elite would furthermore engage in rituals of social interaction where the highest position is held by the emperor who carried the name of the Son of Heaven and who had a task to keep the rituals alive to preserve the cosmic order. Every year, the emperor led the government to worship heaven. This was the most important day in the Confucian religious calendar. Just like in a big family, the Chinese people would worship all the emperor's ancestors, while the Emperor had to worship ancestors from other Chinese royal dynasties. This was done to ensure the continuity of ruling dynasties and the legitimacy of a good and just ruler.

Daoism

The Daoist way of life is expressed individually as an attitude towards health, food, exercise, and wholesome living. Communally, it is practiced through festivals and liturgies that involve the entire village or town in an attempt to create social cohesion and a close relationship with the gods. The Daoist ideal is to transform the people from a being that is drawn to material goods to a being that understands and follows the Dao through rites to important deities. Many Daoist teachers did not condemn inasmuch the Chinese adherence to Buddhism and Confucianism, but to the shamans, which they considered to be a vulgar practice. This may be seen in the veneration of written texts. Communication with deities in Daoism is not through speech but text. All the ceremonies contain written statements (*shu*), prepared by priests, while talismans are also written figures on paper, wood, stone or some other material, or placed on one's body like a magical written tattoo. This strong emphasis on the written word is based on a belief that the earliest scripts were self-generated from original breath or vibration.

From very early periods until today, Daoists cherish two important ritual ceremonies. The Offering (*jiao*) is a renewal of the relationship between community and gods. It is celebrated on all levels of the community – from rural communities to the imperial court. The merit (*gongde*) is a ritual that ensures deceased ascent to heaven. Local communities, however, are in the center of Daoist ritual life. At local levels are lay associations, tasked with keeping the local temple and supporting the *daoshi* (the priest, Daoist master). With time, *daoshi* became a caste, as the function is transmitted within families. They perform the festivities which may have been even ten days long. The inner festival in the temple is contrasted with the outer festival in the streets and homes, where processions with deities' statues, music and theatre celebrations and food gatherings are held.

Those who follow the Dao should nourish their life in a practice called *Yangsheng*. To attain this, a person should exercise *daoyin* or a kind of gymnastics for physical wellbeing. It allows qi to flow freely within one's body. The right kind of breathing is also important and Daoism developed many practices (*xingqi, zhongxi*, etc). Another nourishment of life is the arts of the bedroom (*fangzhong*) or sexual practices which teach men how to avoid ejaculation as it is considered for sperm to have a positive influence on the brain if it is kept in the body. Meditation is yet another form of important everyday ritual for Daoists. The earliest form of Daoist meditation is a visualization of inner gods which helps human to communicate with deities and to protect and perfect their bodies. Meditation on Unity/One was created as a very abstract practice but in time it became a meditation on anthropomorphic One or Three Ones. Daoism tried to have experience with astral journeys to the celestial worlds or the stars and planets. From the 7th century onwards, Daoism was more oriented to contemplation and introspection as Buddhism became more influential in China. From then, Daoism used several books on inner contemplation, clarity of mind and avoidance of cravings.

Alchemy developed early as a remnant of previous shamanic disciplines. External Alchemy or *Waidan* is primarily known for its elixirs made from minerals, metals, herbs and other natural ingredients and then heated with fire. These elixirs release their essence and contribute to transcendence and immortality. The Internal Alchemy or *Neidan* makes an "elixir" within one's body by applying the Daoist doctrine and practices in one's life.

Today, both Confucianism and Daoist are looking to adjust to contemporary societies. Throughout the 20th century, Confucianism has been termed as traditional and backward philosophy, opposed to a progressive society. Its submissive nature and servitude have been seen as anachronistic to modernity and its emphasis on male domination in the public sphere and primacy of older brothers in the family has been condemned as misogynistic and oppressive of women and youth. At the end of the 20th century, there is a revival of Confucianism in politics and economy with the incorporation of Confucian values in societies of Eastern and South-Eastern Asia, where Confucius' teachings about morality, obedience and good leadership still echo within the various polities. Order and harmony have taken place of conflictual patterns of capitalism in Singapore under the leadership of Chinese immigrants, as well as the focus on family, better education and flourishing social bonds. Meritocracy is seen today as a value-driven from Confucianism in China and is presented as a belief system that counters rising voices in favor of liberal democracy based on the "one person, one vote" principle in choosing top leaders. The ideas of Confucianism influences the aging Communist leaders in China who will now quote Confucius' sayings more than those of Marx, Lenin and Mao. Such devotion to the Confucian ideals is seen also in China's soft power and cultural diplomacy through openings of Confucius institutes across the globe. Daoism is also deeply entrenched in Chinese society today, with a rising trend of acceptance in the West.

KEY TERMS AND DEFINITIONS

dantian (dahn'-teen'ən) "Fields for the refinement of the immortal pill"; major nodal points in the human body where the "pill" of immortality can be refined through alchemical means.

dao (dow) A fundamental concept in Chinese religion, literally meaning the "path" or the "way."

In Confucianism, it specifically refers to the entire ideal human order ordained by the numinous Absolute, Tian. In Daoism, it is the primary source of the cosmos, the very ground of all beings.

Daodejing (dow'-duh-jing) Basic Daoist scripture, lit. "The Scripture of the Way and Its Potent Manifestation"; also known as the Book of Laozi, the name of its purported author.

Daozang (dow' zahng) Literally "Treasury of the Dao," this is the Daoist canon that contains the entire corpus of Daoist texts. The most complete version, still in use today, was first published in 1445.

de (duh) Another fundamental concept in Chinese religions, meaning "virtue" or "potency." In Confucianism, it is the charismatic power of the ruler or the man of virtue, while in Daoism it means the concrete manifestation of the dao.

fangshi (fahng-shər) "Magicians" who allegedly possessed the recipe for immortality.

Five Classics The five canonical works of Confucianism designated in the Han Dynasty. They are Book of Odes, Book of History, Book of Changes, Record of Rites, and Spring and Autumn Annals.

Four Books The four texts identified by the Neo-Confucian Zhu Xi as fundamental in understanding the Confucian teaching. Between 1313 and 1905, they made up the curriculum for the civil service examination. They are Analects, Mencius, Great Learning, and Doctrine of the Mean.

gui (gwei) Ghosts and demons, malevolent spirits.

jiao (jee'au) Daoist communal sacrificial offerings to signal cosmic renewal and collective cohesion.

junzi (ju'un zee) The personality ideal in Confucianism; the noble person.

li (lee) Etiquette and proper manners; rituals and holy rites.

ming (see Tianming)

neidan (nay'-dahn) Daoist "Internal" alchemy designed to attain immortality through meditation, breath control, gymnastics, diet, and massage.

neisheng waiwang (nay'-sheng' wi'-wahng) Neo-Confucian ideal of "inner sagely moral perfection and outer political skills."

qi (chee) Breath, force, power, material energy.

ren (rən) Human-heartedness, benevolence; the unique moral inclination of humans.

ru (rōō) Scribes and ritual performers of the Zhou period; later used exclusively to refer to Confucians.

Shangdi (shahng'-dee) The August Lord on High of the Shang period.

shen (shən) Gods and deities; benevolent spirits.

shengren (shəng rən) (or sheng) The Confucian sage, the epitome of humanity.

shi (shər) Men of service; lower-ranking civil and military officials in the Zhou period.

Tian (tee'ən) The transcendent, numinous entity in ancient Chinese religion; the conscious Will that regulates the cosmos and intervenes in human affairs; conventionally translated as "Heaven."

Tianming The mandate or command of Tian that confers political legitimacy to the ruler; also understood by Confucians as the calling to morally improve oneself and to transform the world.

Tianshi (tee'ən shər) "Celestial Master"; reference to a Daoist salvational figure as well as an organized movement.

waidan (wī dahn) Daoist "external" alchemy involving refining of "pills" with herbs and minerals for ingestion so that immortality can be attained.

wuwei (wōō way) Daoist notion of action without intention; actionless action.

wuxing (wōō shing) The five elemental phases of metal, wood, water, fire, and soil that mutually support and overcome one another.

xian (shee'ən) Daoist immortals and perfected individuals.

xiao (shee'au) Filial piety; respect and care for parents and ancestors.

xinzhai (shin jī) "Fasting of the Mind" in the Zhuangzi.

yang (young) Lit. the south-facing side of a mountain, representing the energy that is bright, warm, dry, and masculine.

yangsheng (young shəng) Daoist techniques of nourishing life and attaining immortality.

yin Lit. the north-facing side of a mountain, representing the energy that is dark, cold, wet, and feminine.

zhai (jī) Daoist "fasts" designed to seek redemption of transgressions by the gods.

Zhuangzi (juahng-zee) A fourth century b.c.e. Daoist figure as well as the title of the book attributed to him.

ziran (zee'-rahn) Daoist notion of natural spontaneity.

zuowang (zoh'-wahng) "Sitting and Forgetting" in the Zhuangzi.

ACTIVITIES AND ASSIGNMENTS

1. Who benefits more under Confucianism, those in power or those without? Why might a ruler like a religion that demands obedience from subjects? Why might the ruler's subjects find comfort in the Mandate of Heaven?

2. How does Daoism's deep suspicion of civilization and its produc
social organization and religious practice? Is there a contradiction
of a "socially engaged Daoist"?

3. Daoists utilize a plethora of methods to "return to the Dao," including external alchemy, meditation, physical exercises, internal alchemy, exorcistic rituals, and talismans. With so many different techniques, does anything unite
Daoism as a tradition? If so, what?

4. Do the moral codes outlined in the Nine Practices and Twenty-Seven Precepts of the Celestial Masters represent a radical transformation of earlier
Daoist ideas rejecting the trappings of civilization? Or are they an extension
of earlier Daoist ideas? Why?

Consulted sources and further reading

Confucianism

Confucius (1998) The Original Analects: Sayings of Confucius and his Successors.
E. Bruce Brooks and A. Taeko Brooks (trans/eds), (Translations from the Asian Classics), New York: Columbia University Press

Eno, Robert (1989) The Confucian Creation of Heaven : Philosophy and the Defense
of Ritual Mastery. Albany: State University of New York Press

Ivanhoe, Philip J. and Kim, Sungmoon (eds, 2016) Confucianism. A Habit of the
Heart. Bellah, Civil Religion, and East Asia. Albany: State University of New York
Press

Hunter, Michael J. (2017) Confucius beyond the Analects. Leiden: Brill.

Littlejohn, Ronnie (2010) Confucianism. An Introduction. London and New York:
I.B. Tauris

Richey, Jeffrey L. (ed, 2008) Teaching Confucianism. Oxford: Oxford University
Press

Rosenlee, Li-Hsiang Lisa (2006) Confucianism and Women. A Philosophical Interpretations. Albany: State University of New York Press

Van Norden, Bryan (2007) Virtue Ethics and Consequentialism in Early Chinese
Philosophy. Cambridge: Cambridge University Press

Zhou, Younguang (2012) To Inherit the Ancient Teachings of Confucius and Mencius and Establish Modern Confucianism. Sino-Platonic Papers, 226

Daoism

Bertschinger, Richard (2010) The Secret of Everlasting Life. The Girst Translation of the Ancient Chinese Text on Immortality. London and Philadelphia: Singing Dragon

Chang, Chung-yuan (2011) Creativity and Taoism. A Study of Chinese Philosophy, Art and Poetry. London and Philadelphia: Singing Dragon

Kirkland, Russell (2004) Taoism. The enduring tradition. New York and London: Routledge

Kohn, Livia (2008) Introducing Daoism. London and New York: Routledge

Komjathy, Louis (2013) The Daoist Tradition. An Introduction. London and New York: Bloomsbury

Welch, Holmes and Seidel, Anna (eds, 1979) Facets of Taoism. Essays in Chinese Religions. New Haven and London: Yale University Press

CHAPTER 4

Buddhism

Modern interpretations of Buddhism often ask if it is a religion or a philosophy. This question is often inappropriate and tendentious, but it also avoids a solid definition of the Buddha's teachings. Buddhism may be defined as "philosophical faith", in terms of Karl Jaspers. It may also be a philosophical trust given to Buddha. Despite Buddha's own insistence not to recognize him as a deity or as a founder of a new religion, Buddhism even today carries his name and many people around the world (especially in Asia) venerate him as a deity. Buddha himself defined his teachings as *Visuddhi-maggo* or Cleansing Way. It has no particular theology and no deity – or rather, it did not have any in the Buddhist essence. Although many Buddhists tend to worship the Buddha as a god, there is no conception of God or Supreme Being in Buddhism. Everything that Buddha taught may be summarized as being aware of the world around us by simple examination in order to attain wisdom.

The Teachings of Buddhism

Life and Enlightenment of Siddhartha Gautama – Buddha
Siddhartha Gautama, who will become Buddha, was born in what is today Nepal, around 560 BCE and he died in 480 BCE. Buddha was born in a rich Hindu family of the Kshatriya (warrior) caste. His father was a wealthy local ruler and his son Siddhartha was born and grew up in luxury. It was prophecized to the family that young Siddhartha will either become a wanderer or a mighty king. Because of this prophecy, his father wanted to protect him from the first option,

so he decided to keep his son closed in three castles: one for summer, one for winter, and one for the rainy season. Siddhartha saw there only luxury, happiness, health, and beauty. All the negative things were kept away from him. When he was 19, he married a beautiful girl Yashodara or Gopa that gave birth to a son Rahul. The tradition explains they lived happily ten years, although isolated from the outside world.

Siddhartha's constant interest to see what is beyond the castle walls brought him to secret journeys. On the first of his secret journey outside the castle, he saw an old man, on second a sick man, on third a funeral and on the fourth a poor but happy Hindu monk. He realized that not all people are young and healthy, and no one lives forever. Inspired by the monk he saw, Siddhartha decided to leave the castle and live like a wanderer. He was 29 years old when he made this fateful decision. In the next six years, he will try to find answers to the meaning of life. By following India's ascetic masters (*sadhus*), he began with extreme fasting. The legend has it that he fasted so much that he was only skin and bones and his hairs fell off his arms and legs. However, he did not find the answer he was looking for. He began to eat again and his first five followers left him because of that.

Fairly disappointed, Siddhartha sat beneath a Bodhi tree and decided not to move until he gets enlightened. He sat there, meditated, and was thinking for 49 days. During this time, evil spirits attacked him constantly, trying to draw his attention. Finally, he reached enlightenment and became Buddha. From that day forth, all men who reach this stage retains the name of Buddha – the enlightened one. Buddha spent the next 45 years teaching about his experience. He died when he was 80 years old. In time, myths and legends were written down about Buddha, his life and previous lives. Supernatural beings are present there, such as in the famous Jataka stories. Various canons were made during history to record Buddha's teachings. The earliest canons were originally written in Pali, a vernacular language of Buddha and north of India. They were made in Sri Lanka and consist of "three baskets" (*Tripitaka*): (1) *Sutta Pitaka* or the Discourses, Buddha's sermons divided into five *nikayas* (subdivisions); (2) *Vinaya Pitaka* or the Monastic Rule that guides the life of monks and nuns; and (3) *Abhidhamma Pitaka* as a set of scholarly writings. The Pali Canon is still the most important written document of Buddhist beliefs. All the Buddhist teachings are collectively called *Dharma*.

Four Noble Truths and Eightfold Path

The essence of Buddha's teachings is two main messages given in the holy Indian city of Varanasi/Benares. One is the Four noble truths, and another is Eightfold paths. These truths and ways convey what is the source of human suffering and how to attain freedom from these sufferings. The Four Noble Truths are the following:

(1) The Truth of Suffering - everything in life is suffering (*dukkha*); life inherently includes pain, aging, sickness, and death. We endure physical pain, loneliness, frustrations, fear, shame, disappointment, and anger. This is a realistic notion as Buddhism explains it as a fact and offers a way to avoid this suffering. Suffering occurs because we have a durable relationship with the world.

(2) The Truth of Arising (*Samudaya*) - the source of human suffering is their desires; we will suffer if we expect other people to be exactly as we want them to be, if we would like others to love us, if we do not get what we want, etc. In other words, what we get will not guarantee us happiness. Instead, we should modify our desires. A life filled with the need to exist and to have makes physical suffering as we will be born again as a being that suffers.

(3) The Truth of Cessation (*Nirodha*) - suffering may be gone if people revoke their desires; it also reveals that true happiness and satisfaction are possible. If we revoke our senseless desires and we learn to live day by day (not returning to the past and not thinking too much about our future), then we can reach such happiness. At that moment, we will also have more will and more time to help others and show compassion.

(4) The Truth of the Path (*Magga*) - sufferings are removed through the Middle Way. Men always want something. When they reach what they want, they want more and more. This is the vicious circle of desires but also a circle of suffering. What men need is to be satisfied with what they have. They do not have to be beggars or monks, but they should find the Middle Way – not too little and not too much. To be able to achieve this, a Buddhist has to meditate to achieve mindfulness or awareness (*Shamatal Vipashyana*).

Only a person that can overcome his or her desire and finds the Middle Way may reach *nirvana*. It is a stage when a person has no desires and when wholesome peace is achieved. It is not possible to reach *nirvana* in this life. The real *nirvana* can only be reached in death when a person is united with the cosmos. The Middle Way in this life is achieved through the Eightfold path, based on moral life seen in our talk, our actions, our way of living. It focuses on the mind so that we are conscious of our thoughts and acts. It also involves the development of wisdom through an understanding of the Four Noble Truths and developing compassion for others. The Eightfold Path is the way which a Buddhist should take to release oneself from suffering. It consists of: (1) right view of the world, seeing things as they are, without hope and fear; (2) right intention, without any expectations; (3) right speech, which comes as a consequence of right view and right intention and forms a pure and simple communication; (4) right discipline which is based on simplicity and straightforward relationships; (5) right livelihood which accepts any job we might have; (6) right effort, without any struggle to achieve preconceived goal; (7) right mindfulness, that cherishes precision and clarity, as well as the feeling for details; (8) right concentration, achieved through mediative experiences. They are grouped into divisions of wisdom, morality, and meditation.

Dharma and Buddhist Ethics

Morality is, furthermore, strongly tied to *Dharma* as a universal law that governs both the physical and astral world. *Dharma* is a natural law, to which both people and gods abide. It governs all aspects of life and is above *karma* as the determination of the life cycle. The law is translated into moral duties found in the Five Precepts, i.e., in five sets recognized as: (1) the Five Precepts (*Pancasila*); (2) the Eight Precepts (*atthangasila*); (3) the Ten Precepts (*dasasila*); (4) the Ten Good Paths of Action (*dasakusalakammapatha*); (5) the Monastic Disciplinary Code (*patimokkha*). Buddhist moral codex consists of rules, and five rules (or five precepts) are the basic ones: (1) do not kill or hurt another being; (2) do not take anything that is not given to you freely; (3) relinquish the non-permissible sexual relations and constant quest for the satisfaction of your urges; (4) do not lie, affront or gossip; (5) avoid taking anything that weakens your consciousness, such as alcohol or drugs. Buddhist ethics is formed around the principle of non-harming (*ahimsa*), characterized by vegetarianism and pacifism. The violence of any kind is strongly rejected, although one may see combative Buddhism in everyday life in Asia. Because nothing is permanent, a Buddhist should also be aware that everything one has is just temporary. That is why Buddhism is inherently void of egoism. Just following the precepts is not enough: one has to respect the virtues that form these precepts. There are three cardinal virtues: (1) non-attachment (*araga*); (2) benevolence (*adosa*) and (3) understanding (*amoha*). These three confront also three roots of evil: (1) greed (*raga*); (2) hatred (*dosa*), and delusion (*moha*). Avoidance of every desire will diminish the power of the roots of evil. Another important part of Buddhist ethics is *Ahimsa* or sanctity /inviolability of life. This would go sometimes to an extreme, where Buddhists would wipe with broom their way only not to unintentionally kill some ants or microbes or avoiding any travels during the monsoon season when a lot of creatures would lose their lives in floods.

The foundation of the teaching of the Buddha is his doctrine of Interdependent Origination, according to which all things are interrelated and dependent upon other things for their coming-into-existence and continued existence. Nothing, in fact, has an existence or identity that distinguishes it from all other things. The Buddha also taught that all things are impermanent. Nothing remains the same, even for a moment. Instead, all things are always in a state of becoming. These teachings have two important implications. The first is that, because we human beings are part of the vast web of interrelated things, we have no independent existence as a "self" separate from other things. The second is that suffering will arise whenever we vainly try to grasp or control anything—including the so-called self—in a world that, because it is constantly changing, cannot be grasped. Those who wish to put an end to suffering must learn to live without attachment to things. Letting go of the desire for and attachment to things that cannot be possessed brings an end to suffering and, ultimately, the bliss of *nirvana*. Both notions have a sort of duties imposed on people. This is not seen as such by Buddhists themselves, as they regard these duties as a mirror image of rights that all beings have. For instance, Buddhism forbids enslaving human beings and from this duty emerges a basic human right for freedom. However, Buddhism has no particular accent on the rights of individual human beings or any idea of human rights in the modern sense. Because every human being has the capacity to attain enlightenment and become a Buddha, great respect should be given to every person.

Buddhist (dis)connections with Hinduism

Many of these religious systematic thinking is drawn from Hinduism. In a way, Buddha reformed Hinduism but also kept some of its basic tenets, albeit in a slightly changed way. For instance, Buddhists and Hindus share the idea of reincarnation and the law of *karma*, meaning that everyone will be born in the next life in a form akin to the way of living in this life. However, in many other things, Buddhism is a polar opposite to Hinduism. It retains a negative stand towards the priestly caste of brahmans and against the caste system in general. It refutes the pre-Vedic and pre-Brahman cults with sacrifices, superstitions, and caste subjugations. Classic Buddhism also ridicules the pantheon of gods in Hinduism. In comparison to most other religions, the substantiality of souls is also negated as it would be opposite to Buddha's theses of nothingness (*sunnavada*). The life cycles can be broken with enlightenment. Cycles of everything that exist is another concept shared with Indian religions. The physical universe consists of a container (*bhajana*) and the beings (*sattva*) and is formed in the interaction of five elements (earth, water, fire, air, and space). Such a universe undergoes evolutionary cycles lasting billions of years. *Sattva* determines if this cycle can be fast or slow, with fast cycles occurring when beings are evil and vicious. Beings have their cycles of rebirth occurring in six realms depicted in the wheel of life (*bhavacakra*). The realms are akin to a soul's condition, and it may be the hell, the animal realm, the ghost realm, the titan or demon realm, the human world and the heaven which is again divided into several stages and into various spheres of existence where heavenly beings or gods reside. It is a complex cosmology where the human being is bound by *karma*, a system of rewards and punishments. As a religious concept, *karma* is seen as good or bad luck, but Buddha did not think of it as a preconditioned thing. Instead, he defined it as moral choice and acts based on it. Humans are free to choose which path to take and *karma* can push them forward to the heavenly realm or it may degrade them to the worlds of demons and animals. This cycle is called *samsara* and may transcend into the next life. Good *karma* is achieved through merit (*punya*), mostly in helping the monks by providing them with food and saffron robes. The final goal, however, is not to have a better life condition – although many day-to-day Buddhist have that in mind – but to reach *nirvana*.

Buddhist denominations

In time, Buddhism split into several denominations. Buddha himself did not leave any successor, as something like a succession line would be rather unusual for a religion that strives for nothingness. He left his disciples that will make *Sangha* soon after his death. The three great traditions within Buddhism elaborate on the Buddha's teaching, each in its own way. This occurred mostly when Buddhists started to expand outside the Indian borders and when they encountered new religions and new customs. Already after the death of Buddha, two forms of Buddhism occurred. One is Theravada (known as the Original Teaching), the conservative way which holds fast the Buddha's teachings and emphasizes monasticism and makes a hero of the *arhat*, the person who has attained enlightenment. Theravada is based on the Orthodox Pali canon and is today present almost exclusively in Sri Lanka, Myanmar and Thailand, with a revival in some areas of India as a religion that is particularly relevant for the fight against the caste system. Otherwise, Buddhism became extinct in India at beginning of the 1000s, and Buddhists had to flee to Tibet and other surrounding countries due to threats from Brahman extremists and Islamic invaders. Theravada is in many ways a more scholarly tradition and could not be established as a folk religion. It went through a number of compromises and adjustments to stay compelling religious teachings for those countries where Theravada still prevails.

Another school is Mahayana (the Great Vehicle) which consists of many other kinds of schools like Zen Buddhism or Vajrayana/Lamaism/Tibetan Buddhism. Mahayana was formed between 100 BCE and 100 CE. The spiritual hero in Mahayana Buddhism is the *bodhisattva*, or "enlightenment being," who vows to aid all beings in their quest for enlightenment. *Bodhisattvas* are of typical Buddhist origin, not of Hinduist tradition, and as such a product of Buddhist thinking of compassionate beings that help others to achieve soteriological salvation, even if that means their temporary deceleration in their process of enlightenment. It is compassion that drives these beings to act, although they know it is illusionary to act in this world. However, it also means there is no particular difference between the worldly existential flow (*samsara*) and its end (*nirvana*). Indeed, in a sort of semi-deification of Buddha, Mahayana considers him still to be present as a benevolent force in the world, although he is in the final *nirvana*. Mahayana understands the historical Buddha as an earthly expression of the *Dharma* and teaches a complex cosmology, where Buddha is present in three bodies (*triyaka*), in three dimensions: earthly, heavenly, and transcendent. The first body is *Nirmanakaya*, Buddha's earthly body where he is a mortal as any other human being. The second is *Sambhogakaya* or heavenly body which exists in paradise, and the third is *Dharmakaya* where Buddha is completely identical with ultimate truth. Interestingly, many of such notions are similar to Christian teachings, which occurred around the same time. Until today, this branch of Buddhism is present in China, Japan, Korea, Siberia, Tibet, and some areas of South-Eastern Asia.

Mahayana has a source of "secret knowledge" that was not supposed to be revealed to the world before. These are mostly apocrypha and, in comparison to Theravada, its teachings are more adjusted to popular religious rites and traditions across Asia. Missionaries accepted local beliefs and incorporated them into Buddhism. As a consequence, a myriad of various Buddhist teachings occurred through the Mahayana school, based on several revised scriptures (*sutras*). Among the most famous ones is the Lotus Sutra where a novel idea of Buddha's eternal immortality emerges. Around 150 AD a philosopher Nagarjuna formed a school that would be used as a foundation of Mahayana. His most famous teaching is that all things are void of real existence, at least in a form in which people see things around them. Everything is, in fact, the same in this doctrine of emptiness (*sunyavada*) where even *samsara* and *nirvana* may be understood as the same thing, albeit *nirvana* is substantially more perfect. The objection of material realities calls for more nuanced meditative experiences such as yoga (*Yogacara*).

Another important aspect of Buddhist novelties here is striving to become *bodhisattva* through the Six Perfections: (1) generosity (*dana*); (2) morality (*sila*); (3) patience (*ksnti*); (4) courage (*virya*); (5) meditation (*samadhi*) and (6) wisdom (*prajna*). In advanced stages, bodhisattvas were identified with Buddha's heavenly body. The two most important *bodhisattvas* known to men is Avalokitesvara and Manjushri, the second one being a spiritual father of Tibetan monks. A myriad of other Buddhas and *bodhisattvas* are imagined in Mahayana Buddhism, often depicted in diagrams called a *mandala*. Amitabha Buddha is of particular importance for East Asia, where belief in him coincides with a desire to reach the Pure Land in the west.

Vajrayana Buddhism shares the *bodhisattva* ideal with Mahayana but is distinctive in its emphasis on tantric teachings and rituals. That is why it is also known as Tantra or Mantrayana Buddhism. While adopting Mahayana teachings and cosmology, Vajrayana is also based on arcane treatises from India called Tantras. They are used in forms of mandalas and chants or mantras accessible only through knowing a secret script and language known as the twilight language (*sadhyabhasa*). It is learned in a monastery by a teacher – Lama.

Zen Buddhism is today a favorite kind of Buddhism in the West. It is based on a Buddha's legend. Buddha was approached by a disciple who gave him a flower and asked him to reveal to him the secret of his teachings. Buddha held the flower high in the air and just looked at it in silence. He wanted to show that wisdom is not in smart words but focused reflection of everyday things and events. This gave rise to what we call today Zen Buddhism, the school that teaches its followers not only to read books and think, but also to focus for many years after which enlightenment may occur instantly (*satori*). Because it is not a conscious activity, Zen Buddhism calls for deep meditation, but also humor, artistic expressions, non-conventional behavior. In time, Zen developed two major branches: *Soto*, which is exclusively meditative, and *Rinzai*, which uses other techniques too. Zen is today a Japanese practice that came originally from China and Korea.

The History of Buddhism

Soon after the death of the Buddha, his monks organized the First Buddhist Council (c. 483 BCE) for the purpose of preserving his teachings. It was followed by several additional councils, all of which served to establish the Buddhist tradition. For a time, Buddhism thrived in India—and especially during the third century BCE with the support of King Ashoka. His kingdom was among the largest in the Indian Subcontinent as he was a successful warrior king. His encounter with Buddhism made him repent and accept the peaceful religious lifestyle. During his reign Buddhism became an imperial religion, receiving state support. Ashoka sponsored missionary efforts that brought Buddhism to southern India, Sri Lanka, and Southeast Asia, transferred through a script written in the Pali language. In India, Buddhism had huge schools and universities such as the one at Nalanda.

By 400 CE Buddhism and its teachings had arrived in China and Korea. It continued to spread throughout Asia, though in India its influence began to wane in the eighth century with the emergence of Hindu devotional cults, which proved to be more popular, and with the new Islamic and Arabic conquerors who pushed Buddhism out of Afghanistan and North-West India. Together with Hinduism, the subsequent Islamic rulers in India's north managed to completely oust Buddhism from India. This did not occur in Sri Lanka, where many Indian Buddhists found refuge. Under the leadership of the monk Buddhaghosa, the Pali Canon was made there, and he compiled doctrines and practices of the Theravada Buddhism known as *Visuddhimagga* or Path of Purification. In Sri Lanka, Buddhism was closely attached to political power and remains so until today. The same ideas of politically relevant Buddhism and Theravada doctrines were imported by missionaries to Myanmar and Thailand, where Buddhism remains the official religion. The same occurred in Laos, Cambodia and Vietnam, although with a larger mix with Mahayana and local indigenous religions.

In China, Buddhism was in conflict with Confucianism and Daoism. It was not a potent religion for imperial domination, but it answered many questions of the meaning of life and afterlife which Confucianism did not. Buddhism also had many similarities to Daoism, although Buddhism is more complex philosophically. While being one of three religions in China, particularly favored by the T'ang dynasty, Buddhism did not achieve total "Chinese" character in itself and it was viciously fought against during the Cultural Revolution and hardline Communist power.

From China and through Korea, Buddhism arrived in Japan in the sixth century. Japanese Buddhist were very devotional to the Pure Land school and Amitabha Buddha or Amida as it is known in Japan. In the 13th century, this devotion was reformed by Nichiren and Lotus Sutra became the primary focus of worship and discipline through the mantra *Namu myoho renge kyo* (Honor to the Lotus Sutra of the True Dharma). Japanese Buddhist developed strong ties with the community and discouraged monastic life. As a major counter-school, Zen Buddhism rooted in Japan in the 13th century.

Buddhism was largely unknown in the West until the nineteenth century. It assumed a presence in America in 1893 at the World Parliament of Religions in Chicago, attended by religious leaders from around the world. Another factor that promoted Buddhism in America was the immigration of Asian Buddhists. Today, Western Buddhism has a special character of pure Buddhist teachings, not adorned with history of long cultural and religion additions. Yet, the Western Buddhism also distorts the true meanings of some Buddha's messages due to misunderstanding of relevant conditions and ways of life.

Buddhism contributed largely to Asian art, architecture, music and cuisine. The earliest forms of Buddhist art did not depict Buddha in its human form. Following the early warnings from Buddha himself who did not want to be deified, the Buddhists used signs and symbols that adorned scripts. This is known as the aniconic phase of Buddhist art that lasted until the 1st century CE. After that, iconic art started to emerge with anthropomorphic representations of Buddha, bodhisattvas and other beings of the Buddhist cosmology. This is what Buddhist art is still famous for worldwide, particularly considering the presentation of Buddha sitting in a lotus position as can be seen in various temples, monuments, or *thangka* Tibetan paintings on cotton or silk.

Buddhist countries are adorned with *stupas*, *viharas* and temples. The *stupa* is a closed structure built for veneration or keeping of Buddha's relics or remnants of other famous Buddhist teachers. Later, they would develop into stupa halls (*chaitya-grihas*), where people can also gather and circumnavigate around these stupas. *Vihara* is a Buddhist monastery that contains residence quarters for monks and nuns. It was developed in beautiful local art after the first *Vihara* was built next to the Nalanda University. The third kind of Buddhist architecture are temples which usually contain statues of Buddha in its center and various depictions and frescoes of Buddha's life or various beings and deities.

In the temples, monks and nuns chant prayers. Chanting is an important aspect of Buddhist practice and rituals. Many genres emerged for the musical recitation of sacred texts written in Pali, Sanskrit or Tibetan language. In Tibet, a specific kind of chanting is based on throat singing; in many Theravada countries, repetition of various Buddha's names or magic formula *Om mani padme hum* forms the essence of chanting. In Japan, a specific Shomyo chanting is a major characteristic of local Buddhism. But it is not only chanting that is involved in Buddhist music: the rituals are accompanied by a wide range of instruments, bells, drums, *shakuhachi*, *tingsha*, cymbals and for meditation singing bowls are used. In religious ceremonies, basic chanting has been developed over centuries in various hymns.

Buddhism as a Way of Life

Buddhists identify themselves as such by reciting the Three Refuges: "I take refuge in the *Buddha*. I take refuge in the *Dharma*. I take refuge in the *Sangha*." In doing so, they testify to their commitment to the Buddha and his teachings and their reliance on the entire community of Buddhists. Buddhists also embrace the Five Precepts, prohibitions of killing, stealing, sexual immorality, lying, and the use of intoxicants. Another basic feature of the Buddhist way of life is the Eightfold Path, which the Buddha offered as a prescription for the elimination of suffering. Taken together, these represent the foundation of the Buddhist way of life. It has a very practical meaning. For instance, Buddhists would be ready to endure physical pain with patience and reflection of one's mind but, of course, Buddhism does not forbid any medication. In a general sense, Buddhism recommends vegetarianism as the most potent medication for one's body, which is reflected in Buddhism's radical non-violence.

Buddhist Monasticism

Buddhism was more close to Jainism and in Buddha's own time, the Jain master Mahaviri was reorganizing that faith. Jainism at the time was more drawn to the cult of heroes than the cult of (Hindu) gods and was oriented to ascetic cleansing. They all came from the same dialectic heroism but while Jainism wanted to support moral and ascetic rules in a conservative manner, Buddhism turned to critically check and reform these same presuppositions. Instead of asceticism, Buddhism accepted monasticism as a way of sacred life – the order of monks is called Sangha. Buddhism recognizes both male (*bhikkhu*) and female (*bhikkhuni*) monasticism, although the nuns are often discriminated against and sometimes even not recognized as such in some countries. This discrimination is not theologically contested, as Buddha recognized the *bhikkhuni* order when his stepmother Mahaprajapati asked for his permission to ordain herself. They are to live a simple life of wandering asceticism but in close relation with the local community. They should share compassion and Buddha's teachings and live in monasteries that spread very quickly everywhere where Buddhists dwelt.

A Buddhist monk leaves his family and friends and dedicates his life to mediation and prayer according to certain very detailed rules (*patimokkha*). These rules are part of a larger guidebook of monastic life, i.e. the Buddhist monastic rule known as *Vinaya*. In different areas, *Vinaya* is further developed in regional rules. While Theravada monks would follow the original *Vinaya*, those in East Asia follow *Dharmaguptaka* and those in Tiber and Himalayas stick to Mulasarvastivada.

It is a very long list of how everyday activities should be done, with a particular emphasis on details such as the type of robes monks should wear. Most monks in contemporary Buddhist have to accept celibacy; but in some areas, this is not compulsory, such as in Japan after the Meiji era, when monks and nuns could decide themselves if they want to marry or stay celibate. They live in monasteries and accept the gifts of faithful ones, as a "field of merit", a living example to the ordinary people. The monastic canons ask for no private property and begging for food. Their only "private" things are a saffron robe, sandals, a rosary, a razor for shaving beard and head, one needle and a water colander, which helps them not to swallow a fly by accident. The food they are given has to be eaten by noon. They are vegetarians, although, in theory, they may eat meat if that is given to them. Of course, that seldom happens. Buddhist believers give them regular food as they see it as receiving merits. It often happens that men spend several days, weeks, months or even years in monasteries to be closer to enlightenment or to show gratitude to their parents. After that, they return to normal life.

Those who decide to stay, go through several stages of monastic ordination. First is *Samanera* when novices stay in the monastery and learn about Buddhism. They should observe the Ten Precepts but not the monastic rule. Higher ordinations are called *upasampada* which brings full monastic status and obligation to follow all rules.

Buddhist Meditation

Many Buddhists, both monastics and laypeople, practice meditation in a variety of forms. It is a particularly important part of the Buddhist life, as Buddha attained enlightenment while meditating. This is often depicted in a statue of Buddha in meditating/lotus position. Meditation and yoga are borrowed concepts from the Brahman religion in India, with a significant Buddhist twist. This twist is a new meditation technique called *Vipassana* or Insight meditation, where one makes a deep reflexive analysis of own state of mind. Some techniques, such as *Shamatha* and *Vipassana*, calm and stabilize the mind, allowing one to watch its movements with a nonjudging and detached attitude. Some are more complex, involving the contemplation of mandalas, recitation of mantras, and the visualization of deities. In a broader sense, mediation is *bhavana*, characterized by being abstract, while the term *dhanam* denotes introvert mindfulness of nothingness. In meditation, it is necessary to attain a high degree of control of the mind. The mind should be focused on here and now and it should practice radical mindfulness and consciousness. Meditation is practically possible in the unity of body and mind: while sitting in the lotus position, one can breathe properly and prepare the mind for deep presence. In the beginning stages, a novice may be allowed to look at a particular object and focus on its properties in the most nuanced manner. After that, meditation can focus on present reality without any visual object. Four measureless states are among the most popular meditation subjects: meditation practitioner focus their mind on loving kindness (*metta*), compassion (*karuna*), sympathetic joy (*mudita*) and equanimity (*upekkha*).

A final goal of a Buddhist contemplation is to reach nothingness as the meditation should not be benevolent for one's spirit or soul, but for creating a sense of nothingness, where one can detect things as they are, without a theoretical or practical understanding of these things. A need to internally flee from the world is based on a powerful and intimate understanding of suffering. Meditation practices vary. Still, the Buddhist mediation centers try not to have Buddha's images or statues. Focus on deities, physical position, breathing techniques or yoga are not so much important in a proper Buddhist contemplation. Experience of "out of this world" mediation contributes to one of the essential emotions of Buddhists, but it should be discouraged in the early stages of meditation practise as the mind should exercise focus. The formal Buddhist system of meditations is the Eight stages of Trance (*Jhana*). The first three *jhanas* are sphere of the pure form where the mind is oriented to detach, to focus on rapture and joy and to concentrate. Other *jhanas* are sphere of formlessness where concentration gradually gives place to infinite space and infinite consciousness, to nothingness and a stage which is neither perception nor non-perception. Finally, after the eight *jhana* one can reach the attainment of cessation by touching nirvana with the body. Connected to both spheres are gradually attained psychic powers, telepathy, psychokinesis etc.

Pilgrimages and Rituals

Another Buddhist practice is pilgrimage to holy places and especially the places the Buddha's birth, enlightenment, first sermon, and death. In many cases, pilgrimage destination sites feature stupas containing relics of the Buddha or Buddhist saints. These rituals and practices vary and Buddhism has no clear rites for religious experience. Buddha himself suggested pilgrimages for exercising the sense of spiritual need. Pilgrimage is thus very beneficial in Buddhism and relies on a long tradition of pilgrimages in the Indian Subcontinent. Early Buddhists focused on four main pilgrimage sites, still favorite for Buddhist pilgrims. First is Lumbini, the birthplace of Siddhartha Gautama, which is currently a town in southern Nepal. Second is Bodh Gaya, the central Buddhist place of worship and pilgrimage. It is within the Mahabodhi Temple in the contemporary Indian state of Bihar. Bodhi is a tree under which Buddha meditated and reached enlightenment. Thus, this is also the holiest place for Buddhists because it was here where the first account of reaching Nirvana occurred. The third place of pilgrimage is Sarnath in the Indian state of Uttar

Pradesh. It is the place where Buddha held his first sermon and where he explained the main tenets of Buddhism, including his teachings on the Middle Way, Four Noble Truths and Eightfold Path. Finally, there is Kusinagara, also in Uttar Pradesh, a place where Buddha died and where he finished his recurring cycle of lives. Next to these four, Buddhist canons mention another four pilgrimage sites that make together Eight splendid sites (Attha mahathanani). Additional four are (1) Sravasti, once the capital of old Indian state, and a place where Buddha spent most of his life and also performed miracles; (2) Rajgir, place where Mahavira and Buddha taught and where Nalanda University was founded; (3) Sankassa, where King Ashoka built beautiful temples and where a visit of Buddha is commemorated by a stupa; and (4) Vaishali, where Mahavira was born and which may be said to be among the first Buddhist republics. All eight places are extremely popular pilgrimage destinations for all Buddhists. However, they are situated in a country where Buddhism is a minority religion. Elsewhere, Buddhist pilgrimages are mostly tied to famous monasteries and temples, such as Angkor Wat in Cambodia, the Four Sacred Mountains in China, Mount Kailash and Potala Palace in Tibet, Borobodur in Indonesia, Swayamnhunath in Nepal, Ayutthaya in Thailand and many more. Pilgrims may go there to develop their spirituality as Buddha himself suggested. Others want to fulfil a vow, recover from illness, do merit, or simply travel. Customs and types of pilgrimages vary, but they are mostly connected to chanting, receiving blessings from the monks, walking the circular paths around natural sites or *stupas*.

Perhaps the most popular of all Buddhist practices is the observance of holidays and festivals. The most popular of these is Vesak, a celebration of the birth of the Buddha. It is celebrated on the first full moon day in May, and in many countries, Vesak is also a day of enlightenment and nirvana, although there are special holidays for both. On Vesak day, Buddhist assemble in temples before dawn and hoist yellow flags and sing songs full of praise for the three most important Buddhist concepts in life: Buddha, Dharma and Sangha. They give symbolic and simple offerings to monks. Devotees would also make charities to the poor, elderly, and sick, bringing them gifts or just share happiness. On Vesak, Buddhist eat vegetarian food and should observe the Eight Precepts.

The second most important holiday in the Buddhist religious calendar is the Magha Puja. It celebrates the gathering between Buddha and his 1250 first disciples who will soon form the body of Sangha. That is why Magha is sometimes called the Sangha Day. Buddhist join long processions with candles and it is a day when laypeople make merit by making food, meditating, read Buddhist texts. It is mostly celebrated today in South-Eastern Asia, particularly in Thailand and Laos.

Asala, which commemorates the anniversary of the preaching of the Buddha's first sermon and that is why it is called also Dharma Day. It is mostly celebrated in the Theravada countries. On this day, Buddhist make offerings to the temples and listen to sermons. Parinirvana Day celebrates the day when Buddha reached complete Nirvana or Parinirvana after he died. Meditation and visits to temples are compulsory activity for this day, along with the reading from the Nirvana Sutra. Although this is a day of common Buddhist significance, it is more celebrated in the Mahayana countries. Bodhi Day is furthermore a holiday that commemorates the historical occurrence of the Buddha's enlightenment under the Bodhi tree. Many other holidays exist in the Buddhist religious calendar, some with a more regional or local significance. In general, Theravada Buddhists would celebrate more the holidays connected to the Buddha's life and his teachings, while Mahayana Buddhists would be more keen to join holiday processions dedicated to various bodhisattvas or even syncretistic events in China, Korea and Japan.

SUGGESTED READINGS, WEBLINKS, AND OTHER MEDIA

Readings

- Buswekk, Robert E. Jr., ed. *Encyclopedia of Buddhism.* New York: Macmillan Reference USA, 2004.

- Byrom, Thomas. *The Dhammapada: The Sayings of the Buddha.* New York: Vintage, 1976.

- Gombrich, Richard F. *How Buddhism Began. The Conditioned Genesis of the Early Teachings.* London and New York: Routledge, 1998.

- Gombrich, Richard F. *Theravada Buddhism. A Social History from Ancient Benares to Modern Colombo.* London and New York: Routledge, 2006.

- Prebish, Charles and Keown, Damien. Introducing Buddhism. 2nd ed. New York: Routledge, 2010.

- Keown, Damien. *Buddhism: A Very Short Introduction.* Oxford: Oxford University Press, 1996

- Lopez, Donald. *Buddhist Scriptures.* London: Penguin, 2004.

- Min, Bahadur Shakya. *The Iconography of Nepalese Buddhism.* Buddha Dharma Education Association, 1996

- Phra Brahmapundit. *Common Buddhist Text. Guidance and Insight from Buddha.* Wang Noi: Mahachulalongkornrajavidyalaya University, 2018.

- Skilton, Andrew. *A Concise History of Buddhism*. Birmingham, England: Windhorse, 1994.
- Snelling, John. *The Buddhist Handbook: The Complete Guide to Buddhist Schools, Teaching, Practice and History*. Rochester: Inner Traditions, 1998.
- Strong, John S. *The Buddha: A Short Biography*. Oxford: Oneworld, 2001.
- Suzuki, Shunryu. *Zen Mind, Beginner's Mind*. New York: Weatherhill, 1997.
- Williams, Paul. *Mahayana Buddhism: The Doctrinal Foundations*. 2nd ed. New York: Routledge, 2008.
- Wright, Robert. *Why Buddhism is True. The Science and Philosophy of Meditation and Enlightenment*. New York and London: Simon & Schuster, 2017

Weblinks

- Wikipedia Buddhism Portal—en.wikipedia.org/wiki/Portal:Buddhism
- BuddhaNet—buddhanet.net/pdf_file/deep_ecology.pdf—Buddhist and the environment
- Access to Insight: Readings in Theravada Buddhism—www.accesstoinsight.org/tipitaka/index.html
- The Berzin Archives (Mahayana and Vajrayana Texts from Tibet—www.berzinarchives.com/web/en/index.html

Other Media

- *The Life of the Buddha* (2003), 50 min., www.insight-media.com (also available at www.youtube.com/watch?v=zFbjDcz_CbU)
- *The Buddha* (2010), 120 min., www.pbs.org/thebuddha/ *The Robert A. F. Thurman Collection (On Tibet/On Buddhism)* (1999), 460 min.

SACRED TEXTS

www.sacred-texts.com/bud/milinda.htm
The Questions of King Milinda. A translation of an early Buddhist text in which a monk describes Buddhist teaching on the nature of the self to an ancient Indo-Greek king.

www.sacred-texts.com/bud/jt/index.htm

The Jataka Tales. A charming collection of stories and anecdotes that detail the previous lives of the Buddha.

www.sacred-texts.com/bud/sbe49/index.htm
Buddhist Mahayana Texts. A number of key Mahayana works, including a complete translation of the *Buddhacharita.*

www.sacred-texts.com/bud/glg/index.htm
The Gateless Gate. A presentation on early Zen *koans.*

KEY TERMS AND DEFINITIONS

anatman (un-aat-mun; Sanskrit) The doctrine that there is no independent, eternal self or soul underlying human existence.

arhat (Sanskrit, "one who is worthy") In Theravada Buddhism, one who has attained enlightenment.

bhikku (bi-khu) A Buddhist monk.

bodhicitta (bow-dhi-chit-ta; Sanskrit, "the awakening mind or heart") In Mahayana Buddhism, the wise and compassionate intention to attain Buddhahood for the sake of all other sentient beings.

bodhisattva (bow-dhi-sut-tva; Sanskrit, "the awakening mind or heart") One who is on the verge of enlightenment. In Mahayana Buddhism, a bodhisattva is one who has taken a "bodhisattva vow" to remain in samsara to work for the enlightenment of all sentient beings.

Buddha (bood-dha; Sanskrit, "the Awakened One") A fully enlightened being.

Chan or **Zen** (chah-aahn/Zehn) Respectively, the Chinese and Japanese names for the "meditation" school of Buddhism that values meditative experience far and above doctrine.

Dhammapada (dhur-ma pa-da) A collection of sayings of the Buddha found in the Pali Canon.

Dharma (dhur-mah; Sanskrit, "that which upholds") In the Buddhist context Dharma refers to Buddhist teaching and to Buddhism as a religion.

dukkha (doo-kah; Pali, "suffering") Usually translated as "suffering," it can also be understood as the anxiety, unease, and dissatisfaction caused by desire.

Four Noble Truths The four truths that form the basis of the Dharma: Suffering is inherent in human life, suffering is caused by desire, there can be an end to desire, and the way to end desire is the Noble Eightfold Path.

Impermanence The Buddha's doctrine that all phenomena are in a constant state of change.

Interdependent Origination (Sanskrit: *pratitya-samutpada,* "arising on the ground of a preceding cause") The doctrine that reality is a complex of interrelated and interdependent phenomena in which nothing exists independently; instead, the origination and continuing existences of all things depend on other things.

karma (kur-mah; Sanskrit, "action") Action; also, the consequences of action.

lama (laah-mah; Tibetan) In Tibet, a teacher of the Dharma.

Mahayana (muh-haah-yaah-na; Sanskrit, "great vehicle") Also known as the "Great Vehicle," Mahayana is the form of Buddhism most prominent in China, Japan, Mongolia, Tibet, and Korea.

mandala (muhn-daah-la; Sanskrit "circle") Typically, a circular diagram representing the entire universe, often used as an aid in meditation.

mantra (mun-trah; Sanskrit) A sacred sound or syllable used as a focus for meditation, as an invocation of a deity, or as a protective spell.

Middle Way The Buddha's principle of the path between the extremes of self-indulgence and enlightenment that leads to enlightenment.

nirvana (nihr-vaah-nah; Sanskrit, an "extinguishing" or "blowing out") The ultimate goal of Buddhist practice, nirvana is the extinguishing of desire and the suffering it causes.

Noble Eightfold Path The Buddha's prescription for a way of life that leads to enlightenment. Based on the principle of the Middle Way, it is also defined by eight virtues.

parinirvana (pah-ree-nihr-vaah-nah; Sanskrit, "supreme release") The full entry into nirvana that occurs at the death of one who has achieved nirvana in his or her lifetime.

samsara (sum-saah-ra; Sanskrit, "continuous flow") The cycle of life, death, and rebirth or reincarnation; also, the world of phenomena in which this cycle appears.

sangha (suhn-ghaah; Pali, "community") The worldwide community of Buddhists. Alternatively, the order of Buddhist monks or the membership of a particular Buddhist congregation.

skandhas (skuhn-dhaahs; Sanskrit, "heaps" or "bundles") The five components (body, perceptions, feelings, innate tendencies, and thought) that give rise to a sense of self.

stupa (stooh-puh; Sanskrit, "heap") A reliquary mound in which the relics of the Buddha or of a Buddhist saint are buried and venerated.

sutra (sooh-trah; Sanskrit, "a thread") Verses of text or scripture.

Theravada (thair-ah-vaah-duh; Pali, "the Way of the Elders") The form of Buddhism that is most prominent in Sri Lanka, Cambodia, Laos, and Vietnam.

Three Marks of Existence The Buddha's teachings on impermanence, suffering, and No-Self, the nonexistence of an eternal unchanging self or soul.

Tripitaka (See *Pali Canon.*)

upaya (ooh-paah-ya; Sanskrit, "expedient means") A form of Buddhist practice that encourages the creative application of wisdom to whatever circumstances one is in to assist in easing suffering or cultivating insight.

Vajrayana (vaah-jiraah-yaah-nah; Sanskrit, "Diamond Vehicle," or "Thunderbolt Vehicle") Often described as a form of Mahayana, Vajrayana is the most prominent form of Buddhism in Tibet and Nepal.

ACTIVITIES AND ASSIGNMENTS

1. Is there any comfort to be found in the Buddhist acknowledgment that life is defined by suffering? Does suffering, the first of the Four Noble Truths, mean that Buddhism is a pessimistic religion? Or is it simply more realistic?

2. Buddhism is a tradition that says you have "no-soul," or *anatta*, but that also says nuns are subservient to monks, that one requires bad karma to be reborn as a woman, and that women may cause things to be ritually polluted. Is this a contradiction? How do we make sense of the reality of women in Buddhist countries in light of the doctrine of *anatta*?

3. Tantric Buddhism involves the practice of ritual and sexual yogas, one goal of which is to "transcend dualistic thinking, including the dualisms of proper and improper, male and female, wisdom and compassion, nirvana

and samsara, Buddhas and non-Buddhas." Is this approach an extension of the doctrine of *shunyata* and the idea that everything is empty? Or are Tantric rituals actually a degradation of Buddhist values?

4. "Mindfulness meditation" is often presented as a secular form of mental training to increase focus and reduce anxiety. But some argue that mindfulness meditation is rooted in Buddhist religious practices. Is meditation inherently a Buddhist activity? How do you determine the difference between "Buddhist meditation" and "secular meditation"? Is there a difference at all?

CHAPTER 5

Sikhism

Sikhism is the third largest and youngest of the world religions. Like many religions, there is a general discrepancy in their teachings. While Sikhism is a religion that preaches love, peace, and equality, it also asks its followers to be equipped with swords. Sikhism originates from the Punjab area, which is now partitioned between India and Pakistan. Punjab translates as "area of five rivers" and it is the cradle of one of the oldest civilizations in the world, as well as the birthplace of many cultures and religions. Here the Indus Valley Civilization came to be, one of the oldest in the world. This was also the area where Hinduism, Buddhism, Jainism, Islam and some other local religions left a strong mark which is visible among Sikhs as well.

Sikhs understand their faith as a way of life that follows the teachings of Guru Nanak or the truth, through meditation, sharing, and honest living. Sikhs call for an honest living and honest way of earning for life. Whatever they earn, they should share with other people. Only after that may they meditate on God. Every Sikh believes in one God and thus Sikhism is a monotheistic religion, albeit a pantheistic one. Usual misconceptions about Sikhism is that it is a part of Hinduism, as Guru Nanak was born in a Hindu family. In the Western world, many people perceive Sikhism as part of Islam. Many Muslims do not cut their beard and they also wear turbans, so the physical resemblance makes them think that Sikhs are a form of Islamic school.

There are approximately 25 million Sikhs in the world today, which makes about two per cent of India's population, and so by virtue of its size alone, Sikhism is among the major religions of the world. Sikhs make 60 percent of Punjab's population. Theologically, Sikhism's intermixing of concepts that are common to some Hindu traditions on one hand and Islam on the other make it a very interesting subject for the comparative study of religion. And with nearly 2 million Sikhs living outside of India, it is a global tradition that has a significant impact on the world.

The Teachings of Sikhism

The term "Sikh" is derived from an ancient Sanskrit term that means "disciple." Sikhs call their religion "Sikhi", "Gursikhi" and "Gurmat". Sikhs are thus disciples, specifically of the ten Gurus, beginning with Guru Nanak and ending with Guru Gobind Singh, founder of the Khalsa. Since then, Sikhs have been disciples of Sri Guru Granth Sahib, the traditional name for their most important sacred text, the Adi Granth. The relationship with Gurus is what is at the very core of the Sikh religion. A guru is a teacher or spiritual guide. Guru is able to connect people with God, and thus the God is Gur Prasad or known by the Guru's Grace. That is the aim of Sikhism.

Nanak was born in 1469 c.e. in a small village near Lahore, in today's Pakistan, in a Hindu merchant family. Tradition holds it that Guru Nanak had an adult's man laugh when he was a baby and as a teenager, he listened to Hindu saints and Sufi Muslim preachers. Later, he settled in Sultanpur where he worked for the government. The political life disgusted him because of all the money and power involved. He also developed a strong aversion to the predominant caste system in Indian society. According to tradition, Nanak became recognized as a spiritual leader early in his life. When Nanak was about thirty years old, he experienced a revelation of God, who told him to "rejoice in my name and teach others to do so." He travelled through India and Persia and the Middle East and visited many temples and made many contacts with other religious traditions. The message of his three-day mystical journey was that there is no Hindu nor Muslim, but just God, one who spoke in favor of humanity and against caste, ethnic and religious divisions. Later, Guru Nanak would warn to "accept all humans as your equals, and let them be your only sect". Guru Nanak spent the next twenty years travel-ing and teaching, until at about the age of fifty he built a new settlement called Kartarpur in what is now Pakistan. Here he and his followers formed the first Sikh community, or Panth, and instituted the lifestyle that has characterized Sikhism to this day. He died twenty years later in 1539.

Nine gurus followed Nanak with the same messages about One God and his love for equality among humans. Several of them were martyred. The last, tenth, Guru Gobind Rai is known as the final human guru. He started a new Sikh community called the Khalsa and ended the line of human gurus by making the Guru Granth

Sahib, the Sikh Holy Book, the last living guru. Compiled by Guru Arjan in 1603–1604, the Adi Granth contains the works of his four predecessor Gurus, along with his own hymns and various works by poets. This may be a single holy book of great world religions that is written by its founders. It also contains writings of Muslims, Hindus and references to Judaism, Buddhism, and Christianity. Before his death in 1708, the tenth Guru Gobind Singh ended the line of human gurus by bestowing the name of Guru to the Adi Granth, turning it to Guru Granth Sahib. Thus, it is at the same time the holiest book of Sikhism and the leader of Sikhism. It is considered to be the current living Guru, treated with extreme respect and care. Through the centuries, the Adi Granth has occupied a central place in Sikhism. Whereas the Gurus were once the authorities on religious matters, now Sikhs consult the Adi Granth. Other texts that most Sikhs would classify as scripture include the Dasam Granth and the rahit-namas, collectively called the Rahit, which contains the ideals of the Khalsa that dictate the proper way to live.

Sikhism considers itself monotheistic faith. The Adi Granth's opening consists of only two words: "Ik Onkar", which means "There is only one God". The focus is on One, very much in accordance with the Muslim Tawhid. It is the most important belief in Sikhism. This God is formless, genderless, universal, beyond description and comprehension. It is quite a different concept of God in comparison with the Abrahamic religions. He permeates everything and is all of reality. No image may ever be close to depicting the One God, so Sikhs use the sacred symbol of Ik Onkar. Some Sikhs have a name for One God: Waheguru, the Wondrous God. Guru Nanak and his successors constantly stressed that the One may be understood in many different ways. God is considered to be a Creator, who created the universe with One word (Oang). No religion may claim they possess the complete truth and the One may be called in different names, such as Vishnu, Allah, Yahweh. There is no need to fight over who is the true God, as they were all the same One. In describing the One God, Guru Nanak said: "There is but one God. His name is Truth (…) He is without hate (…) He is beyond the cycle of births and deaths. He is Self Illuminated". It is translated into several names of God: Karta Purakh (the Doer); Nir Bhao (without fear) and Nir Vair (without hate or enmity).

From the idea of One God also stems the need to recognize all mankind, whether Muslim or Hindu as one: "The same God is the creator and nourisher of all; recognize no distinction among them; the temple and the mosque are the same, so are the Hindu worship and Muslim prayer. Human beings are all one", in words of Guru Gobind Singh. As God has no gender, there is also no difference between men and women. In fact, Sikhism was among the first major world religions to make the radical suggestion that women are equal to men as human beings. Women fought in battles, led religious services, and were long-reigning leaders in the Sikh community.

Sikh eschatology does not include preconditions for entering heaven or hell. Some Sikhs consider heaven and hell as part of this world. And while the belief in One God has a tremendous echo of Islam, Sikh eschatology borrows from Indian religions. The soul is constantly reborn in this world, in different forms. Sikhs believe in reincarnation and karma, but this karma is modified by God. One may not choose the life to be born into (this is the act of karma) but God ensures that everyone has an opportunity to become a good person if they try. Sikhism is a religious path to spiritual liberation—"release" from samsara, the cycle of death and rebirth—through devotional praise of God.

God is immanent in creation through hukam, the divine order. It is through hukam, together with God's grace, that God asserts the divine will and communicates truth. Having received God's grace, the task is to respond in loving devotion through meditation on the nature of God. Spiritual liberation, or Mukti (similar to Hindu moksha), the ultimate objective of the religious path, brings about the eternal, infinitely blissful state of being in the presence of God. One does this by realizing being part of God already and letting go of one's ego.

Sikhism is pantheistic religion, as Sikhs believe that God is the universe we exist in. However, God is truth before time (Aad Sach), as the Creator was true and real before time started. With the beginning of time, God became also Jugaad Sach, or Truth when time began. He is also present all the time and sheds the Truth at any time. He will also exist in the future.

Humans, however, have to become aware of it because they are distracted by Maya or illusion. Maya is anything that takes one's mind off God. Maya is the reason for the cycle of death and rebirth. Guru Nanak argued that Maya built a wall between people and God. This wall harbors five "thieves": Lust (Kham); Anger (Krodh); Greed (Lobh); Attachment (Moh); and Pride (Ahankar). Sikhs would do well if one avoids these five thieves. God is believed to dwell within nature and within human beings and thus is imminent, personal, and approachable through loving devotion. Human beings, however, beset by haumai (lit. I-Myself), "self-reliance" or "pride," are inclined to be self-centered. The quest for spiritual liberation is a constant struggle between haumai and the call to live in accordance with the will of God, who plays an essential role in determining the outcome of this struggle. Haumai separates a person from others and blocks them from realizing the oneness of God. This ego causes people to be lonely, to be negative, to crave power and money. Such a person is called manmukh.

Furthermore, all the problems in the world may be traced to the negative effects of ego. All the conflicts and caused by Maya and haumai, as expressed in Adi Granth's message it is not religion or race but the wealth that divides brothers. There is another path, however. Guru Nanak preached about a life full of compassion, truth, contentment, humility, and love. If meditation on God is added to this, a person may become a Gurmukh (instead of Manmukh), meaning he or she is facing to become a guru. This is furthermore possible through the three pillars.

The three pillars are (1) Naam Japo, which is a meditation on God and recitation and chanting of God's name. This is normally done in the morning and before sleeping. Sikhs are supposed to genuinely reflect on qualities of God while they do this; (2) Kirat Karni, working hard and making an honest living. Guru Nanak said: "Only he who earns his living by the sweat of his brow and shares his earnings with others has discovered the path of righteousness"; (3) Wand Chhakna, sharing the fruits of one's labor with others, by providing free food and donating to the community. The communal meal is called langar, particularly in the Sikh religious place (gurdwara). The public kitchen in a gurdwara is open to everyone who visits, regardless of caste, faith or gender. They serve vegetarian food to all, not because Sikhs are necessarily vegetarian, but because all people, of all diets, can partake. In Guru Nanak's time, the idea of different castes sitting together on the floor and sharing a meal was revolutionary. Famously, emperor Akbar the Great could not visit Guru Arjan before the ruler sat with people and shared a meal in a gurdwara. Guru Nanak warned that an enlightened person is those "who view everyone equally, like the air touching king and beggar alike".

Another important part of the Sikh lifestyle is Seva, the selfless service. Through helping and serving their community, Sikhs may become more humble and overcome their ego. It may be any of things in a local community, like cleaning the gurdwara, preparing and serving food, cleaning dishes or volunteering, building houses, etc. Those who follow such rules may hope for a lesser number of rebirth cycles and reach unity with God.

Guru Gobind Rai, the tenth guru of Sikhism, had the trauma of his father being beheaded. The ninth guru's companions fled and were not to be found because they did not have any distinct look that would differentiate them from Muslims or Hindus. That is why Guru Gobind Rai decided to employ a distinctive look of Sikhs in order for them to uphold the Sikh values. A tradition holds it that Guru Gobind Rai gathered a huge crowd and lifted his sword and asked that anyone prepared to give his life for his faith to come forward. There was a big silence, but the Guru went on repeating his demand. One Sikh finally came forward and followed the Guru into a tent. Shortly after, the Guru appeared alone with his sword covered in blood and asked for a second volunteer. Another Sikh stepped forward and again the Guru took him into the tent and reappeared alone with his sword covered in blood. This was repeated until five Sikhs had offered their heads for the Guru. Finally, the Guru reemerged with all five men dressed piously in blue from a tent as Panj Pyare, the Five Beloved Ones.

These five would be the founders of a new Sikh community called the Khalsa. In a ritual, called Pahul, Guru Gobind Singh prepared Amrit (holy water) in a bowl using a short steel sword. Then the Guru's wife, Mata Sundri, added Patashas (sugar crystals) into the Amrit. After completing prayers, Guru Gobind Singh sprinkled the Amrit on each of the Panj Pyare. The Guru then knelt before the five and asked them to baptize him as well. The Guru said the Panj Pyare would be the embodiment of the Guru himself: "Where there are Panj Pyare, he himself would be present". All of them abandoned their surnames or caste names and adopted a single surname – Singh. It means "lion". The Guru then asked the Five Beloved Ones that he joins their Khalsa, drank the Amrit, and took the name, Guru Gobind Singh. The women were admitted to Khalsa in the same way, but drinking Amrit and taking the surname Kaur, meaning Princess. Khalsa would unite Sikhs into one family, with one surname, without any caste, but with the obligation of defending the weak and promoting justice. Even today, many Sikhs partake in the Amrit ceremony and take the surnames of Singh and Kaur.

The teachings of the Khalsa as outlined in the Rahit and include the requirement to don the Panj Kakaar or the Five Ks, each one symbolizing Sikh identity and loyalty to the Panth: (1) Kes - uncut hair, representing discipline; (2) Kargha, a small comb worn in the hair; (3) Kirpan – a sword to uphold justice and protect the weak, and should be used only to destroy tyrants and oppressors, it must not be used for anything else; (4) Kacchera – a pair of underwear with a drawstring that represents the sexual restraint; (5) Kara - a steel wristlet, whose circular shape represents the infinity of God. All five Ks should be worn until death tied to one's body. Although Sikhs are regularly recognized by their turban, it is not part of Five Ks. It is simply worn to cover Sikh's uncut long hair. However, the turban became part of Sikh identity and carries a very special significance for their community.

The mission of Sikhism is to keep the faith within the social level, in family and local community, and to upkeep the principle of equality among all people. It means that Sikhism strives to apply moral principles and life by moral values. Sikhs do not proselytize but they share their belief by their own example. Only upon someone's question is a Sikh permitted to explain its philosophy and teachings of the gurus.

These principles are aimed to be implemented at the national level, which means enacting laws that should reflect moral precepts of equality, freedom, non-discrimination, and justice. While in the Western world many countries already accept the laws Sikhs would have, in other countries it is still a matter of fight. Sikhs should aim to do charitable giving, protect the rights of the weak, feed the hungry, find medicine for the poor and shelter for the homeless. Sikhs support basic needs provision, solid free education focused on providing equality (including widespread literacy), and free health service.

At the global level, Sikhism tries to establish a Haleemi Raj or compassionate rule that would destroy tyranny and oppression, deliver justice for all people and also freedom for everyone. As Sikhism includes a level of violence, Sikhs stress it is a minimum force envisioned as a rapid response to destroy despots and tyrants and to help distribute humanitarian aid, defend people at risk and rescue them from forced slavery. In a political sense, Sikhs are critical of the UN which does not do this. They perceive this international organization as the one that acts in its own interest and not for worldwide causes and this is particularly emphasized through the vetos of five countries in the United Nations Security Council. Apart from Haleemi Raj, the Sikhs aim to establish the Khalsa Raj, a system where there would be a freedom of belief and freedom of choice, i.e. not prohibitionist with regards to alcohol, drugs, smoking, homosexuality, etc, even if some of it may be bad for humans. The current financial and trade system is also being criticized. Sikhs call for a new system based on compassion, rights, companies without ties with politics, and demand of moral behavior of shareholders. A compassionate type of living would include the non-exploitation of animals, by avoiding cruelty and inhumane conditions. It would also include the protection of natural resources from short-term destruction of rainforests and desertification.

The History of Sikhism

Sikhism came into being in the Punjab region of Northern India, at a time when the Mughals came into power. The new religion started in the 15th century with the birth of Guru Nanak (1469-1539). As mentioned earlier, Guru Nanak is born in an area where the majority of the population is Hindu, but where the power is in the hands of Muslims. In Punjab, there were also sizeable Christian and Jain populations. The mid-15th century is also the time when the Bhakti movement was rising, with its devotional love to the god within Hinduism. It is in this context in which Guru Nanak become a follower of the Bhakti movement and later its guru. In his sayings, one may see elements of the core of Hinduism and elements of Islam. At the same time, Guru Nanak was emphasizing the devotional love for God, thus having a strong Bhakti character and is still revered as a major Bhakti guru. Guru Nanak dies in the early 16th century and before his death, he names Guru Angad Dev (1504-1552) as his successor. The line of succession is secured, and the following Sikh gurus are Guru Amar Das (1479-1574); Guru Ram Das (1534-1581), who established in 1574 the city now sacred to Sikhs Amritsar and originally known as Ramdaspur in his honor. He spread Sikhism in North India, organized the structure of Sikh society, and stressed the importance of kirtan (hymn singing) which remains an important part of Sikh worship. There are 638 hymns from Guru Ram Das included in the Guru Granth Sahib.

His successor was Guru Arjan (1563-1606), one of the most important gurus of Sikh history and their first martyr. He was succeeded by his son Guru Hargobind (1595-1644) who, on direction from his father before he would die, took over an important idea that the Sikhs need to protect themselves and adopt a military tradition. Thus, Guru Hargobind is famous for establishing the military tradition of Sikhism and would become akin to a warrior saint. He is famous for wearing two swords, one to represent his authority in the spiritual realm, and another to represent his authority in the temporal realm. After his long tenure, his grandson becomes Guru Har Rai (1630-1661), who was succeeded by his very young son Guru Har Krishan (1656-1664), who died soon after that from smallpox. Guru Hargobind's youngest son becomes Guru Tegh Bahadur (1621-1675), which means "brave sword" or "brave wielder of the sword", as he was known for his unusual bravery and unusual competent warrior skills. Guru Tegh Bahadur continued with the tradition of warrior saint, and especially under the Mughal rule of Shah Jahan and Aurangzeb, representatives of more and more intolerant Mughal dynasty. After his martyrdom, Sikhs had the tenth and the last human leader, Guru Gobind Singh (1666-1708), who formalized the military community.

Guru Nanak has remained the most important of the ten Gurus of the Sikhs, but all of them contributed significantly to the religion. Two deserve special attention: Arjan, the Fifth Guru (from 1581 to 1606), and Gobind Singh, the tenth Guru (from 1675 to 1708). Guru Arjan compiled the scripture that would come to be known as the Adi Granth, and he constructed at the city of Amritsar the Darbar Sahib or Golden Temple. Guru Gobind Singh, revered as the greatest Guru after Nanak, instituted in 1699 the Khalsa, which would redefine the Panth, and he installed the Adi Granth, the sacred scripture, as Guru. The very dramatic event of the founding of the Khalsa involved a display of extreme loyalty by five men who became the Panj

Piare, the "Beloved Ones." Before dying in 1708, Guru Gobind Singh is said to have declared that his successor Guru was not to be another individual but rather the Adi Granth. Khalsa is given a mission to realize God's work (Vaheguru). Everything they do is for the Vaheguru, including serving and chanting (Seva Simran), shaping the soldier's sanctity (Sant Sipahi), be famous for serving (Bhai Kanehiya), etc.

Two fundamental events that shaped Sikh history was the martyrdom of two gurus. The first was of Guru Arjan, the fifth guru of Sikhism, who was roasted alive by the Mughal Emperor Jahangir. The early Mughals were tolerant in beginning and Emperor Akbar was particularly so. But upon his death, his son Jahangir takes power and early in his reign, Jahangir is insecure about his hold on power. As Mughals have their major center in the Sikh are, they witness that the new religion has more and more followers, not only from the Hindu population but also from Muslims. Threatened by this growing following, Jahangir imprisons Guru Arjan and tortures him in an effort to convert him to Islam. Guru Arjan refused despite many days of excruciating torture. Eventually, he died and there are slightly varying accounts of how it happens.

The second Sikh martyr was Guru Tegh Bahadur, who was the ninth guru. In his lifetime, Shahs Jahan and Aurangzeb would lead force conversions to Islam and Guru Tegh Bahadur viewed himself as a protector of the oppressed, not just of the Sikhs but also of other faiths. He was beheaded by the Mughals while attempting to defend not himself or Sikhism, but the religious rights of Hindus.

Over the centuries, Punjab has tended to be a volatile region, marked by political and military strife. Sikhs had to continuously fight against the Mughals. Upon creating the Khalsa, which was also the warrior group, Guru Gobind Singh went to hiding in the woodlands north from Punjab from where he would form the military units of Sikhs. When this guru died, his head general Banda Singh Bahadur would stop the hereditary aristocracy of Punjab and property ownership was granted to people. He was captured, tortured and executed by the Mughals. The Sikhs would then wage a guerilla war against the Mughal Empire. By the early 1730ies, the exhausted Mughals made a peace with Sikhs and allowed them to return to Punjab valley and establish self-rule. In 1738, the Mughal capital of Dehli was ravaged and sacked by the Persian Afsharid Dynasty.

Other competitors would use this opportunity. Vast parts of India were taken by the Hindu Maratha Empire, while Punjab fell under the control of the Afghan Durrani Empire. The Afghans would never fully be able to subdue the Sikhs, despite many massacres. The self-rule was instigated through small Khalsa communities who were also in a state of conflict among themselves whenever an outer enemy was not present. Eventually, they would form the Sikh Confederacy, which would be present for almost the whole 18th century. They were united by a young warrior prince Ranjit Singh who was crowned in 1801 as the maharaja of the Sikh Empire. He repeatedly won in battles against Afghans and drove them all the way to the Khyber Pass, effectively moving them out from the Indian Subcontinent.

During his 30-year old reign, Sikh controlled the whole Punjab. His empire was prosperous and internally peaceful, with inclusive reform government and military that included Sikhs, Muslims, Hindus, European military trainers. The army was professionally trained and modernized in the use of artillery. The Sikh Empire lasted only ten more years after Ranjit Singh died. All three subsequent maharajas were assassinated. The British diplomats declared that Sikh Empire was ruled by a dangerous military democracy and used the opportunity of a weak government. The British East India Company started to station the British soldiers on the Sikh border and started the First Anglo-Sikh War in 1845/6. The peace agreement gave the northern territories of Jammu and Kashmir as well as valuable territories in eastern Punjab to the British. Only two years later, the Second Anglo-Sikh war erupted in 1848/9. At the end of this war, the British East India Company annexed the Sikh Empire. During the time of the British Raj (1858-1947), Sikhs were admired for their warrior skills and abilities. They were noted for their loyalty, skill and bravery, particularly during the First and Second World Wars.

When India gained independence from the British in 1947, most Sikhs living in the western region migrated eastward, favoring Hindu-dominated India over Muslim-dominated Pakistan. In recent times, a new nationalist movement for independence, commonly called "Khalistan," has involved the Sikhs in conflict, the most violent tragedy having taken place in 1984 with the bloody occupation of Sikh holy sites, most notably the Darbar Sahib, by Indian forces. This led to the assassination of Indian Prime Minister Indira Gandhi by two of her Sikh bodyguards on October 31, 1984. Today, the Khalistan movement is not nearly so prevalent as it was in the 1980s. The fact that in 2004 a Sikh, Manmohan Singh, for the first time became India's prime minister perhaps signals a new degree of assimilation of Sikhism within Indian society.

The Sikh diaspora may be found all over the world, with the greatest concentration in the United Kingdom, the United States, Canada, East African countries, Australia, and Malaysia. An interesting fact is that Sikhs make up almost 1,5 percent of Canada's population. Sikhs have been in the United States for over one hundred years and the largest peach, pistachio, okra farms in California are owned by Sikhs. They have helped to build the railroads that connect the east and west coast, they worked in lumbermills and farms. They have also been pioneers in citizenship reforms. The first Asian American elected in Congress was a Sikh, Dalip Singh Saund, representing the 29th California district. They were very active in land ownership rights and California was the first state that promulgated the laws granting the aliens and non-citizens ownership of agricultural land.

Sikhism as a Way of Life

For a long time, there were questions if Sikhism is in fact a syncretic belief made of Hindu and Muslim traditions, or does it retain its individuality and continuity. The first gurus came from Hindu families and had cultural connections to Islam. The political authority in Punjab was marked by the Muslim rulers, first through the Delhi Sultanate, which was in power for over 250 years when Sikhism emerged, and the Mughal Empire. A lot of terminology of Sikhism are borrowed words and ideas from Islam and Hinduism. For instance, the Guru Granth Sahib mentions both Allah and Ram as terms for God. Islamic scholars and Sufi mystics contributed greatly to the Guru Granth Sahib, particularly in its philosophical understandings, while Hinduism was a source for many rituals. For example, when Sikhs pass away, like Hindus, they are cremated.

Guru Nanak emphasized the importance of nam simaran, "remembrance of the Name." This can be done simply by repeating one of the names used to refer to God, or through kirtan, the singing of hymns from the Guru Granth Sahib. A third form involves meditation practices designed to contemplate the divine Name and ultimately to bring one into perfect harmony with God. Daily prayers are another form of devotional practice that can (and should) be done by every Sikh. The most known mantra is the Mool Mantar which says: "One Universal Creator God. The Name Is Truth. Creative Being Personified. No Fear. No Hatred. Image of the Undying, Beyond Birth, Self-Existent. By Guru's Grace".

Daily devotional practices take place at home or the gurdwara, a Sikh house of worship. Gurdwara means "the doorway to the guru". Any building that contains a copy of the Adi Granth is, technically speaking, a gurdwara, and there is at least one in virtually every village in Punjab. Almost every gurdwara has within it a community kitchen, called the langar, where Sikhs gather at various times to share in the preparation and consumption of a meal. Anyone can visit a gurdwara and partake in singing ceremonies and preparing and eating the meals, following the usual etiquette: covering the hair, removing the shoes, washing hands. The most important gurdwara in the world for Sikhs is the Hari Mandir or the Golden Temple, situated in Amritsar, India. In 1604, Guru Arjan completed the work of the Golden Temple and installed the Adi Granth inside it. In order to show tremendous good will, Guru Arjan invited a Muslim Mian Mir to lay the foundation stone of the Golden Temple. The Temple has four doors open on all four sides to show the openness to all peoples of the world, although only one door leads to the inner sanctum, symbolically telling that all paths essentially lead to One God. The Golden Temple has around six million visitors every year and is thus one of the most visited places in the world and serves around 100,000 meals each day, making it the world's largest free serving kitchen, and it is all run and staffed by volunteers.

Important Sikh rituals of the life cycle include the birth and naming of a child; the ceremonial tying of a boy's first turban; marriage, which is arranged by the parents; and the funeral, which centers around the process of cremation. Wearing a turban is a strong part of Sikh identity. It is a symbol of everything Sikhism stands for. The turban reminds Sikhs not only of their religious values but of their duty to the community. The gurus requested of their followers not to cut their hair and to cover it with a turban. The tenth guru, Guru Gobind Singh, said: "Our hair is a stamp of our Guru". He also said that Sikhs are Singh (lion) and turban is their crown. Long beards are considered also as part of the hair, which should not be cut, and this applies to any part of a Sikh physical body. Sikhs wear turban whenever they go outside their home. At home, they wear a small turban, as turban cannot be totally removed from one's head. Even sleeping is not allowed with a bare head.

Three guiding principles of Sikh life are worship, work, and charity, and Sikhs have earned a reputation for helping to improve their communities. With regard to the place and role of women in the tradition, while Sikhism has through the centuries maintained ideals of gender equality when it comes to the most important issue of spiritual liberation, the tradition has tended to be quite patriarchal, with positions of institutional power occupied by men.

Sikhs celebrate several important holidays throughout the year. Sikhs use their own Bikrami calendar. It is a lunisolar calendar, relating to both the Moon and the Sun, that was started in the year 57 BC, meaning it is 57 years ahead of the commonly used Gregorian or Western calendar. The Bikrami calendar is filled with multiple remembrances of the life events of gurus. It mainly involves the Parkash Dhihara, the day when a guru has a second birth in this world; Jyoti Jyotihara is the day when the guru leaves this world and emerges with God, and Gurgadihara is the day when the guruship is passed on from one guru to next guru. Sikhs celebrate also other historical events such as Shahid Dihara (commemoration of a martyrdom anniversary) or Janam Divas (celebration of a birth anniversary). All of these commemorations and holidays are observed because Sikhs want to remember past gurus and events so they could get inspiration and teachings from them. There is a saying about this observance: "I am sacrifice unto those Gursikhs who celebrate the Guru's anniversaries with full devotion. Such Sikhs are blessed by the service of the Guru and progress further successfully". All the gurus have warned their followers of the importance of getting together, celebrating and doing selfless service and strengthening the community.

Maghi is a winter festival that commemorates the Battle of Muktsar and was chosen by Guru Amar Das Ji for Sikhs to attend the gurdwara. Also in January, the commemoration of the birth of Guru Gobind Singh (Parkash Ursav Dasveh Patshah) is celebrated. The Sikh New Year is celebrated on March 13 or 14. Also in March, the festival of Hola Mohalla is held, in the town of Anandpur, the place where Khalsa was made. It is one of the largest gatherings of Sikhs worldwide, as over five million people congregate there during the festival. It was started by Guru Gobind Singh as a gathering where Sikh bravery and valor are shown through the military exercises and mock battles, followed by kirtan and poetry. The contemporary Sikh warriors (Nihang) carry on this tradition and use Hola Mohalla to show their swordsmanship and horse riding, falconry and martial arts (Gatka).

In April, Vaisakhi Day is commemorated. On Vaisakhi day in 1699, Guru Gobind Singh summoned Sikhs from all over India to the city of Anandpur, where he called upon Sikhs to uphold their faith and preserve the Sikh religion. It is here where the Guru made the Khalsa and this counts as one of the most important religious holidays for the Sikhs.

In June, the martyrdom of the Guru Arjan is commemorated, when kirtan and langar are performed in gurdwaras. The beginning of September is the day when the Guru Granth Sahib was bestowed with the title of being the eternal and final Sikh Guru. Large gatherings happen for the Guru Nanak Gurpurab in November. It is the birthday of Guru Nanak when candles and lights are lit and fireworks are made in honor of the first Sikh guru. Also in November, Sikhs commemorate the martyrdom of Guru Tegh Bahadur.

SUGGESTED READINGS, WEBLINKS, AND OTHER MEDIA

Readings

- Cole, W. Owen, and Piara Singh Sambhi. *The Sikhs: Their Religious Beliefs and Practices.* 2nd rev. ed. Brighton, England: Sussex Academic Press, 1995.

- Kaur Singh, Nikky-Guninder, O'Brien Joanne, and Palmer, Martin. *Sikhism.* New York: Chelsea House Publications, 2009.
- Mann, Gurinder Singh. *Sikhism.* Upper Saddle River, NJ: Prentice Hall, 2004.
- McLeod, Hew. *Sikhism.* London: Penguin, 1997.
- McLeod, W. H., ed. and trans. *Textual Sources for the Study of Sikhism.* Totowa, NJ: Barnes & Noble, 1984.
- Nesbitt, Eleanor. *Sikhism. A Very Short Introduction.* Oxford: Oxford University Press, 2005.
- Singh, Khushwant. *A History of the Sikhs.* 2 vols. Princeton, NJ: Princeton University Press, 1963–1966.

Weblinks

- Wabash Center—www.wabashcenter.wabash.edu/resources—The Wabash Center, a trusted resource for all aspects of the academic study of religion, offers links to a wide variety of dependable Internet resources on Sikhism.
- SikhNet—www.sikhnet.com—SikhNet offers an extensive "insiders' view" on Sikhism, with information on many aspects of the religion.
- The Pluralism Project at Harvard University: Sikhism—www.pluralism.org/religions/Sikhism—Thorough and dependable coverage of Sikhism in the United States.

SACRED TEXTS

Sikhs.org/topics2.htm
Provides access to the Sri Guru Granth Sahib, along with other scriptures, in English translation. More generally, the website sets forth a wide array of helpful information from a Sikh's "insider's" perspective.

www.sacred-texts.com/skh/granth/gr01.htm
The *Japji*, the opening section of the Adi Granth, which begins with the *Mul Mantra*.

www.sacred-texts.com/skh/granth/gr05.htm
The Adi Granth on praise of the divine Name.

www.sacred-texts.com/skh/granth/gr04.htm
The Sohila, the prayer recited before retiring for the evening, from the Adi Granth.

KEY TERMS AND DEFINITIONS

Adi Granth (ah'dee gruhnth; Punjabi, "first book") Sikhism's most important sacred text and, since the death of Guru Gobind Singh in 1708, Sikhism's primary earthly authority; traditionally known as Sri Guru Granth Sahib.

amrit (ahm-reet; Punjabi, "immortalizing fluid") A special drink made from water and sugar crystals, used in the Khalsa initiation ceremony.

gurdwara (goor'dwah-ruh; Punjabi, "doorway of the Guru" or "by means of the Guru's [grace]") A building for Sikh worship that houses a copy of the Adi Granth; the central structure of any Sikh community.

Guru (goo'roo; Sanskrit, "venerable person") A spiritual teacher and revealer of truth, common to Hinduism, Sikhism, and some forms of Buddhism. When the word *Guru* is capitalized, it refers to the ten historical leaders of Sikhism, to the sacred text (Sri Guru Granth Sahib, or Adi Granth), and to God (often as True Guru).

haumai (how'may; Punjabi, "self-reliance," "pride," or "egoism") The human inclination toward being self-centered rather than God-centered, which increases the distance between the individual and God.

hukam (huh'kahm; Punjabi, "order") The divine order of the universe.

Khalsa (khal'sah; Punjabi, "pure ones") An order within Sikhism to which the majority of Sikhs belong, founded by Guru Gobind Singh in 1699.

langar A gurdwara's community kitchen that is used to prepare meals for anyone who visits, regardless of religious or caste identity.

Mul Mantra The summary of Sikh doctrine that comprises the opening lines of the *Japji,* Guru Nanak's composition that, in turn, comprises the opening section of the Adi Granth.

mukti (mook'tee; Punjabi, "liberation") Spiritual liberation bringing on the eternal and infinitely blissful state of being in the presence of God; sometimes the Sanskrit term *moksha* is used instead.

Panth (puhnth; Punjabi, Hindi, "path") The Sikh community. In lower case, *panth* ("path") is a term applied to any number of Indian (primarily Hindu) religious traditions.

Rahit (rah-hit'; Punjabi) The *rahit-nāmā,* a collection of scripture that specifies ideals of belief and conduct for members of the Khalsa and, by extension, for Sikhism generally; the current authoritative version, the *Sikh Rahit Maryādā,* was approved in 1950.

ACTIVITIES AND ASSIGNMENTS

1. Guru Nanak famously said, "There is no Hindu, there is no Muslim," and yet a religious institution much like Hinduism and Islam developed around his teachings. Is there a contradiction here? Does anything in the Sikh religious writings or thought address this potential contradiction?

2. The author states, "For decades, scholars have described Sikhism as a Hindu–Islamic hybrid," which offends many Sikhs. Arguably, many religious traditions began by reimagining diverse intellectual and spiritual strains of thought to create something new. Early Christianity incorporated Jewish sacred texts and elements of Greek philosophy, but Christianity is rarely described as Jewish–Greek hybrid. Why, therefore, is Sikhism singled out to be reduced in this way? What are the consequences of explaining Sikhism in this way?

3. Instead of having a person like the Pope as its religious leader, Sikhism designates a text—the Guru Granth Sahib—as the ultimate teacher and leader of its tradition. What consequences might this have for religious tradition? Since the words of the Guru Granth Sahib cannot be changed, does this make the tradition more conservative and less able to change with the times? Or does this allow greater flexibility because each Sikh has the freedom to interpret the text?

4. While the Christian tradition believes that original sin is a mistake or deviation from a divine plan, Sikhism believes that one's own ego [*haumai*]—the source of the Five Thieves—is endowed with humanity by God. How might a Sikh explain this "chronic disease" (GG 466) having ultimately divine origin? Why would God intentionally give humanity the capacity for evil?

CHAPTER 6

Hinduism

Introduction

Hinduism holds a unique place among world religions. It is the third-largest religion in the World. The practitioners of Hinduism consider this religion the oldest in the world. More than 950 million Hindu populations are living around the world. Nearly, 80 percent of the Hindu population lives in India, the birthplace of Hinduism. The remaining 20 percent of Hindus have spread in larger and smaller groups to the various countries worldwide mainly in Nepal, Indonesia, Bangladesh, Pakistan, Sri Lanka, Guyana, Fiji, Africa, Canada, Great Britain and the United States. The followers of Hinduism have contextualized their religion according to the cultures of these countries but at the same time, all Hindus around the globe share a common set of complex, rich and poetic customs. Interestingly, unlike other religions (Christianity, Islam, Buddhism) Hinduism was not founded by any specific personality. Rather, it came into existence through the amalgamation of various religious beliefs and philosophies being practiced in ancient India. There is no concept of central religious authority or central scripture in Hinduism as compare to the Bible and the Quran. Rather, Hinduism deals with the variety of religious influential figures and textual tradition.

Hinduism is a complex religion and with the often difficult translation of terms used in it. For instance, dharma does not give the same meaning as religion and Mandira is not a church. In the restricted sense, Hinduism is not a religion but dharma. The English word 'civilization' is equivalent to the term dharma, as mentioned by Mohan Sen: "Dharma has, thus, more to do with the nature and behavior of men than with their beliefs. It does not necessarily imply any doctrinal agreement except in so far as this influences conduct". Thus, Hinduism is more concerned with conduct than belief and it can be described as a way of life.

In order to appreciate the richness of Hindu culture and religion, it is very important to know the fact that Hindu society is a component of multiple cultures and races. Hinduism contributes to preserving the unity of India for centuries so it is interesting to look into the phases, how this religion has evolved into the present form. Therefore, Hinduism can be compared to a large tree that has so many branches and has been evolving through the synthesis of different civilizations, cultures and religions.

History of Hinduism

Hinduism is an ancient religion and it is rather difficult but not impossible to define its origin and development in India. The ancient civilization in India was named the "Indus Valley" civilization or the "Harappan" civilization which lay geographically in present-day Pakistan. Later, the Indus Valley people were invaded by the Aryans through Persia in about 2000 BC. Earlier the religions and philosophies of the Indus valley were not labelled as Hinduism. Actually, before the 19th century, the word "Hinduism" did not exist. The word Hindu is derived from the Persian language and was used for the people groups living close to the Indus River. Later, the term has been used by the Muslim invaders such as Turks, Afghans and Mughals to India, to refer to those who do not follow Islam. Later this term became territorial, as well as a racial, social, and cultural designation for the people of India. Quite evidently, these manifestations are reflected in the diversity of the religion we now call Hinduism. It can be rightly said that Hinduism was originated in the subcontinent and became mostly curbed to this land on the world's map. Thus, the people belonging to the Indus region and culture without any consistent name for their faith were called Hindus.

Hinduism has been practiced for thousands of years. Some of the practitioners also believe that this religion came into existence from the beginning of the universe. According to the Indologists, the gradual development in culture, language and history caused the ongoing expansion in the practices and beliefs of not only Hinduism but also in the Aryan tradition. According to 19th and 20th-century European scholars, the Indo-Aryan migration was the core event in the development of Hinduism. The archaeological findings, the earliest Hindu scriptures and the Vedas are the main sources that point to the gradual development of the Hindu religion and the Indus Valley culture. Around 5000 years ago, the Indus valley civilization flourished on the banks of the Indus River. The people of this civilization were cultured and literate. By profession, they were merchants and agriculturists and they were keen to have a clean, stable, disciplined environment. These people were familiar with the use of metal and minerals such as gold, silver, lead, copper, tint and bronze but not iron. Planting, weaving and dyeing of cotton were commonly practiced. The fruits, meat, fish, barley, wheat were part of their meals. The well-planned drainage system and streets suggest their efficient social and government structure. The industrial and business system seemed to be also very strong in the Indus Valley Civilization.

The people of Indus were not secular but the temples were rare. Later, the Indus Valley Civilization was invaded by the Aryans, people characterized by non-vegetarianism, sacrifices to gods, a long tradition of oral history, and maybe some forms of caste systems. Moreover, the unique elements of the Indus Civilization such as mother goddess, sexual control and ritual cleanliness were gradually acknowledged and adopted by the Aryans according to the adequacy of their religion. As a result, the blended culture was Aryan in body, but the soul was designed by many local and non-Aryan beliefs and practices. In this period the literature of Hinduism was developed and the writings and interpretation took the form of Hindu Scriptures. Interestingly, the people of the Indus Valley were very literate but they did not produce any literature. On the other hand, the Aryans were illiterate people but they made a great contribution to Indian literature. The literature produced by the Aryans was composed in the Sanskrit language which stands for "perfected" or "well-made". The Aryan period is marked by the development of the ancient literature Vedas or Vedic literature and is also called the Vedic age. Later, Sanskrit became the most preferred and sacred language to perform Hindu rituals and ceremonies. It remained popular among the educated people or elite but could not take its place among the commons.

The sacred Literature in Hinduism

The sacred literature in Hinduism is regarded as Sruti and Smriti. The term Sruti literally means "that which is heard" and serves the same purpose as wahi in Islam. Therefore, Sruti is understood as the revelation of the ultimate reality. Furthermore, it serves as the foundation of all forms of further research or interpretations. Sruti literature consists of Vedas (regarded as the inner and direct experience of revealed truth) and Upanishads (the mystical expression of Vedas compiled between 800 and 300 BCE.) Some other texts are also regarded as Sruti. Those texts include Brahmanas (interpretation of the Brahmins) the collections of priestly literature that explains the Vedic sacrificial rituals. The Aranyakas (texts of the forest) is the mystical descriptions of the great rituals that were taught and shaped in the forest.

Similarly, Smriti is the text which means recollection that is based on the human memory. Therefore the tradition of smriti acts as an interpreter to explain the meaning of the revealed (sruti) text. The two famous epics are Ramayana and the Mahabharata, the 18 Puranas (poetic tales of Shiva and Vishnu), the Dharmasastras and the Dharmasutras (relating to law & social conduct), and the Tantras (ritual to acquire liberation) are part of smriti. Bhagavad Gita was also a part of the smriti but later regarded as sruti.

There is no single most important scripture in Hinduism but there is a huge group of sacred texts in Hinduism which contributes to enhancing the understanding of Hindu beliefs. Popular Hindu literature was also produced in the Aryan period. The word "Vedas" is commonly used to mention all the early Hindu literature. But the four Vedas: Rig, Sama, Atharva and Yajur, are the books that can be referred to as Vedas in a strict sense. First is the Rig Veda (collection of verses), the hymns to the gods. Second is Sama Veda (collection of songs), a handbook for training the person who leads the singing at sacrifices. The third is Yajur Veda (collection of sacrificial formulae). Atharva Veda is the wisdom of the fire priest and collection of incantations and curses. All the other literature of Hinduism derives from or is based on the Vedas. The Vedas are considered to be classified above all the Hindu literature since these are divinely revealed and categorized as sruti. The Vedas are also considered infallible by the Hindus, similar to the Quran is considered infallible by the Muslims. Rig Vedas contains 1,028 hymns and 10,500 verses. Rig Vedas is a composition of many remarkable and significant passages. But, the identical and preferred passage among the Hindus is the Gaytri mantra, a few lines taken from the Rig Veda. It is also the first lesson for the children about Hinduism. Moreover, Rig Veda presents that Indra (also named Durga, Mitra, Varuna and Agni) is the phenomenal form of One Real (Ekam Sat) or Absolute. Other Hindu Scriptures suggest that the creator of the universe That One (Tad Ekam), is only known by the saints.

The Vedas were composed between 2000 and 400 B.C; they are authorless, everlasting and oral authority experienced by the primeval rishis and later being transmitted to the next generation. The understanding of Vedas includes its memorization and the ability to speak the text with the correct accent and meter. The Vedic songs are sung to personify the natural forces or processes (devas) that control the world. The metaphoric Vedas depicts the men's quest to have ultimate union with Brahman. For instance, the great intellects as Buddha or Sankara do not claim to represent a new thought or new path. Instead, they explain their thoughts to retracing a forgotten eternal truth. Similarly, rishi did not produce something new but they created a link between the ordinary things and their forgotten eternal truth.

The Upanishad is thought to be the post-Vedic text which dates back to 1,200 BCE to 200 BCE. The mass of philosophical texts Upanishads helps to reveal and explain the meaning of the Vedas. The Upanishads also presents novel ideas, sometimes tied to the older text, sometimes not. Furthermore, the Upanishads deals with the meditation and mystical experience of the ancient sages. The Vedic period is marked with the tradition of sacrifice which is performed to get connected with the divine. Thus, the sacrificial worldview of the Vedas gave way to the mystical worldview of the Upanishads. Moreover, the Upanishad focuses on the tradition in which a student sat in front of the teacher or guru. The Upanishad reveals a direct, immediate and life-transforming knowledge of God-as-Absolute (Brahman) and self (atman). The collection of 108 Upanishads consists of riddles, debates and dialogues and direct questions about the Ultimate truth and the self.

Brahmanas is another text as well which holds the sruti status. It is the collection of priestly literature to explain the sacrificial rituals related to the Vedas. The Aranyakas (texts of the forest) is the mystical descriptions of the great rituals that were taught in the forest. Some of the later hymns in the Brahmanas refer to the idea that the world was created by sacrifice. Further, this idea also developed into the view that the right way of performing sacrifice standardizes the conservation of the world. Later, the element of the sacrifice to gratify the gods gradually became irrelevant as the act itself took importance. Hence the inner or self-sacrifice became prominent and naturally, the animal offerings became unimportant which became the milestone in the transition from the Brahmanas to the Upanishads.

Upanishad deals with the inner self or inwardness that causes dissatisfaction towards external actions. The main message of the Upanishad is that atman and Brahman are the same. The Supreme reality is manifested in every soul. This concept of the mutual permeate is called atman which means prana or breath. Atman is also perceived as pure consciousness. Prana and its relations to the organs of the self (speech, breath, sight, hearing and thought) are discussed in many of the passages in the Upanishad. Prana corresponds and organs communicate to the five natural forces like fire, wind, sun, the directions and the moon. This correspondence also leads to the identification of atman with Brahman.

The literary meaning of the Puranas is "something very old". The Puranas are written in Sanskrit are also part of the smriti writings. It is commonly believed that the Puranas were composed between 300 BCE and 1000 CE. They are the ancient body of literature that contains information about the creation of the universe, records of genealogies and legacies of gods and deities, description of heaven and hell, rituals and the pilgrims. There is also enormous information about the deities Vishnu and Shiva and the goddesses which is commonly accepted by the people.

The longest epic poem in Hindu scripture Mahabharata contains 90,000 stanzas (Chakra). Mahabharata is said to be dedicated to Ganesha by the sage Vyasa. Ganesha is the elephant-headed god who is associated with good luck and learning. Mahabharata is the tale of the war between the two families. Additionally, the sacred text Bhagavad Gita, which is a dialogue between the god Krishna and the warrior and hero Arjuna, is also part of Mahabharata. Another great epic is the great Ramayana that is associated with the adventure of Rama. Rama is the seventh incarnated form of the Lord Vishnu. The message of the Ramayana is based on faithfulness, loyalty and affection to the family relations such as marriage and brother. Ramayana is a great Indian epic and holds a unique place in Hinduism. The conception of this story is very ancient but it was composed between 400 B.C. and 300 A.D. Rama is broadly worshiped by the Hindus especially in North India. Rama being the principal deity in Hinduism is introduced in many "vernacular" forms. Due to its popularity, it has been translated into many Indian languages. The influence and the impact of Mahabharata and Ramayana on Hindu philosophy have lasted for at least 2000 years. The main theme of the Bhagavad Gita is the Bhakti of humans towards God. Bhagavad Gita (written in 300 B.C.) is a monotheistic exposition of the three fundamental paths for union with the Almighty. First is knowledge (jnana yoga) second is action (karma yoga) and the third is devotion (bhakti yoga).

Caste system in Hinduism

It cannot be rightly said how and when the social caste system was developed in Hinduism, but it was probably introduced by the Aryans. The famous Hymn in Rig Veda (1400-1000 B.C.), Purusha Sukta, means 'Hymn to Man' mentioned the roots of the social structure or four castes of Hindu society. The Vedic period led to the social caste system in the Indus Valley. The Vedas mentioned the Brahmin, Kshatriya, the Vaisya and the Sudra as part of the body. It is mentioned that the Brahmanas were created from the face of the Creator, Kshatriyas were made out of His arms, Vaisyas came out of His thighs and Sudras were created from His feet. As a result, the Brahmins stood as the brain, the Kshatriya as arm, the Vaisya as stomach and the Sudra as feet of the society. The four-caste system is characterized by its duties. The priestly caste of Brahmins was given the responsibility of the religious matters such as performing the rituals and the ceremonial acts. They are also considered the guardians and spreaders of sacred awareness. The second caste was called a Kshatriyas also known as warriors, who were given the duties of kinship, defense and governance. The third caste is known as Vaishyas or professional caste hold the duties of the business. The fourth or the lower caste is created to serve the upper three castes and to do tainted work. Therefore, some of the practitioners argued about Hinduism having an equal social order in which four castes has to perform their obligatory duties.

Some Hindu scholars also view this class division as the law of the social structure, but it has nothing to do with superiority or inferiority. The social law confirms the equal contribution of each class to the welfare of the society because all the body part functions equally to sustain the body. If one organ has stopped working or suffering injury or pain, all bodies will be in trouble. All the parts of the body are equally important. Moreover, the superiority of Brahmin is only determined due to their pure heart and good character. But if Brahmin is spending a life of immorality, then a pious Sudra will be given superiority over him.

The Four Stages

The period of 1000-800 B.C. is remarkable due to the other developments in the Hindu doctrine. The four stages of a Hindu's life called asramas is described in the law book Dharmashastra. Each of these four stages is covering 25 years of one's life. The first stage 'Brahmacharya' refers to the first 25 years of man as a student. The second stage is called Grhastha which refers to the married life and children. The third stage is called 'Vanaprastha' that is a period of abandonment and retirement. The complete departure from life is called 'Sannyasa' which is the last stage.

Core beliefs in Hinduism

The natural rebirth in Hinduism is believed to occur according to the individual's deeds or Karma. The bad karma is reduced when someone is born and spent a life of happiness which later determines the improved status and good luck. If the human has spent an ideal life then the rebirth will bring good tidings and prosperity for him (karma, Samsara, moksha). But, the person's immoral actions will automatically lead him to the moral consequences of Karma. The immoral person may be born again but lead a life with less prosperity or face cruelty or may be born as an animal, dog or insect. Therefore, Karma is the true renunciation of each and every desire without any expectation of getting a personal reward. However, those who are attached to the personal reward will get the remuneration according to their actions such as pleasant, unpleasant or some mixed outcome.

In Hinduism, the fundamental idea is the eternal self which is also called atman. It is further believed that Atman and Brahman are the same. Atman exists in all sentient things and is born repeatedly into this world because of constant action (karma) or as the result of that action. When the atman realizes its true nature, it is released from this cycle (samsara) and union with the Ultimate is achieved.

The cycle of rebirth due to karma is called samsara. The continuous cycle of rebirth can be continuous and without any limits. Escape and freedom can be the only desire by humans to take them out of the tiring rebirth cycle. The longing to get freedom from the cycle of life and rebirth is called moksha. Moksha means 'freedom' or 'liberation'. Such freedom or liberation can only be attained when the person is free from all the human desires of envy, resentment, arrogance and love of money. Furthermore, when an individual is free from all the immoralities and grasps the reality of the world as a temporary place to do good deeds and to show kindness to others, is a way to moksha. Finally, by attaining moksha, the cycle of rebirth ends. The individual's quest for liberation is played out in a life situation that is determined by caste status, the four stages of life, and the four aims of life. These factors help to establish an individual's dharma. This is the main theme of the great epics of the Ramayana and the Mahabharata, of which the Bhagavad Gita is a small but highly influential part.

Dharma is practiced to achieve the comprehension of the Almighty and finally reaching the moksha. The fruit or the reward of practicing the dharma is peace, joy, strength, and tranquillity. Hinduism has assigned different duties to both men and women. However, the rules for the acts like non-violence, truth, non-stealing, cleanliness and control of the senses, are the same for all mankind. The concept of right and wrong is followed in Hinduism as in other World religions. An individual has to adjust his or her conduct to meet the standards of the moral law. While explaining the ethical teachings of Hinduism, Sivananda mentions the Sermon on the Mount of Jesus and the Ten Commandments in the Bible and the ethical teachings of Buddha.

The concept of ahimsa is considered very important in Hinduism and means not to kill or harm other creatures such as humans, animals and the environment. Moreover, Hindus believe that helping other humans is equal to helping Brahman. In Hinduism, the term charity or selfless service is called dana or sewa. Therefore, all living creatures share the soul or spirit of Brahman which is called atman, should be treated well without the expectation of any reward. These selfless services are seen to be part of karma yoga. The protection of forests and trees is also considered a sacred act because Lord Krishna (the eighth incarnation or avatar of Lord Vishnu) spend many years in the forest.

Hinduism is the religion of freedom. But, it does not support the idea that freedom or salvation can be achieved through only one mean. Rather, it approves every means which ultimately leads to the end. According to Sivananda, Hinduism never put any restraints upon human reason, thoughts, feelings and will of man. The Hindus can practice a wide range of freedom in the matter of faith and worship that allows absolute diversity within Hinduism. Moreover, Hinduism cannot be limited to the particular form of worship or human responses to the nature of creator or creation. Rather it allows a wide range of freedom to the human to investigate the core of the dogma. Hence diversity of worship and faiths and practices is warmly welcomed in Hinduism on the condition that it should all lead to the ultimate reality. Sivananda states that "Despite all the differences of metaphysical doctrines, modes of religious discipline and forms of ritualistic practices and social habits prevalent in the Hindu society, there is an essential uniformity in the conception of religion and the outlook on life and the world, among all sections of Hindus."

In Hinduism Yuga refers to the four ages of the world which have a continuous cycle. These cycles are given specific names as Satya Yuga (age of truth), Treta Yuga, Dvapara Yuga, and Kali Yuga. The last age kali Yuga refers to the present age in which the evil or bad forces have dominated the world. However, the first age Satya yuga refers to the good and purest age. In the cosmical cycles, these Yugas are in constant rise and fall.

Different school of thought in Hinduism

Hinduism is identified by Sanatana Dharma and Vaidika-Dharma. Sanatana Dharma means that Hinduism is the eternal and oldest religion on earth. It is universal and it existed from the start of the universe. Sanatana Dharma is eternal because God Himself is the guardian of this religion. Vaidika-Dharma means that Hinduism is derived from the Vedas, with the Upanishads that presents the intuitive spiritual experiences of the ancient Sages and Rishis. These experiences (Aparoksha-Anubhuti) are considered to be valuable as they are direct and fallible. In this regard, the Vedas are revealed to the Rishis by the Almighty and took the form of Vedas. Therefore, the Vedas are the most powerful and the authorized scripture in Hinduism.

Hinduism is the religion of freedom. But, it does not support the idea that freedom or salvation can be achieved through only one mean. Rather, it approves every means which ultimately leads to the end. All Hindu worshippers believe in the main concepts of Hinduism. But there is a difference between the followers of Lord Vishnu and Lord Shiva. The Hindus who worship Vishnu as the most important god are called Vaishnava Hindus. The Vaishnavites focus on the ten incarnations (that include Rama and Krishna) of Lord Vishnu to substantiate his importance. Similarly, Shaivism is the kind of Hinduism in which people mainly focus on Shiva as worshippers and practice raja yoga. The practitioners of Shaivism are called Shaivites.

The Upanishads contains some of the contradictory passages that refer to the relationship of the world and individual souls with the Brahman. Later, to resolve this issue the different schools of Vedanta such as Advaita Vedanta and Dvaita Vedanta were established. The Advaita Vedanta resolves the matter by explaining that certain passages proclaim the non-difference between the world and the individual soul with the Brahman. On the other hand, Dvaita Vedanta clarifies how certain passages proclaim the difference of the world and individual souls from Brahman (Jayaram). All schools of Vedanta acknowledge three primary sourcebooks: the Upanishads, Bhagavad Gita and Brahmasutra (sutra: aphorism; composed c. 400 BC). All Schools of Vedanta agree that the central teaching of the Upanishads is that Brahman is the ultimate principle underlying the universe and individual souls.

Concept of God

It is commonly perceived that Hindus believe in many gods or Hinduism is a polytheist religion. But it is not completely true because Hinduism is also monotheist as they believe in the one ultimate reality of Brahman. Hinduism like Christianity refers to the fundamental similarity between divinity and humanity which is incarnation. Rosen advocates that to understand the concept of God in Hinduism, we should look beyond the terms monotheist or polytheist. He further says that Christians believe that God assumes three forms (trinity) but they never think of trinity as a polytheistic approach. Similarly, the complexity of Hinduism refers to that God can have unlimited forms.

One of the most significant differences in Hinduism is the split between monistic and dualistic (or devotional) viewpoints. Some monistic Hindus also believe in various gods and goddesses. Furthermore, the divine reality resides not just in icons housed in grand temples or simple shrines in the home, but in all things, and is especially venerated in the natural world as trees, rivers, and mountains. Dualistic or devotional Hindus conceive of God as embodied in specific deities. Vishnu, Shiva and Brahman are the most popular gods among the Hindus. However, other gods and goddesses are also admired and worshipped by the Hindus such as Saraswati, Mahadevi, Parvati, Ganesha, Agni and Varuna.

Whenever God takes a physical form or descent into the world in order to resolve any suffering, that incarnation is called Avatar. In Christianity, the incarnation of a divine person in human nature has occurred once, and only once, in all of history (through Jesus Christ). However, in Vaishnavite Hinduism, there has been a series of incarnations of Lord Vishnu: "For the salvation of those who are good, for the destruction of evil in men, for the fulfilment of the kingdom of righteousness, I come to this world in the ages that pass" (Bagawat Gita, 4.8). Hindus call these incarnations, the ten avatars of Vishnu.

In Hinduism murti is not considered an idol but a source of blessings. The Shilpa Shastras (Treatises on Art) dating from 1st or 2nd cent. BCE contains all the instructions on how a murti or statue should be formed. All the information about posture, shape, hand gestures, color, symbols, type of wood or stone, rituals when carving and painting can be found here. Later the image is purified with honey and butter. Then through breathing into the statue the Divine power is installed and the special ritual of uncovering of the eyes is performed. In this way, the murti becomes the divine icon or the source of divine blessings. Later the murti is placed in the heart of the temple, called garbha-griha, the "womb-house" or "egg-house". The worshipping of the murti may consider idolatry by the monotheists. But, Hindus believe that man is a finite being who cannot reach the infinite through murti or statue. The murti is just the physical channel or symbol of divine energy. It is just a point of access between heaven and earth. Hindus believe that the Absolute can be encountered through symbols and images, although it is beyond all forms. Believing murti as the divine image does not mean that God is only limited to the image. The Divine and Ultimate reality is infinite and is not limited to any specific form or number. Rather the physical form as an image or murti is just for the sake of devotee (Shattuck 67). Sometimes the image is non-anthropomorphic such as in stones or the linga of Shiva. The non-human or super-human features can take the shape of an elephant head (Ganesha) or the many arms of Durga. This is also a reminder of the difference between the divine and the human.

Niguna and Saguna are the two forms that explain the way the Absolute is perceived or worshipped in Hinduism. Niguna means that the nature of the Absolute is completely transcendent, elusive, ineffable and incomprehensible and remains a mystery for humans. On the other hand, Saguna means that humans can comprehend and worship the true nature of the Absolute through concrete forms and symbols. The deities as Vishnu, Shiva or Mother Goddess are worshipped in the identifiable form whether abstract or transcendent. These images are the concrete form is the artistic representation of the Absolute, although it will always transcend the image.

The concept of Trimurti refers to the cosmic energies of creation, preservation and destruction. Brahma signifies the world of creation. The sustenance of the world and the process of maintenance is the responsibility of Lord Vishnu. Shiva assures the process of dissolution, which is an ongoing cycle. The personified form of the impersonal Absolute and supreme reality Brahman is Brahma.

It is quite difficult to comprehend the meaning of Brahman. God is presented as the "one Divine being hidden in all beings, all-pervading, the self within all beings, watching over all works, dwelling in all beings, the witness, the perceiver, the only one, free from qualities. He is the one ruler of many who (seem to act, but really) do not act; he makes the one seed manifold" (Svetasvatra Upanishad VI, 11-12). The word Brahman in Hinduism is considered the holiest and highest as it is mentioned in the Upanishad. Brahman is the one ultimate veracity, one vital ground for all existing. The cluster of the gods leads to the one ultimate reality that is Brahman.

Language in Hinduism

Language is of great importance in Hinduism. It covers and highlights all worldly matters and human experiences. The outer aspects of language such as composition, grammar, poetic expression have a significant role in Hinduism. Moreover, the inner aspects of language were also picked and reduced keeping in view the scientific or factual importance. The oral form of the language is given significant prominence as thought to be a fully and truly experienced form. On the other hand, the written tradition is seen as a secondary thing that is merely developed for the investigation purpose. The written word also provides assistance to those who are not able to remember the important text by heart. The understanding of Vedas does not just include its memorization but also comprises the ability to speak the text with the correct accent and meter.

Poem and poetry serve a special purpose in Hinduism. Its bold metaphor, sensuous imagery and profound philosophical insights carry a special power. The poetry covers and inspires every mood from passionate devotion to cynical satire through chanting meditation dance and music. Mantras mean the special sequence of words. These words serve the purpose to connect the practitioner to the Ultimate. Mantras in Hinduism are thought to be powerful as they remove ignorance (avidya), reveal the truth (dharma), and realize release (moksha). Repeating of mantras appropriately removes all impurities which leads to the purification of the knowledge and finally to the release. Moreover, the mantra has the catalytic function as it turned the ritual setting into reality through its sacred potential.

Worship in Hinduism

Hinduism allows free will in the matter of worship. God can be reached through work (karma), or meditation, knowledge (jnana), or simply through devotion (Bakhti). All these paths or ways are equally legal. As already mentioned, religious practices can vary from person to people but one thing is common that all these lead toward the Ultimate. The worship in Hinduism is mainly performed to show bhakti or devotion to the deity. Various kinds of worship are focused on and followed in Hinduism. Different modes of worship serve different purposes. Hindus mainly perform four types of worship namely: puja, aarti, darshan, parsad and havan in the temple or at home.

Puja ceremony in Hinduism involves worshiping and showing respect to Brahman and one or two of the thousands of Hindu deities. Aarti worship includes an aarti lamp which is passed around in front of all worshippers present in the ceremony. The ceremony ends when the worshippers wave their hands over the flame and then over their heads in order to get blessings from Brahman. Darshan as a term comes from the darsana which means the sight of some sacred object, holy person and especially the image of a deity. In this sense, Darshan means interaction between the worshiper and the image of the deity during worship which serves the purpose of spiritual fulfillment. Parsad means 'grace'. It contained fruits and flowers. Milk and other liquids are also used in the ritual bathing of the murti. Havan is the traditional fire that was used to sacrifice the animals to god Agni in ancient times but no longer happens in the present era. At present time, the Havan fire is flamed during weddings for the couple to walk seven times around the fire. The temple experience is altogether personal or individual. The people individually watch the activities of a priest, offer prayer and receive darshan and then parsad. Home worship is almost similar to temple worship. Each of the Hindu families dedicates an area such as a shelf or special room to the household deity. The deity can be one or more according to the devotedness of the family members.

Yoga

The word Yoga is derived from the Sanskrit word Yuj which means 'to join'. Yoga is a discipline that controls the mind and calms the body. It also improves concentration. The basic aim of Yoga is to attain complete union with the supreme. With the passage of time, Yoga practice became very popular not only in India but around the World.

Ritual and Festivals in Hinduism

Hinduism is the most diverse religion as far as its festivals and rituals are concerned. It can also be rightly said that it is a product of the amalgamation of the different cultures and civilizations from Vedic Aryan to primitive animist tribes. It is quite a difficult task to give an exact list of Hindu rituals and festivals. In Hinduism, the annual festivals are connected with the seasons. But amidst these varieties and diversities, there is no conflict in believing that God is all-embracing, all-pervading, omnipresent. The puja of gods and goddesses of the Hindu pantheon is also not contradictory.

Some of the Hindu rituals are mentioned just to give an idea about Hindu culture and religion. However, these are enormous in numbers and it is a difficult task to mention all. Moreover, Hindus can limit themselves to perform a few of the rituals otherwise they will not have time for the other tasks of life. It is also true that Hindu religious practices are performed according to cultural background, social status, caste, sex, age and sect.

Religious observance such as fasting is performed on a specific weekday. Other prayers and penances are observed according to the lunar calendar at the time of the full moon and new moon. Other adherences are followed as occasional or can also be dependent on the desires of the performer. For example, the women occasionally observe vartas (vows) for the welfare of their husband, family or community such as Savitri Vrata, Shashthi Vrata, Maghamandala Vrata, Pausha Vrata. Savitri Vrata is observed for the well-being of the Husband. Shashthi Vrata is observed for the well-being and happiness of the children. Maghamandala Vrata is observed for the blessings of sunshine in the cold winter months. Pausha Vrata is observed for the full harvest. Some of the religious ceremonies are connected with the different phases of life. The birth rituals and their performance differ between castes.

The welcoming ceremony of the newborn child is called jatakarma. The father of the child whisper Mantra or religious verses into the infant's ear to ensure the child safety and comfort. He also touches and smells the child. The dot of Kajal (a black carbon substance commonly used by women for eye makeup) is used behind the ear often in the Om shape. Later Namakarana ceremony is performed to the child to whom a name is given. The puja ceremony is arranged in the local temple and the prayers and petitions are offered for the child's long life and good future.

Death Ritual in Hinduism involves the washing of the dead body with special ingredients such as honey, ghee, yogurt, milk and essential oils. The essential oils are used to anoint the body and it includes sandalwood for a man's body and turmeric for a women body. The white simple dress or cloth is used to cover the dead body but other clothes according to the contemporary style or choice can also be used. A garland full of flowers and rice balls is placed around the body by the family members or the attendees of the funeral. Moreover, basil leaves are also used to embellish the body. In addition, the water as a symbol of purification is sprinkled over the body and the placement of a lamp near the head of the body is also common practice in Hindu funerals. The cremation ceremony is referred to as mukhagni. The cremation is supposed to be performed 24 to 48 hours after the death and unnecessary touching is not allowed as it is considered impure. It is performed in the presence of friends and family members and the Hindu priest and lasts for 30 minutes. At the end of the ceremony, the cremated ashes are scattered or poured into the Ganges River or other important places. The family mourning period and certain rituals continues lasts for ten days to 30 days in which they are also considered impure and are not allowed visiting temple or shrine at home. The mourning family also displays the picture of the dead with a garland around it. By performing all the rituals, the family helps the dead person in the process of gaining moksha from the birth cycle to attain nirvana.

In Hinduism, rituals related to weddings or vivah are also very important. However, marriage rites vary from person to person and caste to caste. The horoscope of the bride and groom must match each other. The other marriage rituals include walking around the fire altar and the utterance of mantras by the priest. The marriage unites the bride and groom into one household dharma. Marriage celebrations are dependent on the social status of the bride and grooms family social status.

The festival of Shivratri, the night of Shiva, is held in February or March. The Hindu people fast for the whole day and night. They worship and pray during the night and they break their fast the next morning. Shiva is considered to be a quick-tempered god, so soothing food items such as milk, water, honey, and the leaves of the wood apple tree (Aegle marmelos), are offered to make Shiva happy. In addition, a drink made of almond, hemp seeds and milk is called 'thandai' has also become the part of festive because hemp seeds are said to be dear to Shiva.

Holi is a festival of colors that is celebrated by coating others with dry and water-colours. The festival of Holi is celebrated with joy, singing and dancing in spring for two days in February or March. The people mostly wear white outfits so the different colors thrown on the clothes can be visible. This festival is associated with the gods Krishna and Shiva. The marriage procession of Shiva is retreated and celebrated as Holi. The food such as malpua (fresh bread soaked in sugar syrup), Puran Poli (unleavened wheat bread stuffed with lentils and jaggery and baked on a griddle), and gujjiyas (flour patties stuffed with milk solids, sugar, almonds, and raisins and then deep-fried). Holi is observed as a public holiday in most of India.

The festival of Onam is associated with the harvest season which is celebrated between August and September mostly in Kerala. Ganesha, the son of Shiva and

Parvati, is an elephant-headed god. He is worshiped as the god of good luck and prosperity who removes all obstacles in men' life. His image or murti is installed at home for a few hours or few days until the festival finishes. Later, these same images placed at homes were brought into the procession while dancing and singing continues. Modak is a kind of food that consists of wheat flour pastry stuffed with coconut and jaggery and baked on a griddle is eaten and offered to Ganesha throughout the festivals.

Dussehra is the festival that proclaims the victory of good over evil. Each year Dussehra is celebrated in the month of October. The celebration of Dussehra varies from place to place throughout India. Mostly, it is celebrated while dancing and singing. Finally, the celebration ends with the burning of the statue of Rama (who represents evil) and proclaiming the victory of Rama (who represents good). Moreover, the story of the Rama called Ramlila (part of the Hindu epic Ramayana) is presented or performed during Dussehra celebrations (Practices in Hinduism).

Navaratri or Sharad Navaratri also known as Durga Puja is another one of the major festivals held in the respect of female deity. This festival is held in September or October. Navaratri lasts for nine days and ends with the celebration of Dussehra on the tenth day. But sometimes it may last for eight days with Dussehra on the ninth day depending on the lunar calendar.

Diwali is celebrated after twenty-one days. Where Dussehra is celebrated as Rama victory over Ravan, similarly Diwali is celebrated as Rama's return to his birthplace Ayodhya, after 14 years of exile. Diwali is the festival of lights and happiness. During this festival, the homes are decorated with lights. In the same way, the use of fireworks and the exchange of sweets between family and friends are also very common. The deity Lakshmi, who is the goddess of wealth, is worshiped and venerated.

The most sacred city in Hinduism is Varanasi. It is believed to be the city where Shiva, the god of destruction, lived a long time ago. The River Ganges, which is one of the most sacred rivers in the world, runs through the city and Hindus bathe in it with the hope that they can wash their sins away. A lot of Hindus believe that people who die in the city of Varanasi can achieve moksha. Hindus believed that a bird Garuda was flying over the Gages River. The bird carried a jar full of immortality nectar, and four drops from the jar fell into the Ganges. For this reason, Hindus make a pilgrimage to the Ganges to take bath into it, so that their sins can be washed away.

Kumbh Mela is one of the greatest gatherings of Hindu pilgrims on the river Ganges. It continues for fifty-five days and took place after twelve years on a large scale (Practices in Hinduism). People from different parts of India gather at four different locations. Allahabad and Hardwar are the most famous among these four locations.

During this event, Hindus wear garlands around their neck and then throw these into the river Ganges as an offering. The processions to the Ganges River are led by the Holy man and hope to get moksha by showing their devotion to the Brahman.

Cultural Synthesis and its influence on Hinduism

Between the 5th and 6th BCE brought the more personal and practical ways of salvation through Jainism and Buddhism. Through the influence of these new movements, Vedic religion developed into Brahmanism, which began to recognize Brahma, Vishnu and Shiva as personifications of Brahman. The later centuries saw a wave of the new synthesis in theism, yoga practices and caste duties. According to Gandhi, Hinduism teaches the following: "God exists. He is without beginning, immaculate, and without any attribute or form. He is omnipresent and omnipotent. His original form is Brahman. It neither does nor causes to be done. It does not govern. It is bliss incarnate, and by it, all this is sustained".

Around 800 BC the amalgamation of many Vedic and non-Vedic cultures give way to new cultural norms and trends. In this period the intellectual creeds and opinions were also shaped and the ideas about the existence of God, life after death and reincarnation were challenged. The religious leaders and others also reconsidered their religious position and eliminated some of the uncertain practices. This situation of intellectual experiments gives way to Buddhism and Jainism. The founders of these religions were both Kshatriyas. It is interesting to note that although Hinduism gave birth to these two religions, their influence on Hinduism is also very prominent. Jainism has a considerable effect on Hindu thoughts and practices such as Jain ascetics and vegetarianism are the best examples. Similarly, Buddha gave a new turn to the Upanishad teachings and practices, though Upanishad itself has influence over Buddhism. When king Ashoka was converted to Buddhism, he promoted this religion across India. At this time Hinduism was greatly influenced by Buddhism. Buddha is regarded as the avatar of Enlightenment. For religious instruction, Hindus also use the parable method common in Buddhism. Moreover, Buddhist art put a visible influence on Hindu sculpture or iconography.

The Bhakti movement revolves around the idea of devotion to God. The Bhakti movement started in south India in the sixth century under the influence of the religious experiences of the poet-saints. These saints had been singing hymns while travelling from one place to other. The Bhakti literature consists of devotional songs. The southern and northern areas of India are the birthplace of these Bhakti songs. The common language of love and appreciation is used for the gods and goddesses by the sages. These Bhakti songs were being commonly used and composed in the sixth century. Moreover, these songs are still sung and written by the Hindus. The men and women from all spheres of society joined the Bhakti movement by singing the hymns in their vernacular languages instead of Sanskrit in order to show devotion to God. Later, this devotional pattern was also admitted and appreciated by the Hindu theologians that even these poems became part of the worship along with the temple liturgies. In this connection, the teachings and poetic works of Alvars and Nayanar were compiled in the 10th century. During this era, great names appeared in world history as great practitioners of the Bakhti movement namely: Kabir, Guru Nanak, Mirabai, Surdas, Tulsi Das, Chaitanya (Sonali). Later, Islam enters India around the Eighth century. Along with Islam, the great Sufi orders were also introduced which later spread throughout north India. It is noteworthy that Islam and Hinduism equally influenced each other as far as their practices, social structure, art, architecture and religious practices.

However, the interaction between Islam and Hinduism was not completely peaceful. The Hindu temples were destroyed during Mughal rule (1526-1757) in northern and west India. In the middle of this tension, the Hindu poets-saints focused on the personal relationship with God through devotion. The Bhakti movement also proved a relief for the Hindus who had been suffering the hardships of the Muslim rule in India. Open-mindedness was promoted and fanaticism was condemned. Moreover, it brought the tidings of hope and salvation for the Hindu community. Furthermore, this movement proved fruitful in order to bring Hindus and Muslims closer. The Muslim Sufi contributed to this movement with the idea of love, devotion, brotherhood and equality. In reality, the efforts were made by the promoters of this movement to eliminate the differences between the two communities by stressing that Rama and Rahim are the different terms used by Hindus and Muslims for the same God. The social reforms and the attitude towards women were improved. The Bhakti movement later gave way to Sikhism.

The nineteenth century is known as the period of revival and reform movements within Indian religious traditions. The Hindu revivalist movements such as Brahmo Samaj, Arya Samaj and Ramakrishna Mission flourished during the British period in India. As a result, Hindus like other communities also felt the need to define their religious traditions and practices in order to distinguish them from the other contemporary religions i.e. Buddhism, Islam and Christianity. Consequently, a number of factors such as Christian missionary activities in colonial India, the Western style of education of Indians and their journeys to the Western world, Hindu culture, philosophy and belief system, encourage Hindu scholars to redefine their religion. Many scholars are agreed that due to the low caste mass conversion toward Christianity in India, the Hindu leaders started redefining and reconsidering their relationship with the low castes. Moreover, the status of women in Hindu society was also improved due to these reform movements.

Religious Pluralism and Hinduism

In terms of cultures and religions, India has been a pluralist society for centuries. It was home to the major religions of the world such as Hinduism, Buddhism, Jainism, Christianity, Zoroastrianism and Islam. Religious pluralism means that a person has the complete right to follow his belief even though it is not acceptable for others. In the same manner, Hinduism gives respect to different religious paths of spiritual realization. Rig Veda says: "Truth is one; people call it by various names" (Easwaran, Gita, 20). In the same way, the Upanishads are also inclusive in so far as they mention different gods after the Vedic period. Likewise, Gita promotes religious inclusivism, for example: "Whoever comes to Me (Krishna), through whatsoever form, I reach him; all men are struggling through paths which in the end lead to me." This attitude of religious tolerance in the Vedas (shruti) continued to be present in the remembered tradition (smriti) that followed the Vedas. A text from the 11th century CE found inscribed on a temple in India express pluralism which reads as follows: "The Vedas, the Samkhya, the Yoga, the Pasupata and the Vaisnava creeds, each of them is encouraged in some place or another. Some think that this is better, or that is better owing to differences of taste, but all men reach you, the Supreme, even as rivers, however, zigzag their courses may be, reach the sea". Jayanta Bhatta, a 9th century Brahmin logician and the author of the well-known work Nyāyamañjarī ('Blooms of Nyāya'), concluded that "the scriptures of all faiths – Buddhist, Jaina, Samkhya, etc. – are true and authoritative either because God is directly the author of each, in his several incarnations, or because they are ultimately based on one Vedic revelation".

On the other hand, religious tolerance and social exclusivism in Hinduism can appear at the same time as some smriti literature excludes women and Sudras from the direct study of the Vedic texts which is a kind of exclusivism. But there are other ways for women and Sudras to reach salvation, for instance, through karma and yoga bhakti. In addition to this, the great Muslim scholar, Al Biruni (973-1048), noted the social exclusivism of the Hindus towards foreigners (non-Hindus) because they could not be included in any of the official castes. He noted the presence of religious tolerance for the different schools of thought within Hinduism. Similarly, many travelers in India like Barbosa (1480-1521) and Bernier (17th century) observed the same kind of tolerance that Hindus had for other Hindus (Sharma 271-73).

In the Medieval period (1000 to 1800 CE) before the arrival of the Muslims, foreign invaders were absorbed into Hindu society. But the encounter of Islam with the Hindus was different. Muslims had not been absorbed into Indian society because their religious identity was too strong. Arvind Sharma is of the view that although Muslims were excluded from the social caste system, still Hindus showed religious tolerance for Islam as a religion. The important question is what Sharma mean by religious tolerance? With the passage of time in the Modern period (c.1800 to the present), Hinduism became inclusive and pluralistic after its encounter with the West through British rule in India. The first Hindu response was to reject the values and ideals of the West. But most modern Hindu writers advocated religious tolerance and (moral) pluralism e.g. Ram Mohan Roy (1772-1833) and others. Ram Mohan Roy was the founder of the Brahma Samaj. He interpreted the Vedic texts in a theistic sense and wanted to restore the tradition of the Upanishads. He sought to establish the figure of Brahman as the supreme reality. He fought vigorously against the cult of images, claiming that it was the purest superstition and contrary both to reason and common sense. He rejected Hindu polytheism, and never ceased to affirm his belief in a single God, inaccessible and eternal, who could only be addressed in worship.

Mul Sankar (1824-1833) or Dayananda Sarasvati, was the founder of the Arya Samaj. He taught that the 4 Vedas (Rig Veda, Yajur Veda, Sama Veda, Atharva Veda) are infallible and that their superiority over all other Hindu texts is unchallengeable. He presented the Vedic religion as a rigorous monotheism allowing no place for polytheism or the Hindu cult of images because the supreme deity was perceived as Absolute. The 33 deities (devatas) mentioned in the Veda, are only the forces of nature or activities with useful benefits for humanity (cosmic forces).

In the 1960s, many Hindu gurus left India and settled in the West where they taught about the philosophy of inclusivism. They taught the classical themes of neo-Vedantism: the oneness of the human soul and the divine, the transcendent unity of the religions and religious universalism, the spiritual superiority of India as the sacred civilization and the cradle of various religions. They accepted the validity and unity of all religions from a Hindu perspective. They integrated the other religions inclusively into their system in order to neutralize them, without giving them the supreme place in the hierarchy, which always falls to Hinduism. Swami Vivekananda (1863-1902) took part in the first meeting of the World's Parliament of Religions held in Chicago back in 1893, where he introduced Hindu beliefs and practices to the western world.

Hinduism absorbs everything that enters into it and raises it to a higher level. Every God accepted by Hinduism is elevated and ultimately identified with the central Reality. Hindu scholars claim the Supremacy of Vedanta Hinduism over other faith traditions by saying that the truth which other religions were seeking was the truth first revealed to the Hindus. They claimed that this truth was to be found in the Vedanta – India's spiritual treasure, which other religions need for their survival and regeneration. Radhakrishnan is not open and tolerant toward other faiths. Underneath his charitable exterior lies confidence and pride in Upanishadic spirituality and belief that India is the world's spiritual home. Where he differed from the current Hindutva propagandists was in his dislike for their aggressive and violent methods as the means for achieving Hindu superiority. The word Hindutva was coined in 1923 by V.D. Savarkar (d. 1942) to refer to Hindu nationalism. The view of Savarkar was that only the religions of Indian origin were to shape India. Such a position does not necessarily compromise Hinduism's soteriological pluralism. But the alignment of religion with power creates a problem for tolerance.

Religious pluralism is also associated with Gandhi and was influential from the 1920s to 1948. Gandhi (1869-1948) was actively involved in promoting good relations between Hindus, Sikhs, Muslims and Christians in India. He felt that religions had a positive role to play in public but that India should be a secular state (not aligned with any one religion). Nehru thought that Indian nationhood should avoid any connection with religion except in a reformist capacity. This view persisted till the 1980s. Nehru's secularism was more European and was this view was included in the Constitution (1950).

Lal, Vinay. And   Borin van Loon. *Introducing Hinduism. A Graphic Guide*, Icon publishers, 2013 p. 3-9 13, 16-15,57,25

Wangu, Madu. B. *World Religions Hinduism*. Chelsea House, 2009.New York, ed.4, p. 7,10, 18, 13-14,41,114,43

Warrier, Maya. *Faith Guides for Higher Education: A Guide to Hinduism*.university of Leeds, 2007, p.1

Sen, K. Mohan, *Hinduism*, Penguin book, 2005, P. 4, 34, 28-29, 22-23, 52-56

Rosen, Steven. J. Essential Hinduism. Green Wood publishing group, United States of America,2006. p. 20

Flood, Gavin, *Religion ,History of Hinduism*, , 2009 http://www.bbc.co.uk/religion/religions/hinduism/history/history_1.shtml

Mittal, Sushil and Thursby, Gene, *Religions of South Asia*: *An introduction*, Routledge, New York, 2006. P 35-36, 38, 40, 49,

Coward, H., *Scripture in the World Religions, A Short Introduction*, Oxford: Oneworld, 2000. P. 116,113, 115-116

Markham, I. (ed.), *A World Religions Reader,* Chichester, UK: Wiley-Blackwell, 2009, p. 35,61

Shattuck, Cybelle. Religion of the World: Hinduism. Routledge London, 2003, p. 39-41, 20-21,38-39,29, 43,67, 71,82, 60-61,91,110

Brockington, J.L., *The Sacred Thread, Hinduism in its Continuity and Diversity,* Edinburgh: University Press, 1998. P 36, 41,43

Charkra, Hyden, *Epic Hindu literature: Mahabharata, Ramayana, etc.. – With Over 200 000 Verses, About History.* https://about-history.com/epic-hindu-literature-mahabharata-ramayana-etc-with-over-200-000-verses/

Sivananda. Sri, Swami. *All About Hinduism. The Divine Life Society*, 1999. p. 31,32,41, 24,28,26,1,2,121

Charities, Practices in Hinduism. BBC. https://www.bbc.co.uk/bitesize/guides/zvrsv9q/revision/9

Subramanian. Sriram, G. Ghojogh, B. *Introduction to the Non-dualism Approach in Hinduism and its Connection to Other Religions and Philosophies.* Research Gate, 2020, p.11, 3-4 https://www.researchgate.net/publication/342503023_Introduction_to_the_Nondualism_Approach_in_Hinduism_and_its_Connection_to_Other_Religions_and_Philosophies

Jayaram V , Brahman According to Advaita and Dvaita in Hinduism : Hinduwebsite.com https://www.hinduwebsite.com/hinduism/essays/brahman_duality.asp

Easwaran, E. (trans.), *The Bhagavad Gita,* New York: Vintage Books, 2000, p. 20

Iconography: Hindu Iconography. Encycolopedia.com.

https://www.encyclopedia.com/environment/encyclopedias-almanacs-transcripts-and-maps/iconography-hindu-iconography

Easwaran, E., The Upanishads, Mumbai: Jaico Publishing House, 2016. 11-12
Chawla , Puneet. What is Parsad. Live Vastu : A way of Good Life https://www.livevaastu.com/dr-chawla-corner/what-is-prasad

Miles, J. *The Norton Anthology of World Religions,* New York: Norton & Co., Vol. 1, 2015. P .63

Moore, A.C., *Iconography of Religions – an Introduction.* SCM press, 1977.p. 105

Sonali. *Bhakti Movement: Meaning, Features and Impact*
https://www.historydiscussion.net/history-of-india/bhakti-movement-meaning-features-and-impact/2734

Walsh, Judith, E. A brief History of India, Infobase publishing USA, second edition, 2010 p.68

Jones, Constance, A. and Ryan. James D. *Encyclopedia of Hinduism.* Infobase publishing. 2007, p.23

Sharma, A. *Religious Tolerance – a History,* Uttar Pradesh, India: HarperCollins, 2019. P.256-257, 263-265, 270-71, 281-82, 286-287, 285-286

Demariaux, J, B. *How to Understand Hinduism. SCM press, 1995. p. 90,102*

CHAPTER 7

Judaism

Judaism is the oldest of three monotheistic and Abrahamic religions and one of the oldest monotheistic religions in general. It is also a national religion of the Israelites, specific by its belief that Jews are God's Chosen People, symbolized through the Covenant with God.

The Teachings of Judaism

Judaism is commonly described as a religion rooted in ethical monotheism: that is, a belief system that assumes the existence of a single (and singular) deity whose creative agency brought the universe into being and who directs all life toward ethical goals. The singular God is not a theoretical affirmation, but a soteriological experience of the Jewish people. He is an all-knowing, all-powerful creator, who has no children, no rivals and no equals. More specifically, Judaism assumes that a special covenant relationship exists between the Jewish people and the Creator-God and that the history of that relationship can be found, in part, in the pages of Jewish scripture. God is also historically the only Savior for the people that are chosen in a unique way.

Judaism is a special religion in the Middle East because it is not monolatry, which means that Israelites did not choose to worship the One God while accepting the existence of other gods. This may have been the case in the early Jewish state in Kanaan. From the very start, Judaism had a united cult that rests upon the possibility of choice. A mission is given to the whole nation, and it is upon them if they want to cherish it or not. The whole history of the Jewish people is, thus, a history of loving and caring God for those who accept the mission and of annihilation for those who do otherwise. As such, Judaism is monotheistic in an abstract way but for a concrete covenant. It describes more than explains ontologically. This connection contains a restrictive aspect, often arbitrary.

At the heart of all religious practice in Judaism is the concept of the mitzvot, or divinely revealed commandments, that embody a life of ethical purpose, and reflect the spiritual and moral discipline that is expected of all observant Jews. Monogamous marriage is a symbol of a strong connection with the One God who calls also other people to unite in Jerusalem. That is why Judaism is often described as centralized universalism. In the oldest part of Torah, Abraham's El (or Elohim) is YHWH (Tetragrammaton), which is ordinarily translated as Yahweh, meaning most probably "I am who I am". Although it is a matter of many theological discussions, the essence of being is contained in this name. God is the life force, creator of everything that is. Many Orthodox Jews would not even pronounce the name Yahweh loud and would just use HaShem (the Name) or Adonai (My Lord) instead. Many Orthodox Jews will not even write words like God and would use G-D instead.

God is a person. He created the world in six days and rested on the seventh, traditionally being held as Saturday, the holiest day in the Jewish week. In the Hebrew Bible, God reveals himself as "God of Abraham" and then "God of Israel". God speaks directly to a man and promises constant presence, posterity, land, and progress. For patriarchs, he was a very personal God who interacts directly with chosen persons. He accepts Abel's offerings and saves Noah from floods. He talks directly to Abraham who often calls him El. It is the name of the highest god in Mesopotamia; without his permission, none of the other deities could have been worshipped. It was a covenant with Abraham who was requested to leave Mesopotamia and settle in Kanaan. The covenant was symbolized through the practice of circumcision of every male child until this day both in Judaism and in Islam. This god was not tied to a place, cosmic events or political powers and it was easy for Abraham to accept such a notion of the highest God. Abraham's descendants Isaac and Jacob called him "God of the fathers" and later he will not be known only as "God of Abraham", but also "God of Isaac" and "God of Jacob", the one who sends Joseph and Israelites to Egypt to survive and who rescues them through Moses from the Egyptian slavery. God of Moses and the prophets will soon become a leader of Israelites. All of this divine history shows that God takes an active interest in human affairs and interacts with humans on Earth. Humans can develop a personal relationship with God, while God granted humanity free will.

With Moses Yahweh will become a moral God, who gives laws, customs and priesthood. The morality requests come in form of Ten Commandments given to the chosen people on Mount Sinai, together with 613 mitzvahs. These are normative moral requests of 2nd millennia cultures: respecting the personal god and not adoring any other deity; respecting other persons, their family and property. God, in turn, respects human freedom, manifested through many rebellions in the desert. He is ever-forgiving and ever-loving but is also a warrior god, who will help Israelites to brutally conquer the Kanaan and destroy their cities. Old cosmic deities of water, wind, sun, or some local deities, are now male'akim, the angels or messengers. They carry God's words. By following these commandments, a further covenant with God is made, through which the Jews arrive back to the Kanaana and for a state that would eventually become a kingdom.

For Saul and David, he is far more than that. The Jewish kings will position Yahweh as the national god. The unified kingdom under the Davidian dynasty was stable enough to produce a number of texts written by the religious elite from the main Temple in Jerusalem. The Temple housed the Ark of the Covenant, which contained two stone tablets written by God himself, and thus became the sacred heart of Jewish worship. There is a clear break in textual development around the 8th century in the Israelite kingdom when the codification of Jewish religion began. The first part of the Hebrew Bible may have been written around this time. Soon after Solomon, ten Jewish tribes would form the Kingdom of Israel in the north, while two tribes established the Kingdom of Judah in the south. This was the time of great prophets (of which Isaiah, Ezekiel, Jeremiah and Daniel are the most known) would stir and warn the Jewish society of their injustice and break of the covenant with God, which would surely have consequences. They came in 722 BCE with the attack of Assyrians who conquered the Northern Kingdom. In 586 BCE the Babylonian Kingdom conquered Judah, destroyed Jerusalem and brought Jews into slavery. This was a heartbreaking historical event for the Jewish people, but in 539 BCE Cyrus the Great decides to allow Jews to go home. With political and religious leaders like Ezra and Nehemiah, and with Persian help in rebuilding the Temple, a new age for Judaism began, focused on certain liturgical and essential reforms.

The Jewish eschatology is quite different from the ones contained in Christianity and Islam. Tanakh barely mentions heaven and hell. Heaven is considered just where God lives. Sheol or hell is just a vague underworld where souls go after death. While not giving any details about it, Tanakh makes it certain that the soul lives after one dies. The wording in Tanakh is that a good person is gathered to his or her people; while bad ones are cut off from their people. Thus, the only certain "reward" is that soul will be reunited with their ancestors, but Tanakh does not explain what the afterlife will be like nor if any rewards or punishments await. For most rabbis, it will be a consequence of the type of life on the Earth, so it is necessary to follow God's commandments as close as possible, if nothing else then because of doing good in this world. The type of doing good is Tzedakah, justice or charity, often visible in the donation of 10% of income to the needy, poor and sick.

Jewish soteriology includes the person of the Messiah. Many Jews throughout history have hoped for the coming of a Mashiach, which is prophesized in Tanakh. He will bring a Messianic age. As a leader, he will rebuild the Holy Temple in Jerusalem, bring all the Jews back into the Promised Land, and will bring about the perfection of the world and end all the sufferings. All Jews will be resurrected to return to Jerusalem and they will be present when God creates new heaven on Earth. That is why the Jewish law forbids cremation, to keep the physical body intact for when it is resurrected by God after the arrival of the Messiah.

The History of Judaism

The origins of Judaism are interwoven with the origins of the Jewish people, and those origins can be traced back at least to the late thirteenth century b.c.e. when the Egyptian Pharaoh Merneptah claimed to have wiped "Israel" out forever. However, most of our information about Jews or Judaism derives from the Hebrew Bible—known to Christians as the Old Testament—and its record of interaction between a people who called themselves Israelites and their one god, known in Hebrew as YHWH. The twenty-four books that make up the Hebrew Bible constitute the sacred scriptures of the Jews, and these books record the history and religious thought of these people from its remote beginnings until the sixth-century BCE. when a significant portion of the nation of Israel was driven into exile in Babylonia. While there is no clear founder of Judaism, one may point to Abraham, Isaac and Jacob as the three sources from which Jewish religion came; Jacob even gets the name Israel, whose meaning abounds but was accepted by the whole nation. Judaism, on the other hand, stems from Judah, one of 12 Jacob's sons and subsequent tribe who populated Judea. Lastly, the name Hebrews means either "nomads" or "decedents of Heber", which is mentioned in the Bible.

The subsequent history of the Jews, and the further development of Judaism, can be traced through distinct periods of cultural change and geographical displacement, as much of the Jewish population of Israel dispersed by the sixth-century CE throughout the Middle East, the Mediterranean, and Europe, forming a Jewish diaspora. It is during this period that the Talmud, the second most important scriptural work was compiled, a work of voluminous commentary and legal codification based on the laws and teachings of the Hebrew Bible.

The Bible is, arguably, the most well-known literature in history. The Hebrew Bible is probably the most universally accepted version of the Bible, known to the Christians as Old Testament and to Jews as Tanakh. It is not one unified book, but a collection of many different books, such as Torah (the Five Books of Moses), Nevi'im or Prophetic Books, and Ketuvim or Writings. While all of them are considered sacred, the most exalted is Torah, which includes Genesis, Exodus, Leviticus, Numbers and Deuteronomy. They explain the creation of the world and first men, covers patriarchs and the creation of the nation of Israel. It is the very basis of all Abrahamic religions. According to the tradition, Torah was received or revealed to Moses by God on Mt Sinai and written down by him. Historians are not sure about this tradition; most Biblical scholars agree that Torah was not written by one single person but was written in fragments by different people over a long period of time. Historically, many Biblical "facts" about Israelites is uncertain due to lack of evidence outside the Bible. The Torah was finished around the 8th century BCE, containing stories and beliefs of previous generations.

Mainstream theology suggests four main sources of the Hebrew Bible. First is the J-source or Yahwist source (around 9th and 8th century BCE, time of David and his descendants), characterized by the use of this name for God. The second is the E-source of Elohim source, characterized by the use of this name for God and is written a short time after the J-source. These two sources were soon combined. The third is the D-source or Deuteronomy source, responsible for the whole book of Deuteronomy and some writings outside the Torah, like Samuel and 1 and 2 Kings. This happened sometime in the 7th or 6th century BCE and is characterized by a heavy accent on morality and laws. Lastly, there is a P-source of Priestly source, written in 6th and 5th century BCE by priests and is characterized by purity and rituals. It has an obvious accent on a need to rebuild a new religious identity while in Babylonian exile. Here, the personal prayer and an image of modern Judaism comes about, as a result of a change in living conditions, environment and sudden minority status. A strong accent on the monotheism of this reformed Judaism may point to possible monolatry in the old homeland. Different sources can be easily seen in the texts of the Torah.

The Biblical history of Judaism lasts until the 4th century BCE. Possibly the most important event is the building of Solomon's Temple, which will serve as the center of global Judaism. it was the main religious center, place of rituals and sacrifices, built in 10th century BCE and destroyed by Babylonians in 586 BCE. In the same place, the Second Temple was erected in 516 BCE. It was destroyed by the Roman emperor Titus in 70 CE and only the Western Wall survived. Until today, this is one of the most sacred sites in Judaism. Jewish eschatology mentions the building of the Third Temple as the announcement of end times.

The Biblical time is followed by the Hellenistic period (4th BCE-2nd CE) when Talmud was formed. After Tanakh, Talmud is the most sacred text of Judaism, compiled in 38 volumes. It is the primary source of the Jewish law (Halakha) and Jewish theology in its many forms, as it also contains rules on how the Torah or the Commandments should be interpreted. It is filled with debate, legal interpretations, history, ethics, philosophy and legends. It consists of two parts: Mishnah – the first written compilation of Jewish oral law and is thus known as the Oral Torah; Gemara is the rabbinic interpretation of Mishnah. Talmud is the basis for all Jewish laws in history from that time and is widely used in Rabbinic Judaism. This was also the time when the Second Temple and Jerusalem were destroyed by the Romans and ended all hopes of Jews to liberate themselves from Roman rule. The Jews moved all across Europe, North Africa and the Middle East, which would periodically suffer from persecutions.

Rabbinic Judaism is a historical period between the 2nd and 18th centuries. A rabbi is a scholar and teacher of the Torah. By the 6th century, Rabbinic Judaism became the dominant type of faith and is the foundation of all Judaic traditions today. A large emphasis is given to the Torah studies, which was conducted through the creation of Yeshiva. These religious and educational institutions focused on daily lectures (shiurim) and study pairs (chavrutas). Rabbinic Judaism also opened synagogues as the place of prayer. This long period is characterized by the thriving Jewish communities in the Islamic world (including Spain), institutionalization of Kabbalah, division between Ashkenazi and Sephardi Jews, occasional pogroms and trading successes in Europe.

Modern Judaism begins in the 18th century and lasts until today. It was characterized by the splitting of Judaism into several groups, pogroms and genocides, but also the creation of the modern State of Israel in 1948 by the partition of Palestine. About six million Jews were systematically murdered during the Shoah, the Hebrew term for the Holocaust.

The Encounter with Christianity and Islam

The evolution of Judaism was affected, in part, by interaction with two world religions that derive a portion of their theology and worldview from Judaism: Christianity and Islam. For Judaism, the Creator-God remains a transcendent figure who has not incarnated God's self in the person of Jesus of Nazareth, nor has God chosen

Muhammad as one of God's prophets. Still, Judaism influenced beliefs in such a great manner that nearly everyone in the Middle East, Europe and North Africa follows a monotheistic religion. Like Christianity and Islam, however, Judaism looks forward to a time of divine judgment and world redemption—the Messianic Age—when peace and justice will exist for all peoples. Distinctive to Judaism is the belief that the one God has established a special covenanted relationship with the Jewish people, and that they have been commanded by God to carry out God's teachings (Torah) and religious practices (Mitzvot). The global interreligious dialogue often involves the three monotheistic religions, where many features of both theological discussions and peace efforts may found a common ground and the same Semitic roots of understanding God and the world we inhabit.

The Modern Era: Reform Movements

In the modern era, Judaism has assumed a number of denominational forms, distinguished from one another by the rigor of their religious observances and differences over their understanding of Judaism's most basic beliefs. Arranged as a continuum, these denominations can be classified from the most rigorous and traditional in observance (Orthodoxy), to the somewhat more lenient and adaptive (Conservatism), to the most innovative and culturally assimilated (Reform and Reconstruction). In the 1800s, each bigger city in Europe had one chief rabbi who had the authority to amend common laws and to guide the Jewish community. With democratic processes and enlightenment ideas in Europe, such a rule did not sit well with many Jews. They wanted to apply a more scientific background to their lives and to promote morality on basis of a "reform" and "modernized" Jewish tradition. Some of the first changes occurred in references. Some changed the prayerbooks, rejecting Jerusalem as their home, as they were living for generations in Europe. For instance, Reform Jews stopped wearing a kippah, had shorter services, and introduced organ music to synagogues. In the 1830ies, a group of young German Jews, headed by Rabbi Abraham Geiger, decided which rituals still have a meaning and which do not, particularly due to the unclearness of some rules. They also changed the kosher rules and tend to think that the purpose of religion was to feel holy and spiritual and to be moral. This was the very start of the Reform Movement.

Traditional rabbis rejected all of these changes. They started to call themselves Orthodox, as they stuck to the laws of Torah and Talmud, warning that the Jews cannot just reject what was written for them and explained by the rabbis through centuries. A splinter group of modern Orthodox allowed some smaller concessions.

For instance, Samson Rafael Hirsch, who was the leader of this group, allowed men to shave their beards. Far more importantly, Hirsch (who was the rabbi of Frankfurt) decided it was time to split organizationally and to form separate synagogues and communities, rather than arguing only one way in Judaism. Zechariah Frankel, another critique of reform, was important for the arguments for and against the use of German language in liturgy instead of Hebrew, which was seldomly known by ordinary Jews. He was the founder of Conservative Judaism, formed around the Jewish Theological Seminary in Wroclaw, Poland. This seminary would later become the heart of the Conservative Jews in the United States. In the late 19th century, both Conservative and Reform Jews migrated to the United States, where they form the two largest and most influential communities.

In the European East, Rabbi Israel ben Eliezer was using kabbalistic knowledge to spread a new form of Judaism. He introduced kabbalistic rituals in everyday life, saying there is nothing without a God's spark. He wanted to find the true meaning in everything and everyone. Like all kabbalists, he travelled around, without an intention to gather students. His disciple Rabbi Dav Baer did not travel but asked listeners to come to his home. From them, a whole new group came to be. They would soon be known as Hasidic Jews. From a small group in 1730, Hasidism became the major form of Judaism in the whole of Eastern Europe until 1815. Their success was tremendous, as they looked like a charismatic movement, where they danced, clapped, sang religious songs, and were enthusiastically spiritual. Instead of focusing only on the law, Hasidim gave blessings and cared for the spiritual state of people. They would focus more on prayer than on studying, although they were printing more books than any other Jewish group at the time. On local levels, they would form Chavurot, small groups of people who would facilitate communal mitzvot, from dowry to funerals. With the arrival of reform ideas, Hasidim would join other more conservative Jews and together they formed the Jewish Orthodoxy. They are recognizable for their heavy hats and black clothes, and also by long curly hair on the sides of their head (Payot) and they do not cut it because of a Commandment in the Torah.

Many Jews use and favor Kabbalah as a daily practice. As an ancient mystic stream of Judaism, Kabbalah is centered around the Book of Zohar (the Book of Radiance), which is a book that collects knowledge from even older mystical works. By tradition, knowledge of Kabbalah was received by Moses and kept secret in an elite circle, which was only rediscovered by the Spanish Jews. It looks at the Tanakh through ten sefirot, ways to interact with an aspect of God. Through Zohar, Jews are encouraged to understand deeper what God's message is and what is Judaism all about. Zohar was written in the 13th century, as a mix of intellectual upgrading through the Muslim scholars and deep religious feelings among the European Jewish diaspora. Its creation was influenced by Maimonides, a Jewish philosopher, who claimed no one can ever know what God does, just what God does not do. Other influential Kabbalists of the time were Isaac the Blind, Nachmanides, and Abraham Abulafia. However, it is a religious feeling that says about God's everyday influence in personal life. Kabbalah answers this challenge with multiple aspects of God through ten sefirot. Zohar was written and developed in northern Spain. In times of the Spanish Inquisition, Isaac Luria argued that the world was a perfect pot that was destroyed and it is up to good men to collect all of the pieces. This is done through the good deeds or sparks that makes us one step closer to the Messiah. Luria also developed some of the most typical Jewish rituals today. His ideas became very popular and helped in the spreading of Kabbalah. While there are many misconceptions of Kabbalah, as mystical and magical practice of Jews throughout centuries, only with Zohar the main characteristics of Kabbalah are revealed. Besides ten divine powers or sefirot, these are ideas that one of the divine power is feminine, which will later introduce the gender dualism in Kabbalah; and that divine powers can be described by an allegory of a tree. An idea shared by almost all Kabbalists is Ein Sof (Infinite, No-End), the main characteristic of God whom we cannot describe otherwise and is inconceivable by thinking. The only way to approach understanding God is through sefirot. Finding the secrets and going deeper to sefirot is done through a number of ways, mostly by mystical meanings of each of 22 letters of the Hebrew alphabet. Writing them in a specific way achieves special knowledge and this was used in decoding the Torah.

Like many other faiths, Judaism faces a number of challenges. One of the weightiest of these challenges, philosophically viewed, is the need to respond religiously to the mass slaughter of Jews by the Nazis during World War II (the Shoah), while preserving some measure of belief in a Deity who is both compassionate and just. In addition, as Judaism seeks to adapt to the transformative values and mores of the contemporary period, it has sought to accommodate the changing roles of women in synagogue worship and community leadership. Even Jews who cannot accept the faith claims of traditional Judaism have found a place within the worldwide Jewish community as secular or "ethnic" Jews, for whom Judaism remains an important cultural force and influence.

Global Snapshot

There are around 15 million Jews today in the world, making it the tenth most popular religion globally. The largest concentration of Jews is in Israel, the United States and France, followed by large groups living in Palestine, Canada, the United

Kingdom, Iran, Russia, Germany, and Australia. Judaism is specific as it is not only a religion: it is also a people, nation, culture, and civilization. However, it is not a race, as there are Black, Asian and White Jews, as a consequence of both descendants and converts. According to Jewish law, a Jew is a child born of a Jewish mother or a person who converts to Judaism, although some modern Jewish denominations now accept descent through the father. Judaism is tightly connected to ethnic origin, so all Jews are at the same time ethnically Jews and religiously Jews.

Since the Middle Ages, two distinct groups of Jews are Ashkenazi and Sephardi. The Ashkenazi are the Jewish community that developed in Central and Eastern Europe and speak Yiddish, a combination of Hebrew and the languages of Central Europe, mostly German and Russian. Most Jewish immigrants to the United States are Ashkenazi and many Yiddish words are now part of the US English slang. The Sephardi Jews are descendants of the Jews of Spain and those who fled from Spain to the Mediterranean countries of Levant, North Africa and Europe. Their language is Ladino, a combination of Hebrew and Old Spanish, a tongue under a threat of extinction.

There are many Jews who are not Ashkenazi nor Sephardi. The most famous ones are Jews of Iran, Iraq, Yemen, Ethiopia, China and Georgia. They all make up a diverse range of Jewish beliefs and cultures. Even in one area, there may be several Jewish identities. This is the case with the Jews in India. Three distinctive Jewish communities are known to have migrated to the Indian subcontinent: the Bene Israel, the Cochin Jews, and the Baghdadi Jews. Of these three, the Bene Israel were the largest and most successfully acculturated, and like the Cochin Jews, they traced their origins in India to biblical antiquity. All three communities have seen their numbers diminish during the latter part of the twentieth century, and many of their members have emigrated to Israel.

Religious Violence and the Future of Zionism

In 1898, the World Zionist Congress came to be a political body of Jews worldwide. The term "Zion" is associated with a part of Jerusalem. Jews were always considering Jerusalem their sacred center and pilgrimages to the land of their ancestors was called "return to Zion". The growing Zionist political movement called for a massive migration to Israel at the end of the 19th century. This modern Zionism, created by Theodor Herzl, centered around the belief that all Jews belong to a single nation, and that they should establish a sovereign Jewish state. The World Zionist Congress discussed where this state should be. Proposals ranged from Alaska to Uganda, but Jerusalem, in Palestine, was the area that held the most significance for Jews. In 1019,

Great Britain accepted an idea of a Jewish state in Palestine, and after the Holocaust, many other Western countries supported it as well. The state of Israel gained its independence in 1948. After the establishment of the Israeli government, the World Zionist Congress lost some of its power but is still alive through the World Zionist Organization. They have access to a large budget and together with the Israeli government, they encourage further Jewish settlement in Palestine.

Today, some 45% of Jews affiliate with religious Zionism, which is an idea that original Jewish traditions should be preserved, and Jews should have a sovereign state in the Promised Land. However, many Palestinians call this area also their home, they too have religious claims over Jerusalem, and they resent the influx of Jewish immigrants there. While Zionists secured land for Jews, it also flared territorial disputes and conflicts in the Middle East and contributed to the Israeli-Palestinian conflict. And while some more Orthodox Jews consider violence to be a legitimate tool to fulfil the Jewish aims, other Orthodox are even against the Zionist state in general. This messianic interpretation of Zionism is at odds with both mainstream political views in Israel and the perception of Israel in most of the Jewish Diaspora.

The politics of appeasement and interreligious dialogue for peace is not easily achievable in Israel. The assassination of Yitzchak Rabin, Israel's Prime Minister, on November 4, 1995, pointed up more than political differences in Israel: Rabin's assassin, Yigal Amir, had aligned himself with a community of ultra-Orthodox Jews who viewed Rabin's peace diplomacy as a religious crime. In their eyes, Rabin had become an enemy of the Jewish people by offering to give away territories captured by Israel during the 1967 war in exchange for a peace treaty with the Palestinians.

In contemporary times, religious Jews may accept violence as a way of preserving Israel and/or spreading the state authority in the West Bank, where the Palestinian Authority has the power. While the violence is readily condemned as such, some Jewish rabbis consider the use of violence in Israel as self-defence, even if it means destroying Palestinian homes and building new Jewish settlements. One major exception is the Jewish Defense League, founded in 1969 by Rabbi Meir Kahane in New York. There are now many Kahanist groups in Israel and the world, and they are listed as terrorist organizations by both the United States and Israel.

Judaism as a Way of Life

Jewish religious practices are designed to give meaning and direction to every facet of human life, from birth to death. Every newborn child within the Jewish community is welcomed into the covenant of Abraham and given a Hebrew name that often recalls the biblical origins of the Jewish people. At every critical juncture in the life cycle, the covenant relationship with God is renewed and celebrated: at a Bar or Bat mitzvah, at a wedding, during the mourning for a parent or near relative, prayers are recited that affirm Judaism's belief in the divine purpose that infuses all of human existence.

Like many other religious cultures, Judaism has developed a calendar of sacred festivals and life-cycle events that allow Jews to express their thanks for divine gifts and to commemorate significant events in their history. Chief among these holy days are the pilgrimage festivals, Pesach (Passover), Shavuot (Pentecost), and Sukkot (Tabernacles), and the "Days of Awe": Rosh Hashanah (New Year) and Yom Kippur (Day of Atonement). Two of traditional Judaism's signature religious practices are the weekly Sabbath (Shabbat) and the Dietary Code (Kashrut), both of which set Jews off from the rest of society. The yearly religious calendar reflects a similar awareness of divine purposefulness. The calendar is lunisolar, meaning that months are based on the phases of the moon but adjusted in average length to fit the length of the solar cycle. Years are numbered according to the rabbinical calculation of the start of the world. In 1178, Maimonides calculated it was the year 4938 from the creation of the world and the religious calendar is using this reference until today. Three of the major Jewish festivals—Pesach, Shavuot, and Sukkot—are occasions of thanksgiving, celebrating both the biblical narrative of the Exodus from Egyptian slavery and the fruitfulness of the earth. The two remaining critical sacred occasions—Rosh HaShanah and Yom Kippur—are primarily days of self-reflection and repentance, rather than occasions for the celebration of harvests or acts of historical deliverance. Rosh Hashanah is the first day of the Jewish calendar, a traditional anniversary celebrating the creation of Adam and Eve by blowing the shofar, a hollowed ram's horn. Yom Kippur is the Day of Atonement, when fasting is requested, as well as prayer in the synagogues. These two holidays are the High Holy Days, which refers to the ten days starting with Rosh HaShanah and ending with Yom Kippur, known as the Days of Repentance (Yamim Noraim, or the Days of Awe).

Shabbat or the Sabbath or Saturday is the seventh day of the Hebrew week and the most important day for the Jews. Since God rested on the seventh day, according to the account of Genesis, Jews do the same. It is a day of physical and spiritual rejuvenation. Halakha forbids any work on Shabbat, like doing business, spending money, shopping, housework, driving, using electricity or even using a phone are strongly discouraged. On Shabbat, a Jew should focus on reading and prayer. Observant Jews pray three times a day, in the morning after sunrise (Shaharit), in the afternoon before sunset (Minhah), and at night (Maariv), after the stars come out. In the prayers, Jews face towards Jerusalem. Prayer routines reflect ancient traditions of religious expression, rooted in biblical and rabbinic practice. While the Jews can pray alone, it is considered better to pray in a group of ten people. The denominational differences that characterize modern Judaism are reflected in both the liturgies and the distinct rituals that define and differentiate each of the principal communities that make up global Judaism. Some of the common things in Jewish prayer include covering one's eyes while praying Shema Israel which speaks of the love of God and adherence to his commandments; the Standing Prayer or Amida, when Jews have to stand still and not be touched by anything around them; and the praying clothes which includes kippah, tallit or the Jewish prayer shawl, and tefillin which are two leather boxes with prayers inside them. One goes on the hand and the other on the head.

The Kosher laws regulate the Jewish diet. All vegetables, fruits, grains and nuts are kosher. Regarding meat, the kosher animal is the one that both chews its cud and has a cloven hoof, like beef or sheep. Non-Kosher animals include pigs, dogs, rabbits, shellfish, birds of prey, whales and dolphins. Kosher animals should also be killed in a certain way called shechita. A trained professional with a very sharp knife delivers a quick death to the animal, best in one cut. All blood must be drained from the animal because blood is not kosher. One cannot combine milk and meat, which brings a lot of dietary restraints. For instance, one cannot eat cheeseburger or butter on mash potato served with meat. This rule realizes in "milk meals" and "meat meals", where the main feature is either milk or meat. That is why most Kosher restaurants are either "milk" or "meat" restaurants. Today, the kosher industry is a worldwide business, recognized by special kosher symbols on the products which have to be labeled if they are kosher or not (food items such as fruits, vegetables, and honey are instantly kosher). It may not only involve the food, but also services and lifestyles.

All the Jewish rituals are regularly done in a synagogue. Every synagogue contains a handwritten Torah Scroll, which is read aloud at every ceremony. A synagogue is led by a rabbi, a trained Jewish scholar and interpreter of Jewish law. Rabbis also conduct many Jewish events such as circumcisions, Bar and Bat Mitzvahs, weddings, and funerals. While in the synagogue, male Jews wear a kippah or yarmulka, as a sign of respect to God with covering the head. Orthodox Jews believe they are always in the presence of God and thus wear a kippah all the time. Whenever ten Jews assemble in the synagogue, they can have a prayer (minyan). There is no need to wait for the communal prayer to be organized. In every synagogue, one would find a bimah, which is a table from which Torah is read loud, and a desk for the prayer leader (hazzan). The Torah scrolls are kept in the Torah's Arc, a casket or a cabinet that resembles the Ark of the Covenant.

SUGGESTED READINGS, WEBLINKS, AND OTHER MEDIA

Scholarly Texts

- Adler, Rachel. *Engendering Judaism: An Inclusive Theology and Ethics*. Boston, MA: Beacon Press, 1999.

- Cohen, Shaye J. D. *The Beginnings of Jewishness: Boundaries, Varieties, Uncertainties*. Berkeley: University of California Press, 1999.

- Elazar, Daniel J. and Geffen, Rela Mintz. *Conservative Movement in Judaism: Dilemmas and Opportunities*. New York: SUNY Press, 2012.

- Galambush, Julie. *The Reluctant Parting: How the New Testament's Jewish Writers Created a Christian Book*. San Francisco, CA: HarperCollins, 2005.

- Goodman, Martin. *A History of Judaism*. Princeton, NJ: Princeton University Press, 2018.

- Jacobs, Louis. *The Jewish Religion: A Companion*. Oxford: Oxford University Press. 1995

- Plaut, W. Gunther. *The Rise of Reform Judaism: A Sourcebook of its European Origins*. New York: World Union for Progressive Judaism, 1963.

- Raphael, Marc Lee. *Judaism in America*. Columbia University Press, 2003

Weblinks

- www.jewfaq.org—Judaism 101
- www.aish.com—The Jewish website
- www.myjewishlearning.com
- www.beingjewish.com
- Union for Reform Judaism—www.urj.org
- United Synagogue of Conservative Judaism—www.uscj.org

Educational Documentaries

- *The Forbidden Garden: Piercing the Veil of the Kabbalah*, 2000, 63 min., www.insight-media.com

- *Essentials of Faith: Judaism*, 2006, 24 min., www.insight-media.com

- *Introduction to Judaism*, 2004, 30 min., www.insight-media.com

- *Keepers of the Faith: Hasidim in the New World and Beyond*, 2000, 53 min., www.insight-media.com

Popular Films

- *The Chosen* (1981). Directed by Jeremy Paul Kagan—A sentimental but historically sensitive portrayal of Hasidic life and the struggle to preserve a traditional legacy in the modern world.

- *Schindler's List* (1993). Directed by Steven Spielberg—A powerful dramatization of the rescue of over 1,000 Polish Jews from the Nazi death camps by an ex-Nazi war profiteer.

- *Ushpizin* (2005). Directed by Gidi Dar—An Israeli film that offers a sympathetic and somewhat whimsical view of ultra-Orthodox life in contemporary Jerusalem.

- *The Women's Balcony* (2017). Directed by Emil Ben-Shimon—a satiric comedy, set in Israel, that takes on misogyny and fanaticism in an Orthodox community.

Literature

- *The Chosen* by Chaim Potok (1987)—Potok's best-known novel, about a Hasidic dynasty in New York.

- *The Diary of a Young Girl* by Anne Frank (1947/1997)—A classic account of a young Jewish girl's experiences during the Holocaust.

- *Souls on Fire: Portraits and Legends of Hasidic Masters* by Elie Wiesel (1982)—An evocative account of some of Hasidism's leading figures.

SACRED TEXTS

http://www.sacred-texts.com/bib/bas/deu.htm
Deuteronomy 30:9–20
This passage is God's final comment on the covenant promise, as related by Moses before his death and imparted to the Israelites before their conquest of the Promised Land, the biblical Land of Israel. It repeats the language of the *Shema* (Deuteronomy 6:4–9) and reminds the people that YHWH ("the Lord") will reward their faithfulness and punish them if they worship other deities.

www.sacred-texts.com/jud/sjf/sjf04.htm
Pirke Avot (The Sayings of the Fathers), Chapter 2
The "Fathers" whose sayings are collected in this portion of the Talmud are rabbinical sages of the first and second centuries c.e. These maxims, and many others like them,

were so popular they were often incorporated into the daily/Sabbath prayer book and read on Shabbat. Consider especially this section:

Rabban Gamliel, son of Rabbi Jehudah ha-Nasi, said, . . . Do His will as if it were thy will, that He may do thy will as if it were His will. Annul thy will before His will, that He may annul the will of others before thy will.

Hillel said, separate not thyself from the congregation, and trust not in thyself until the day of thy death; and judge not thy friend until thou comest into his place ... and say not when I have leisure I will study; perchance thou mayest not have leisure.

Rabbi Tarphon said, the day is short, and the task is great, and the workmen are sluggish, and the reward is much, and the Master of the house is urgent. He said, it is not for thee to finish the work, nor art thou free to desist therefrom; if thou hast learned much Torah, they give thee much reward; and faithful is the Master of thy work, who will pay thee the reward of thy work, and know that the recompense of the reward of the righteous is for the time to come.

KEY TERMS AND DEFINITIONS

Baal Shem Tov (1698–1760) A charismatic faith healer, mystic, and teacher (whose given name was Israel ben Eliezer) who is generally regarded as the founder of the Hasidic movement.

Bar/Bat Mitzvah A rite of passage for adolescents in Judaism, the *Bar Mitzvah* (for thirteen-year-old boys) and the *Bat Mitzvah* (for twelve- to thirteen-year-old girls) signal their coming of age and the beginning of adult religious responsibility.

covenant A biblical concept that describes the relationship between God and the Jews in contractual terms, often thought of as an eternal bond between the Creator and the descendants of the ancient Israelites.

Dead Sea Scrolls Religious literature hidden in caves near the shores of the Dead Sea (c. second century B.C.E. to first century c.e.)

Diaspora A Greek word in origin, it refers to those Jewish communities that live outside of the historical land of Israel.

election The belief that the biblical God "chose" the people of Israel to be God's "kingdom of priests" and a "holy nation." This biblical concept is logically connected to the idea of the Covenant, and it entails the belief that the Jews' relationship with God obliges them to conform to His laws and fulfill God's purposes in the world.

eschatological Any belief in an "End-Time" of divine judgment and world destruction.

ethical monotheism A core concept of Judaism: it is the belief that the world was created and governed by only one transcendent Being, whose ethical attributes provide an ideal model for human behavior.

Exodus The escape (or departure) of Israelite slaves from Egypt as described in the Hebrew Bible (c. 1250 b.c.e.)

halacha An authoritative formulation of traditional Jewish law.

Hasidism A popular movement within eighteenth-century Eastern European Judaism, Hasidism stressed the need for spiritual restoration and deepened individual piety. In the course of the 19th and 20th centuries the Hasidic movement spawned a number of distinctive communities that have physically separated themselves from the rest of the Jewish and non-Jewish worlds, and who are often recognized by their attire and their devotion to a dynasty of hereditary spiritual leaders.

Holocaust The genocidal destruction of approximately 6 million European Jews by the government of Nazi Germany during World War II. This mass slaughter is referred to in Hebrew as the *Shoah*.

immanence The divine attribute of in-dwelling, or God being present to human consciousness.

Kabbalah One of the dominant forms of Jewish mysticism, kabbalistic texts begin to appear in Europe during the twelfth and thirteenth centuries. Mystics belonging to this tradition focus on the emanative powers of God—referred to in Hebrew as *Sephirot*—and on their role within the Godhead as well as within the human personality.

Luria, Isaac A sixteenth-century mystic who settled in Safed (Israel) and gathered around him a community of disciples. Lurianic mysticism seeks to explain the mystery surrounding both the creation of the world and its redemption from sin.

Maimonides A twelfth-century philosopher and rabbinic scholar whose codification of Jewish beliefs and religious practices set the standard for both in subsequent centuries.

Messiah A possibly supernatural figure who will judge and transform the world.

mikveh A ritual bath in which married Jewish women immerse themselves each month, after the end of their menstrual cycle and before resuming sexual relations with their husbands.

mitzvot Literally translated, the Hebrew word "mitzvot" means "commandments," and it refers to the 613 commandments that the biblical God imparted to the Israelites in the Torah (i.e., the first five books of the Hebrew Bible).

Moses The legendary leader and prophet who led the Israelite slaves out of Egypt. Moses serves as a mediator between the people of Israel and God in the Torah, and is later viewed as Israel's greatest prophet. It is to Moses that God imparts the Ten Commandments and the teachings that later became the Torah.

omnipotence The divine attribute of total and eternal power.

omniscience The divine attribute of total and eternal knowledge.

Pesach An early spring harvest festival that celebrates the liberation of the Israelites from Egypt, Pesach (better known as "Passover" in English) is celebrated for seven days in Israel and eight days in the Diaspora. The first two nights are celebrated within a family setting.

Rosh Hashanah The Jewish New Year, it is celebrated for two days in the fall (on the first day of the month of Tishri) and accompanied by the blowing of a ram's horn (a *shofar*, in Hebrew). It signals the beginning of the "ten days of repentance" that culminates with Yom Kippur.

Seder a ritualized meal, observed on the first two nights of Pesach, that recalls the Exodus from Egypt.

Shavuot A later spring harvest festival that is celebrated for two days, and is associated with the giving of the Torah at Mt. Sinai. Along with Pesach and Sukkot it was one of the "pilgrimage" festivals in ancient times.

Siddur The prayer book that is used on weekdays and on the Sabbath.

Sukkot A fall harvest festival that is associated with huts (in Hebrew, **sukkot**) in which the ancient Israelites sought shelter during the Exodus. It is celebrated for seven days in Israel (eight days in the Diaspora). During that time Jews take their meals, and if possible sleep, in huts that are partly open to the sky.

synagogue Jewish house of worship. The focal point of every synagogue is the Ark, a large cabinet where scrolls of the Torah are stored.

tallit A prayer shawl that is worn during morning prayers (traditionally by men). The fringes of this shawl represent, symbolically, the 613 *mitzvot* found in the Torah.

Talmud A multivolume work of commentary on the laws of the Torah and on the teachings of the entire Hebrew Bible, composed in two stages: the Mishnah (edited in approximately 200 c.e.) and the Gemara (edited, in its Babylonian version, around 500 c.e.). Traditionally, Jews refer to the Talmud as the "Oral Torah," and regard it as an extension of sacred scripture.

Tanakh An acronym standing for the entire Hebrew Bible: Torah (the first five books of the Hebrew Bible); Neviim (or "Prophets," which includes works of both prophecy and history); and Khetuvim (or "Writings," a miscellaneous gathering of works in poetry and prose). Taken together, the twenty-four books that make up this collection constitute the core "scriptures" of Judaism.

tefillin Taken from the word for "prayer," tefillin refers to two small boxes to which leather straps are attached. Traditionally, Jewish males from the age of thirteen wear tefillin during weekday morning prayers. Inside each of these boxes is a miniature parchment containing biblical verses. One box is placed on the forehead and the other is placed on the left arm, signifying that the individual's mind and will are devoted to God.

Torah Literally, the word *Torah* means "teaching," and in its most restrictive sense it refers to the first five books of the Hebrew Bible. Less restrictively, it signifies the totality of God's revelations to the Jewish people, which includes not only the remaining books of the Hebrew Bible but also the writings contained in the Talmud.

transcendence The divine attribute of being above and beyond anything human beings can know or imagine.

YHWH These four consonants constitute the most sacred of names associated with the biblical God. The exact pronunciation of this name, according to ancient Jewish tradition, was known only to the High Priest, but after the destruction of the Second Temple the precise vocalization of these letters was lost—only to be recovered in the days of the Messiah.

Yom Kippur Referred to as the "Day of Atonement," it is the most solemn of all of the fast days in the Jewish religious calendar.

Zionism A modern political philosophy that asserts a belief in Jewish national identity and in the necessity of resuming national life within the historic Land of Israel.

Zohar A kabbalistic *midrash* based on the biblical Book of Genesis (c. 1280 C.E.).

CHAPTER 8

Christianity

hristianity is the world's largest religion with about 2,4 billion followers. It is the
major religion in North and South America, in Europe, Australia, and many African countries, while it has a rising membership in some Asian countries as well.
The basic belief of Christianity is that Jesus is the Christ or Messiah from the Hebrew
Bible. That is why Christianity cherishes and shares some basic beliefs about God with
Judaism, as expressed in the Old Testament. However, the New Testament chronicles
the life of Jesus as a man and the revelation of him as the Son of God. This is differential
specific that characterizes Christianity and distinguish it from other monotheistic religions in such a way that some scholars from Judaism and Islam consider Christianity
as polytheistic in its nature. In the subsequent centuries, Christian beliefs influenced
the creation of the Western world, including many ideas that still form our societies
and policies.

The Teachings of Christianity

Christianity began with Jesus of Nazareth, a first-century Jewish teacher whose
message about the kingdom of God, repentance, and love was grounded in the
Jewish scriptures but differed in important ways from their traditional interpretation. After his crucifixion by the Roman rulers of Judea (in modern Israel), Jesus'
followers proclaimed his resurrection and identity as God's Messiah. The most
notable was Paul of Tarsus, whose letters to early Christian churches are included
in the New Testament. According to Paul, Jesus' death had been a sacrifice that
atoned for the sin of all who had faith that God had worked through him for this
purpose.

Christianity teaches that the Church, the worldwide community of Christians, is the spiritual communion of those who are united in Christ. The Church is sustained by scripture, which consists of the Old Testament (the Jewish Scriptures) and the New Testament, a collection of early Christian texts. Together, they make the Bible. Within the New Testament, four Gospels are accepted by all churches as relevant documentation of Jesus' life and teachings. The word Gospel comes from the Greek original Evangelion – meaning the Good News. There were many gospels and accounts about Jesus. Most of them are now lost, but some 50 are still considered valid. However, the church authorities recognized four of them as the most authoritative and needed for one's salvation. These are the Gospels of Matthew, Mark, Luke and John, written between 60 and 150 CE. Sometimes they differ significantly in details, but their message remains the same. According to them, Jesus was born in Bethlehem and was raised in the town of Nazareth on the shores of Lake Galilee in the impoverished province of the same name in the north of Israel. Although a son of a carpenter, Jesus became a Jewish teacher (a rabbi), supported by his cousin John the Evangelist who even baptized Jesus. For a vast period between his early childhood and baptism when he was 30 years old, we do not have any records of Jesus' life. Some Apocrypha suggests Jesus ventured throughout the Orient, visiting areas as far as India and Tibet, but there is no clear evidence about that. After his baptism, Jesus began with preaching and practising miracles in Galilee and surrounding areas. He gathered his followers and among them, twelve would become most famous, named apostles. A radical interpretation of the Jewish faith favors those who are poor and in need, while critiques the political and especially religious elites. A high point of Jesus' life is when he arrives in Jerusalem and makes a clear protest against the ruling powers. This eventually leads to his arrest, torture and crucifixion. But the writers do not stop here: Jesus miraculously comes back to life and gives his final messages. The Acts of Apostles and various epistles at the end of the New Testament testify of miracles performed by Jesus' followers and their final understanding of God's plans, while Apocalypse is the last book of the Bible that explains the Christian eschatology.

All of this is also supported by tradition, which can be broadly defined as the sum of doctrines and customs that reach back to the time of Jesus. The Holy Tradition is the only direct evidence of Jesus' existence and work. The apostles wrote down whatever they saw or heard about Jesus, while those who followed the apostles carried these messages on as the apostolic fathers. In a chain of scripts, their written memories were kept and widely discussed by the church fathers. The main messages of Christ are kept within such a chain called the apostolic succession, together with the ordination of priests as the descendants of apostles.

In many ways, the Old Testament announced the New one, while the New Testament validates the Old. This may be a feature of what unites these two very different religious accounts. The Old Testament is a collection of books stemming from over two thousand years of history and is an extremely complex collection of books, styles, messages and experiences. However, it has a leading idea of God's plan for the world and particularly for the Jews as the Chosen People. Jesus teaches about the validity of the Old Testament, calls God Father, and respects the Law (Torah). He reminds of the prophets who over time encouraged people with a faith in a savior – a messiah, and finally reveals himself as such a savior albeit not in the manner and style preferred by the Jews oppressed under the Roman rule. Jesus teaches Jews that they have to be ready and aware of the Law, not to be strict followers of its word but feel it with their souls. The biggest command is love without limits. One must love perfectly and without limitations, just as God does. Such love consists not only in care for our loved ones, but includes also love for one's enemy, for God's creation, for everything that exists. Everything else has succumbed to this understanding of love. This includes also love beyond kin, ethnic group or even religion. Christianity is, thus, a very egalitarian religion that calls for the unity of all people as brothers and sisters.

Jesus did not only teach, he performed miracles as well. These are accounts of his extraordinarily status which would suffice for his sayings that he is the Son of God, or God incarnate as later theology would posit. Gospels describe miracles in great detail. Jesus was able to heal people beyond the medical possibilities of those times. He could also control natural phenomena and break the rules of physics. Even his enemies acknowledged the miracles, although they suggested it is the work of the devil. None of these miracles, however, were strong enough for all his disciples to understand Jesus' divine nature. This would only come after his resurrection as the greatest Evangelion so far – the good news that death is not the end and that men can beat death. Jesus' resurrection was a sign that he indeed really is the Son of God as only God can resurrect dead ones and that would happen only at the end of time. The resurrection of Christ announces a divine plan for the world and the arrival of the Kingdom of God. Finally, all the Gospels do not raise any doubt in Jesus' divinity, however, the nature of that divinity has been questioned and debated ever since.

Not all believed in these basic Christian teachings. A vast majority of Jews refused to believe Jesus was something more than a mere human. A deep trust in worldly gains against the Roman Empire was the essence of the Jewish understanding of the Messiah. Also in other areas of the Mediterranean, the faith in Jesus' teachings was gained by marginalized members of society and some elites. It would be needed several centuries to establish the doctrine of Christianity and particularly of

Christ himself. That was achieved through the seven ecumenical councils of the early church, convened by the Christian emperors. The First Ecumenical Council in Nicea in year 325 confirmed Christ's divinity, proclaimed Arius' heresy of "created and not born Jesus" and consubstantiality of Father and Son. The Second Ecumenical Council in Constantinople in 381 made the Constantinople-Nicean Creed of Faith and confirmed the Trinity with Holy Spirit as same as Father and Son. The Third Ecumenical Council in Ephesus in 431 accepted Mary as the Mother of God (Theotokos) and refuses the Nestorian belief that human and divine nature are separated in Christ. Nestorians made their own church, while some other church fathers from Ephesus promoted monophysitism, a belief that Christ has only divine nature and not a human one. Such a belief was condemned on the Fourth Ecumenical Council in Chalcedon in 451 which confirmed the dogma of diophysitism, i.e. the two nature of Christ. This led to another schism, as the Alexandrian and Antiochian patriarchies were split over this matter. Some Oriental churches are still Monophysite and they are sometimes called the non-Chalcedonian churches. The schism was not immediate and different ideas were still present in the Christian realm. For clarification of the Church's standpoints, the Fifth Ecumenical Council in Constantinople in 533 confirmed all previous teachings and tried to make peace with the monophysites. This did not happen. Another understanding of Jesus is Monothelitism that defines one will in Christ – the divine one. The Sixth Ecumenical Council in Constantinople in 680/681 condemned this teaching and proclaimed two wills – divine and human; Christ as a morally perfect human being could not act against the divine will. In Seventh Ecumenical Council in Nicea in 787 icons are accepted as veneration but not adoration of God. And while Christology has been grasped in its totality from the New Testament, God the Father is left as an elusive "person" within the Holy Trinity and the Holy Spirit has been dogmatically understood only centuries after Christianity began with the theological discipline of pneumatology.

In the letters of Paul, the other New Testament texts, and later Christian writings we see a Christian system of thought based on the teachings of Jesus and the Jewish scriptures. Christians believe that God is the omnipotent, omniscient, and omnipresent Creator of the universe, whose immensity, beauty, and design reflect divine nature. According to the Christian doctrine of the Trinity, God is triune; that is, divinity is one in its essence but expresses itself eternally in the three "persons" of Father, Son, and Holy Spirit. Many tried to compare this Trinity with the Hindu trinity of Vishnu, Shiva, and Brahma, or to point to the significance of number three in Indo-European thought. The incarnation of God the Son in Jesus Christ (Jesus the Christos, or Messiah) was the supreme expression of God's grace, or love for humanity, for Jesus suffered and died to save human beings from sin, which separates them from God. This is so distinctive that none of previous religions or concepts could jeopardize the Christian revelation as non-original. Trinity is real and not imagined, as Christ himself is talking about his Father. This makes a mystery and tensions in understanding how come God can be incarnated and separate but still united and plural.

Christianity did not only problematize the question of knowing God who is transcendental and above everything we know: it professed the coming of God among the people. It can be traced throughout the Old Testament, with anthropomorphic meetings of God and Abraham, just as the visible signs of God in times of Moses. Later, God is in direct contact with numerous Jewish prophets. However, the culmination of God's presence among the people is in the incarnation in the body of Jesus. He is at this time indeed Emannuel – God with us. As humans cannot understand God in its cosmic reality, he is revealed in Jesus Christ and through the Holy Spirit. Revelation is made in three ways, each for one person of the Trinity, but still, the utter mystery of God remains. In the end, Christianity suggests accepting the eternal and limitless love from God and to keep faith in Trinity without much questioning. The faith includes the revelation of the Trinity and none of the rational understanding may help in finding proof for its existence.

God's love is countered by human's sin. The concept of sin, and particularly of the Fall or Sin of First Men Adam and Eve, was developed by St Augustine of Hippo, who positioned an idea that their action has corrupted man's nature and created fall from the image of God. This is further inherited by every human. While the concept of sin diverges among scholars, the Augustinian idea gained ground in the belief that humans cannot save themselves. The one who will save them is Soter – the Savior. Christ saves in an act of atonement, as he becomes a substitute for humanity and takes over all our sins. Salvation is not a passive condition. We are not perfect because of Jesus' act, but we are called to participate in the love and mercy of God through sacraments and save ourselves from the last judgment through a pious life, learning and reading about Christ's message, participating at the Holy Liturgy and forming the Christian community. Christians hope for an end to suffering and injustice in this world, but they differ in their views on the form that end will take. Similarly, Christians believe that there must be consequences for the choices people make. While some believe in heaven and hell as concrete realities, others see them more vaguely as spiritual states of eternal union with or separation from God.

All Christians make together with the Church. It is a community of those who believe in Christ and who have been baptized as a visible sign of their connection with Christ. St Peter very plastically explains what is the Church. It is a living body whose head is Christ himself and soul is the Holy Spirit. Physically, this body is receiving love and mercy from God through their belief in Jesus and the acts of the Holy Spirit. It is manifested in sacraments, while the Eucharist is the highest ritual where Christ is even physically present.

The History of Christianity

Christianity demonstrated a remarkable ability to attract converts during its early centuries, but the new religion also had its critics. Rome suspected Christians of disloyalty and pagan citizens of its empire objected to certain Christian beliefs and practices. This situation was made more difficult by the emergence of diverse forms of Christianity. To promote uniformity of belief among Christians, the Church (a) put authority into the hands of bishops, (b) established a canon of scripture, and (c) held councils at which orthodoxy was defined. The conversion of the emperor Constantine was a turning point in Christian history. Constantine and his Christian successors promoted Christianity and made it the official religion of the empire by the end of the fourth century. In the next several hundred years, Christianity is formed as a coherent religion with its dogmas confirmed on seven ecumenical councils. The time of these councils formed a dogmatic system characteristic for the Eastern Churches and made a supra-metropolitan ecclesial system which would later transform itself into four eastern patriarchies: Constantinople, Alexandria, Antioch, and Jerusalem. Rome had a differentiated position as the main authority in honor and teaching of Peter and Paul. The political position of Rome and its influence was also relevant for Rome to be the first of all patriarchies. Other apostles made other patriarchies in the East which would be a contentious fact over centuries for Rome.

Early Church councils formed several Christian communities that found their way of existence. These were the first schism in Christianity, mostly tied to the Christological debates. They form Oriental Orthodoxy, characterized by miaphysite Christology and some 60 million adherents. They are still the oldest church institutions in the world and consists of six autonomous churches: (1) Coptic Orthodox Church of Alexandria; (2) Syriac Orthodox Church of Antioch; (3) Armenian Apostolic Church; (4) Malankara Orthodox Syrian Church or Indian Orthodox Church; (5) Ethiopian Orthodox Tewahedo Church, and (6) Eritrean Orthodox Tewahedo Church. These churches share much of theology with the Eastern Orthodox Churches and they accept three ecumenical councils, but they differ in understanding the human and divine natures of Christ as united and not separated. This closeness was a ground on which several historical attempts for better relations were tried. A unity of some Oriental and Orthodox churches was partially made on Council of Florence (1431-1445) but it never took effect. In the 20th century, this schism was approached from other vantage points. Problems were seen not as theological and Christological in nature but a matter of culture, mentality, and different translations. This is true for the relations with the Eastern Orthodox churches as much as with the Roman Catholic church, particularly after the pontificate of John Paul II. The churches understand that the schism does not change nor touches the core of the Christian faith. The terminology and semiotics of the Christian creed were understood differently and it provoked a misunderstanding in defining theologically the same thing.

By the early Middle Ages, two great traditions were beginning to take shape within the Church. Western Christians followed the lead of the bishop of Rome or pope. Eastern Christians followed the bishop, or patriarch, of Constantinople. Although they were in agreement on essential features of Christianity, political conflicts and theological differences gradually separated the West and East. A final split in 1054 divided the once catholic (universal) church into the Roman Catholic and Orthodox churches. From that time on, the two branches of Christianity have developed different approaches to understanding the Christian faith. Catholic scholasticism, encouraged with the work of St Thomas Aquinas, put a large emphasis on rationalism and logic, considering pure mental activity and philosophy as an essential part of knowing God. The East never accepted such a way and instead called for an inner and mystical experience of God, with traces of ancient Greek philosophical heritage. The East also did not accept the Western formula of the Holy Spirit in the Christian creed. Until the 7th century, the Church was united in claiming that the Spirit comes from the Father, but later some Western areas included it comes also from the Son (Filioque). The Eastern tradition refused to accept that and this also led to numerous theological debates but also to largely developed pneumatology in the Orthodox churches. The Roman Catholic Church continued its existence as a coherent hierarchy and numerous monastic orders such as the Benedictines, Dominicans, Franciscans, Cistercians, Jesuits, Carmelites, etc. with a single exception of the Old-Catholic Church which emerged as an opposition to the papal authority, celibacy and use of Latin in the liturgy after the First Vatican Council. Roman Catholic Church considers itself as One Church (one body) consisting of the Latin Church, with the Roman/Western rite and 22 Eastern Catholic Churches. The difference is in rites, liturgical language, church discipline and customs, while creed, sacraments and union under the Pope tie these churches together. Roman Catholicism is today very hierarchically structured. There are three hierarchical levels: priest level (bishop, priest, deacon), canonical level (pope, ordinary, dean, parish priest and chaplain) and honorary level (cardinal, metropolitan, archbishop, prelate, canon and prebendary). It is a centralized and supranational institution whose supreme leader is the Pope, the bishop of Rome, that rules over the church with the help of the Holy See and its bodies. Bishops rule over the local churches and bishoprics, further structured as deaneries and parishes. Catholics accept dogma formed on the first eight ecumenical councils but it had 13 more councils which are not accepted by other Christian churches. These councils determined specific Catholic teachings and beliefs such as the definition of purgatory, sacraments, the link between written revelation and tradition, the immaculate conception of Virgin Mary, papal infallibility, Mary's ascension to heaven, etc.

The Eastern Orthodox Churches are now the second biggest Christian church, with some 220 million adherents. Their Orthodoxy stems from their belief in the right understanding of the Christian faith and struggles against heresies. Cultural and political antagonism between Rome and Constantinople, policies of the Byzantine emperors who defined even theological questions and differences in rites, language, church discipline such as celibacy, were instrumental for the great schism between the Eastern and Western churches. They are united in the liturgy but divided in jurisdictions (autocephality) and the power is exercised through a synod. Although Eastern Orthodoxy does not have a figure powerful like a pope, they have the ecumenical patriarch of Constantinople as their representative and spiritual leader. Other autocephalous churches have a patriarch as a figure of unity, but the church is ruled by the Bishopric council. Every autocephalous church is divided into eparchies with a bishop (episcope) and the lowest level are the parishes. They follow seven councils of the early church and are close dogmatically to Roman Catholicism but diverge in liturgy, hierarchy, celibacy and other issues. There are Orthodox churches of Constantinople; Alexandria; Antioch; Jerusalem; Georgia; Cyprus; Bulgaria; Serbia; Russia; Greece; Romania; Albania; Poland; and the Czech Republic and Slovakia. Contested positions of the Orthodox Church in America, formed in 1970, and the Orthodox Church of Ukraine, formed in 2019, are among many other self-proclaimed or semi-autonomous churches, among which is also the Macedonian Orthodox Church. Most of these churches were under the Ottoman rule for a long time. Historically, they formed a special bond with the state powers in a concept termed Symphonia, or the separation of political power for the emperor and spiritual power for the Church. In such a connection, the Church was still disadvantaged as many emperors were keen to ask for specific rules to be determined, but the bishops were satisfied with the protection of their properties and monastic life, as well as with the official position of Church teachings. With state protection, the bishops could easily act against various heresies and new teachings. This is valid for the Eastern church as much as it was for the Western one until the late Middle Ages. In comparison to the Roman Catholic Church, the Orthodoxy was based on local ethnic churches which later transformed themselves into national and state churches, although the nationalistic standpoints are considered heretical (ethnophiletism).

In the sixteenth century, Protestantism emerged as a third great Christian tradition. Founded by Martin Luther, Protestantism is based on Luther's principles of salvation by faith alone, the unique authority of scripture, and the priesthood of all believers. When Reformation struck in Germany, it rejected the papal supremacy but very soon the new Christian denomination had major disagreements over almost everything else. It also had the large political support of local rulers who did not want to support their competitive peers who had good relations with local bishops or with Rome. Luther did not envision the complete separation or schism from the Roman Catholic Church and he was blamed for being a secret papist by many of his radical followers. With Jean Calvin in Switzerland, the Protestant branch of Christianity gained clear contours. Protestants are united by several major concepts: (1) priesthood of all believers and not through a special sacrament for a religious elite; (2) justification by faith (sola fide) rather than by good works; (3) salvation comes through pure grace and not through merit (sola gratia); (4) Bible is the highest authority in everything (sola scriptura). Beyond this, the Protestant churches have very different approaches and concepts about Christian life. That is why there are many sub denominations in Protestantism: Adventists, Anabaptists, Anglicans/Episcopalians, Baptists, Calvinists/Reformists, Lutherans, Methodists, Moravians/Hussites, Pentecostals, Quakers, Waldensians. From the 18th/19th centuries onwards, this list includes also Non-denominational, Charismatic movements, Evangelical churches, independent and free churches, etc. Historically, they are divided into five groups. First are Evangelic-Lutheran churches, closest to Catholicism and with the original teaching of Martin Luther. Also close to both Lutherans and Catholics are Anglicans, which even has branches that embrace apostolic succession. Anglicans were made in 1534 under the influence of English king Henry VIII who called for a break of union with Rome. In subsequent centuries, Anglicans accepted many influences of Protestant theology. Reformed churches are those that reformed the teachings of Luther, following Jean Calvin. Evangelical free churches consider themselves as successors of Reformation and include the Adventist, Baptist, Methodist and Evangelical-Pentecostal churches. The fifth Protestant group are smaller and novel religious groups such as Anabaptists, Independent, Quakers, etc. While not being overly interested in ecclesiology, Protestantism puts Jesus Christ in its center. As numerous denominations may show, Protestantism is in fact a general name for all Christian beliefs separated from Catholicism in the 16th century. The name stems from political and historical circumstances in Germany. It is connected primarily with Martin Luther and Philipp Melanchthon, as founders of Lutheranism, and Huldrych Zwingli and Jean Calvin as founders of Reformation/Calvinism in Switzerland.

By the nineteenth century, the forces of liberalism, secularism, science, and industrialization had forged a modern culture that challenged religion in general and Christianity in particular. Initially, the Roman Catholic Church took a defensive stance against modern culture, but it adopted a more open attitude after the Second Vatican Council (1962–1965). For Orthodox Christians, the modern era brought limits on religious freedom under the Ottoman Empire in the fifteenth through nineteenth centuries and outright persecution by communist regimes in Eastern Europe and Russia in the twentieth. The modern era also saw the division of Orthodoxy into fifteen autonomous national churches. Protestant Christians responded to modern culture in different ways. Liberals saw progress as a sign of God's work in history and emphasized the importance of social activism. Conservatives resisted social and intellectual trends they considered threatening to essential tenets of the faith. By the end of the twentieth century, there were thousands of Protestant denominations.

The future of Christianity will depend on how it both shapes and responds to a rapidly changing world. It is a world in which the demographic center of Christianity is shifting toward Africa, Latin America, and Asia; women and other marginalized groups are calling for larger roles in their churches; new Christian groups and ideologies are beginning to compete with older ones. A rather conservative understanding of the Church is that it cannot function if it does not accept at least the first four councils, essentially confirming early Christology, Trinity, and Holy Mary as Theotokos. This leaves some communities that call themselves Christian outside the Christian acceptance. They are not churches, but sects. Christianity sees Jehovah's Witnesses and Latter-day Saints as sects and not churches because the former do not accept Trinity, do not regard Jesus as Son of God, and consider the Holy Spirit to be invisible and functional God's power, while the latter understand the Trinity as three bodily creatures that are separated and different, thus confirming their polytheistic belief. Still, the fundamental dogma of Christianity has not been challenged by anyone and it still remains a common basis of all Christians worldwide, no matter how different they might be in other issues.

After the Second Vatican Council, the Church began its approach to ecumenism, the unity of all Christian churches. However, the term itself is contested. The World Council of Churches thinks Christian unity is the work of the whole Church in evangelization. The Second Vatican Council defines the ecumenical movement as activities in accordance with various needs of the Church and signs of the time that call for deeper unity among Christians. There is no single or interconfessional definition of ecumenism. In fact, some regard it the first task of the Church today, while others tend to think it is Satan's work. Respecting each others' sacraments as valid and having concelebrations of the Holy Eucharist are the two most visible approaches to unity. They are also challenges because not all churches accept the same religious creed, there is a problem of apostolic succession between apostolic and Protestant churches, and there are different understandings of Christ's presence in the Eucharist.

Christianity as a Way of Life

The foundation of the Christian way of life is worship. It is a dedication to the teachings of Christ instead of indulging in a lustful lifestyle. For Roman Catholic and Orthodox Christians, worship is based on ancient liturgies in which congregations hear and respond to readings of scripture and a sermon or homily and then join in a celebration of the Eucharist. Most Protestant congregations follow the general outline of the liturgy but eliminate most of its ritual, focus attention on the sermon, and simplify or eliminate the celebration of the Eucharist. Another feature of Christianity is that it is utterly hierarchical, although it teaches egalitarianism. For much of history, the Christian clergy had a privileged position in society due to their task of preaching, teaching, evangelization and healing. The role of the apostles and adherence to their successors, the bishops and priests, has been a postulate of the Church life for centuries. This was an exclusively male position and only with recent Protestant movements could women be ordained as priests too. While preserving uniformity of original apostolic creeds, such a system also supported non-egalitarian society. It resembles in names of Catholic (universal) and Orthodox churches. This also gives power to the shepherds of the Christian flock to warn of and ask for a specific way of life, going from sexual life to diet.

The sacraments also have an important place in Christian life. As outward and visible symbols of God's invisible grace, they offer spiritual nourishment and bring the individual into a deeper experience of God. All Christian churches recognize Baptism and Eucharist as the sacraments, while Orthodox and Catholics, together with Old-Catholics, Anglicans, and some Lutherans, recognize seven sacraments. They are divided into several groups. Sacraments of initiation or the fundamental sacraments are: (1) Baptism, the basic sacrament through which a person officially becomes a Christian; it is done by pouring water three times or by submersion in the water, with the accompanying formula "I baptize you in the name of the Father and of the Son and of the Holy Spirit"; (2) Confirmation, through which baptismal grace is confirmed and strengthen through anointing with the holy oil or chrism, taken as a symbol of Holy Spirit's gift; (3) Eucharist is taking part in the Holy Communion by eating the Body and Blood of Christ in the manner of leaven or unleavened bread and wine; these are miraculously changed in its substance by evoking the Holy Spirit. Sacraments of healing include (1) Penance or Reconciliation or spiritual healing of a baptized person from the distancing from God through a sinful act; it includes remorse, confession to the priest, absolution by the priest, and satisfaction or penance. (2) Anointing of the Sick is done by the priest who anoints a sick or dying person with the holy oil. Both sacraments of healing may be repeated. Sacraments of service are: (1) Holy Orders, whereby a layperson becomes a deacon, and then hierarchically a priest and a bishop; the sacrament can be given only by a bishop; (2) Matrimony establishes a bond between the spouses in love, provides them with God's grace and blessing for children. All sacraments are valid if the person truly believes in them and if the present priest has the necessary administrative power. This notion is called sacerdotalism, as the sacraments cannot be physically fulfilled without the presence of ordained priests. As sacerdotalism is not present in the majority of Protestant churches, they only do communal baptism and gather at the Communion that has symbolic and not the real transformation of bread and wine into body and blood of Christ.

Eucharist is a constant reminder of Easter, an act of gratitude and prayer when the real (or symbolic in eyes of some Protestants) presence of Christ is met through bread and wine. The Holy Eucharist is the center of church life, its source and the highest act human can make. It is also a reminder that Jesus guarantees his followers an eternal life in heaven, with Virgin Many and all saints. Jesus himself says he is a living bread that came from the heavens and whoever will eat his body will have eternal life and will be resurrected on the final day. In a way, the Church is also a sacrament, a sign of salvation through time. At the end of times, Lord Jesus Christ will judge living and dead and the Church will then become a heavenly Jerusalem. This soteriology ends with the eternal life of people together with God.

Prayer is another important part of the Christian life. Attributed to Jesus himself, the "Lord's Prayer" found in the Gospel of Matthew serves as a model of Christian prayer, but more specialized forms have been developed. These include the Roman Catholic rosary and the "Jesus Prayer" of the Orthodox tradition. Much more than just a rite for everyday use, Christianity also embodies the specific mysticism of finding God and Christ within oneself. Early Church fathers had to explain their understanding of mysticism against gnostic movements influenced by the Persian and Greek mystical traditions. Gnosticism was highly developed all over the Roman Empire in its late years and also in the early Middle Ages. It claimed it has preserved secret knowledge that could be passed on to new disciples through special orders and ceremonies. Their teachings were called heresies and were viciously fought against. But those who accepted the original church teachings (and especially St. Paul) were still very much keen to see the rituals and social life as something irrelevant. At the end of the 3rd century, they started to live in isolation, choosing deserts and caves as their habitat. This is how Christian monasticism came to be and we can trace it back to the Egyptian Desert Fathers such as St. Anthony the Great, St. Pachomius and St. Macarius. They established a cenobite way of communal living for both male and female monks and the first rules of monastic life. In the East, these rules were supplemented by St Basil the Great and it still serves as the main principle of consecrated life for the Orthodox monks and nuns. In the West, the eastern rules were transformed into the Rule of St Benedict for his order. With the creation of subsequent Catholic orders, the rules were adjusted to their charismas and aims. The rules and monastic communities gave chance to those who want to live a mystical experience of their faith free from any side attacks or claims for heresies. Following the rules and living together with the brothers and sisters would also guarantee one does not deviate too much from the accepted path.

Christianity was not conceived as an abstract religion. Despite that, the earliest images of Christ are made only in the 4th century. This image remains today, and we know Jesus as a slim, bearded, long-haired and robed person. From the early traditions, he is Mediterranean but pale-looking, and as such is depicted in the icons. While respected and venerated in Roman Catholicism as well, icons are predominant in the Orthodox churches. It is a sacred image used in religious veneration – but not adoration as an object. The most common icons depict Jesus, Mary, saints and angels. They are placed around the church and form an iconostasis that divides priests from people in the traditional Orthodox church designs. Icons are kissed by the believers. The Christian art includes also frescoes depicting the life of Jesus and saints, with Christ Pantocrator featured always in the highest place. Catholic tradition was more concentrated on the images of Jesus' life and most prominent was his suffering and crucifixion, while Protestants were more focused on his messages in a visual form. The Virgin Mary is prominent in the Orthodox and Catholic art, but far less in Protestant one.

Another important practice is the observation of the holy days and seasons of the liturgical year, an annual cycle of events that recapitulates the life of Jesus. Every day begins with sunset, as a leftover from the Jewish tradition. Most Christian holidays are not fixed but change due to Easter. The only bigger holiday which is fixed is Christmas, although the fixed character of the birth of Christ makes troubles for the liturgical calendar because sometimes it moves Easter drastically too early or too late in spring. The liturgical calendar consists of several liturgical seasons. First is Advent, a time of preparation for Christmas, characterized by solemnity and fasting. It begins on Sunday closest to St. Andrew's Day (November 30) and lasts until Christmas Eve on December 24, with four Sundays. Advent is followed by Christmas Season that begins with Christmas. It is the second most important Christian holiday. it celebrates the birth of Jesus Christ and his incarnation. The celebration lasts eight days, until January 1st. It contains holidays of St Stephen, of Holy Family, and Virgin Mary. January 6th is a holiday of Epiphany or Theophany when God revealed his message to men. One week after that is a holiday of Christ's baptism, which ends the Christmas season.

Between Christmas season and Lent and after Easter season all the way to the end of the liturgical year is Ordinary Time. It is a season without specific meaning in liturgies and is dedicated to various topics of the Christian life. It contains 34 weeks. It still has some important holidays for Christians like the Holy Trinity, followed by the Feast of Corpus Christi dedicated to the act of Eucharist. The last Sunday of the liturgical calendar is the Feast of Christ the King.

Lent is a solemn time of preparing for Easter when Christians are called for more prayer, repentance and good deeds. It lasts 40 days, as a reminder of Jesus' fasting for 40 days in the desert before he was baptized. The Lent begins on Ash Wednesday and lasts until Maundy Thursday. Big celebrations are avoided, and the faithful should also do spiritual exercises. A week before Christmas is called Holy Week that begins on Palm Sunday, that celebrates Jesus' Messianic arrival to Jerusalem and commemorates his sufferings. On Maundy Thursday, holy oil is consecrated: it will be used in liturgies for the whole year. During Lent, the Way of the Cross is often performed.

The most important part of the year is Paschal Triduum when kerygma is commemorated: suffering, death and resurrection of Jesus Christ. It consists of Good Friday, Holy Saturday, and Easter. It begins on Maundy Thursday in the evening (already Friday in the old way of reckoning time) with the mass that celebrates the Last Supper, when sacraments of Holy Eucharist and Holy Orders are conceived.

Priest cleans the feet of 12 men, in memory of Jesus' act to the apostles. Good Friday is a day of Jesus' suffering and death on the cross. It is a day of fasting. There is no mass, but there is a ritual commemorating Christ's suffering that should be done before 3 pm when Christians traditionally believe Jesus died. On Holy Saturday there is no mass and no activity. In the night, Christians start to celebrate the biggest holiday of the year – Easter, the resurrection of Christ. His victory over death is fundamental to Christianity. Easter is celebrated for further 50 days. It is a season of joy and celebrations. On the 40th day after Easter, Christians celebrate Jesus' assumption to heaven, while on the 50th day is the Pentecost, the third most important Christian holiday, when the arrival of the Holy Spirit among apostles is remembered and the birthday of the Church is celebrated.

SUGGESTED READINGS, WEBLINKS, AND OTHER MEDIA

Readings

- Dowley, Tim. *Introduction to the History of Christianity.* Minneapolis: Fortress Press, 1995.

- Ehrman, Bart D. *The New Testament: A Historical Introduction to the Early Christian Writings.* New York: Oxford University Press, 2000.

- McGrath, Alister E. *Theology: The Basics.* 3rd ed. Malden, MA: Blackwell, 2004.

- Ware, Timothy. *The Orthodox Church.* London: Penguin Books, 1993.

Weblinks

- www.catholic.org—Catholic Online

- www.christianitytoday.com—evangelical Protestantism

- www.vatican.va

- www.orthodoxwiki.orgwww.theopedia.com—evangelical Protestant encyclopedia of Christianity

Other Media

5. *Understanding the Apocalypse: The Vision of the End* (2005), 60 min., www.insight-media.com

6. *This Far by Faith: African-American Spiritual Journeys* (2003), 360 min., www.insight-media.com

7. Fountain of Immortality: Meditations on the Orthodox Divine Liturgy, 30 min., https://www.youtube.com/watch?v=hm2qSeiTCfI

8. Draw Near: A Video Guide to the Catholic Mass, 24 min., https://www.youtube.com/watch?v=hm2qSeiTCfI

SACRED TEXTS

The Gospel of Luke
http://www.sacred-texts.com/bib/bas/luk.htm
This gospel contains two of the most famous of Jesus' parables: the Parable of the Good Samaritan (10:25–37) and the Parable of the Prodigal Son (15:11–32).

Paul's Letter to the Romans
http://www.sacred-texts.com/bib/lbob/lbob13.htm
This is the best source for his thought about God, human nature, sin, and salvation.

The "Apostles' Creed"
www.creeds.net/ancient/apostles.htm
According to ancient tradition, the Apostles' Creed was composed by the apostles under the inspiration of the Holy Spirit. Today, the Creed appears in slightly different forms in the many Christian churches that make use of it in worship. Although scholars cannot assign a definite date to its original form, it is clear that it was composed well before the Nicene Creed.

The Philokalia
www.archive.org/details/Philokalia-TheCompleteText
This is one of the great texts of the Orthodox tradition. Written by monastic mystics between the fourth and fifteenth centuries, it is the best primary source for the hesychast tradition.

The Little Flowers of Saint Francis
www.ccel.org/ccel/ugolino/flowers.html
This text is a collection of tales about St. Francis of Assisi, perhaps the most beloved of medieval saints. These stories about Francis's life, teaching, and miracles have much to say about medieval piety and the qualities Western Christians admired in the saints.

Martin Luther's "Ninety-Five Theses"
www.sacred-texts.com/chr/the9510.txt
According to tradition, Luther posted his theses on the door of the church at Wittenberg, Germany, thereby sparking the Protestant Reformation.

KEY TERMS AND DEFINITIONS

apostle In the New Testament, Jesus' disciples, sent out to preach and baptize, are called apostles (Greek *apostolos,* "one who is sent out"). Paul of Tarsus and some other early Christian leaders also claimed this title. Because of their close association with Jesus, the apostles were accorded a place of honor in the early Church.

apostolic succession According to this Roman Catholic and Orthodox doctrine, the spiritual authority conferred by Jesus on the apostles has been transmitted through an unbroken line of bishops, who are their successors.

baptism Performed by immersion in water or a sprinkling with water, baptism is a sacrament in which an individual is cleansed of sin and admitted into the Church.

bishop Responsible for supervising other priests and their congregations within specific regions known as dioceses, bishops (from the Greek *episkopos,* "overseer") are regarded by Roman Catholic and Orthodox Christians as successors of the apostles.

Calvin, John (1509–1564) One of the leading figures of the Protestant Reformation, Calvin is notable for his *Institutes of the Christian Religion* and his emphasis on the absolute power of God, the absolute depravity of human nature, and the absolute dependence of human beings on divine grace for salvation.

Christmas An annual holiday commemorating the birth of Jesus, Christmas is observed by Western Christians on December 25. Most Orthodox Christians, who follow the Julian calendar (an older form of the Western calendar) for religious festivals celebrate Christmas on January 7.

church In the broadest sense, "church" refers to the universal community of Christians, but the term can also refer to a particular tradition within Christianity (such as the Roman Catholic Church or the Lutheran Church) or to an individual congregation of Christians.

Easter An annual holiday commemorating the resurrection of Christ, Easter is a "moveable feast" whose date changes from year to year, though it is always celebrated in spring (as early as March 22 and as late as May 8).

Epiphany An annual holiday commemorating the "manifestation" of the divinity of the infant Jesus, Epiphany is celebrated by most Western Christians on January 6. Most Eastern Christians observe it on January 19.

Eucharist (yoó-ka-rist) Also known as the Lord's Supper and Holy Communion, the Eucharist is a sacrament celebrated with consecrated bread and wine in commemoration of Jesus' "Last Supper" with his disciples.

evangelicalism This Protestant movement stresses the importance of the conversion experience, the Bible as the only reliable authority in matters of faith, and preaching the gospel. In recent decades, evangelicalism has become a major force in North American Christianity.

fundamentalism Originating in the early 1900s, this movement in American Protestantism was dedicated to defending doctrines it identified as fundamental to Christianity against perceived threats posed by modern culture.

gospel In its most general sense, "gospel" means the "good news" (from Old English *godspel,* which translates the Greek *evangelion*) about Jesus Christ. The New Testament gospels of Matthew, Mark, Luke, and John are proclamations of the good news concerning the life, teachings, death, and resurrection of Jesus Christ.

grace Derived from the Latin *gratia* (a "gift" or "love"), grace refers to God's love for humanity, expressed in Jesus Christ and through the sacraments.

icons Painted images of Christ and the saints, icons are used extensively in the Orthodox Church.

Inquisition The investigation and suppression of heresy by the Roman Catholic Church, the Inquisition began in the twelfth century and was formally concluded in the middle of the nineteenth century.

kingdom of God God's rule or dominion over the universe and human affairs. The kingdom of God is one of the primary themes in the teaching of Jesus.

liturgy The liturgy (from the Greek *leitourgia,* "a work of the people" in honor of God) is the basic order of worship in Christian churches. It consists of prescribed prayers, readings, and rituals.

logos In its most basic sense, the Greek *logos* means "word," but it also means "rational principle," "reason," or "divine reason." The Gospel of John uses *logos* in the sense of the "divine reason" through which God created and sustains the universe when it states that "the Word became flesh" (John 1:14).

Lord's Prayer A prayer attributed to Jesus, the Lord's Prayer serves as a model of prayer for Christians. Also known as the "Our Father" (since it begins with these words), its most familiar form is found in the Gospel of Matthew (6:9–13).

Luther, Martin (1483–1536) A German monk who criticized Roman Catholic doctrines and practices in his Ninety-Five Theses (1517), Luther was the original leader and one of the seminal thinkers of the Protestant Reformation.

Messiah In the Jewish Scriptures (Old Testament), the Hebrew messiah ("anointed one") refers to kings and priests, who were anointed with consecrated oil. In later Jewish literature, the Messiah is sometimes understood as a figure—in some cases, a supernatural figure—who, having been "anointed by God," rescues the Jewish people and the world from evil. Christianity understands Jesus of Nazareth as the Messiah.

Nicene Creed A profession of faith formulated by the Councils of Nicea (325) and Constantinople (381), the Nicene Creed articulates the Christian doctrine of the Trinity.

original sin Formulated by St. Augustine in the fourth century, the doctrine of Original Sin states that the sin of Adam and Eve affected all of humanity, so that all human beings are born with a sinful nature.

Orthodox Church Also known as the Eastern Orthodox Church and the Orthodox Catholic Church, the Orthodox Church is the Eastern branch of Christianity that separated from the Western branch (the Roman Catholic Church) in 1054.

parable According to the gospels of Matthew, Mark, and Luke, Jesus made extensive use of parables—short, fictional stories that use the language and imagery of everyday life to illustrate moral and religious truths.

Paul of Tarsus A first-century apostle who founded churches throughout Asia Minor, Macedonia, and Greece. Paul was also the author of many of the letters, or epistles, found in the New Testament.

Pentecost A holiday celebrated by Christians in commemoration of the outpouring of the Holy Spirit on the disciples of Jesus as described in the second chapter of the New Testament book of Acts.

Pentecostalism A movement that emphasizes the importance of spiritual renewal and the experience of God through baptism in the Holy Spirit, Pentecostalism is a primarily Protestant movement that has become extremely popular in recent decades.

Protestant Christianity One of the three major traditions in Christianity (along with Roman Catholicism and Orthodoxy), Protestantism began in the sixteenth century as a reaction against medieval Roman Catholic doctrines and practices.

purgatory In Roman Catholicism, purgatory is an intermediate state between earthly life and heaven in which the debt for unconfessed sin is expiated.

Roman Catholic Church One of the three major traditions within Christianity (along with Orthodoxy and Protestantism), the Roman Catholic Church, which recognizes the primacy of the bishop of Rome, or pope, has historically been the dominant church in the West.

rosary Taking its name from the Latin *rosarium*, "garland of roses," the rosary is a traditional form of Roman Catholic devotion in which practitioners make use of a string of beads in reciting prayers.

sacraments The sacraments are rituals in which material elements such as bread, wine, water, and oil serve as visible symbols of an invisible grace conveyed to recipients.

saint A saint is a holy person (Latin, *sanctus*). Veneration of the saints and belief in their intercession on behalf of the living is an important feature of Roman Catholic and Orthodox Christianity.

scholasticism Represented by figures such as Peter Abelard, Thomas Aquinas, and William of Ockham, scholasticism was the medieval effort to reconcile faith and reason using the philosophy of Aristotle.

sin The violation of God's will in thought or action.

transubstantiation According to this Roman Catholic doctrine, the bread and wine consecrated by a priest in the Eucharist become the body and blood of Christ.

Trinity According to the Christian doctrine of the Trinity, God is a single divine substance or essence consisting in three "persons."

ACTIVITIES AND ASSIGNMENTS

1. Not all religions have creeds, but Christians have historically been uniquely preoccupied with creating creeds. Why has belief and having the correct beliefs been so important for Christianity? What are the historical and theological factors that have made Christianity different in this way?

2. Why do some American Protestants feel "let down" when they visit the Church of the Holy Sepulchre? What do these disappointed visitors think the tomb is supposed to look like? And why don't they enjoy the holy site the way some other Christians do?

3. In the United States, Christians are more divided by their political views than by their theological beliefs. Why do you think this is? What are some contemporary political issues that divide American Christians?

4. Why is Paul a controversial figure? Explain why some praise Paul's contributions to Christianity and others consider him a "corrupter" of Jesus's doctrines. Do these issues still matter today? Why or why not?

5. With help from the emperor Constantine, Christianity went from being a "religion of martyrs" to a "religion of rulers." How might having political power have affected the lives of Christians? What consequences might this change have had for other religious groups in the Roman Empire such as Jews and pagans?

6. Compare and contrast the "Great Schism" that separated Catholicism from Orthodox Christianity with the Protestant Reformation that separated Catholics from Protestants. From the evidence presented, were these splits more about theological beliefs and religious practices or more about power and politics? How can you tell?

CHAPTER 9

Islam

slam is an Arabic term which literally means 'submission to the will of God'. The followers of Islam are called Muslims. The creation of Islam goes back to the 7th century which makes it the youngest of the major world religions. Islam began in Mecca, present day Saudi Arabia, during the lifetime of Muhammad. Islam is the second largest religion after Christianity in the number of adherents worldwide. Today, there are around 1.8 billion Muslims living around the world, more precisely in the broader Middle East and North Africa, South Asia, West Africa, Southeastern Asia, Central Asia, Siberia, China.

Islam retained its emphasis on an uncompromising monotheism and strict adherence to its beliefs and practices. With the expansion of Islam from Mecca, Muslims began to practice, understand, and interpret Islam in diverse ways in many different countries, cultures, and communities. As a result, many sectarian movements have arisen within Islam which have their own interpretation however, Muslims are bound by a common faith and a sense of belonging to a single community (*ummah*).

Islam shares a worldview similar to other monotheistic religions that there is one God. However, Islam is believed to be a religion that follows strict monotheism and the word used to denote it is *Tawhid* (the oneness of Allah). *Tawhid* is the most important belief, as the entire religious adherence is centered around this idea and Muslims' life is based on submission to the will of one and only God (in Arabic, Allah). In Islam, a great emphasis is put on the oneness, uniqueness, transcendence, and utter otherness of God. It is believed that God is unique and beyond human perception and imagination. God encompasses all creation, and no mind can completely encompass or grasp him. Attributing an equal partner to Allah or associating anyone or anything to him is *shirk* which means 'to share with someone' or implies associating God with other gods or deities or idols. Shirk is considered to be a grave sin in Islam. In minds of some Muslim scholars, Christianity borders with *shirk*, as the Holy Trinity may be understood as polytheism. *Tawhid* is reflected in the daily lives of Muslims where it is forbidden to represent God and the prophets in any kind of art and architecture. That is why Islamic art mainly consists of a variety of decorative patterns, later formalized as arabesques and Arabic calligraphy.

Muhammad, who received the message of the Quran from God, is recognized as the last and final prophet in the line of prophets sent to humanity by God. Muslims believe that Muhammad was the last of seven greatest prophets or messengers sent by God to humanity and most of them are shared with the tradition of Christianity and Judaism. However, not all of these religions agree on who is and who is not a prophet. For example, in Christianity, John the Baptist is believed to be a prophet but, in Islam and Judaism he is not believed to be a prophet.

The Teachings of Islam

The major teachings of Islam are contained in the Qur'an, the holy text that was revealed to prophet Muhammad. The Qur'an which means 'recitation', and is believed to be the word of God on which the Islamic doctrine is established. It is also believed that the Qur'an was enunciated by the archangel Gabriel to prophet Muhammad. Revelation of Qur'an is compared to embodiment of Logos in Christ in Christianity. In the life of Muhammad, the Qur'an was only in verbal arrangement which was later complied as a book in the caliphate of Abu Bakr, the first caliph of Islam. The Qur'an consists of 114 *surahs* (chapters), arranged from the longest to the shortest. The *surahs* of the Quran contain the major teachings of the Qur'an. *Tawhid*, the oneness of God is the most significant teachings of the Qur'an.

Islam is based on five pillars (arkan al-Islam): (1) Shahada, the tenet of faith; (2) Obligatory prayer (salat); (3) compulsory giving (zakat); (4) fasting in the month of Ramadan; (5) Pilgrimage to Mecca (hajj). There are also three essential beliefs (usul al-din): (1) Tawhid; (2) Nubuwwat or prophethood; (3) Resurrection. Shi'a and Ibadi Muslims add to this also Justice of God ('adl) and Imamate.

As both part of Shahada and Tawhid, Allah is believed to be eternal, uncreated, all knowing and all powerful. Muslims believe in the supremacy, eternity, and omnipotence of Allah. They have the belief that He sees everything and is present everywhere. Moreover, it is believed that He has created and is sustaining this universe and controls life and death for all creatures. The Qur'an identifies a wide range of attributes of God, which describe His many qualities. He is presented, for instance, as the Merciful and the Forgiving, but also as the Judge and the Avenger. In the Islamic tradition, these attributes came to be known as *al-asma al-husna*, 'the Beautiful Names of Allah'. In Islamic vocabulary ar-Rahman and al-Rahim are the names of Allah which signifies mercy, compassion and loving tenderness. Many contradictions depend on how one interprets the word God and the names attributed to Him. There is a lengthy debate among theologians centered on whether God had certain human features or qualities, or whether He was beyond all human description. One such interpretation is that human beings enjoy a personal relationship with the Loving, Merciful God, ever ready to forgive sins and respond to prayers, but He is not merciful in the human sense of feeling sorrow and pity for one in distress. God does not become human to understand suffering. Rather, God's mercy is an attribute befitting His holiness, bringing divine aid and favors.

Allah is the first and nothing can precede Him and He is the last whose existence persists without end. This is a belief which humbles Muslims and reminds them of the evitable end of themselves and this world. These divine attributes remind believers of their relationship with God. They help to guide the actions of those who reflect on the Beautiful Names. As God is Merciful, believers seek His forgiveness, and also show mercy to people around them. As He is the Protector, they seek safety in Him, and strive to shield the vulnerable. As He is the Wise, they too endeavor to gain and share wisdom. Muslims believe that knowing and remembering these names is another way by which they can call upon their Creator and have their prayers answered. These attributes also establish a relationship between God and human beings. For example, He is presented as the One who gives guidance, bestows mercy, and dispenses justice. These aspects are an integral part of God's acts of creating and sustaining the universe.

Islam teaches the reality of prophets as those who received revelations or major messages from God. This is principle of prophethood (nubuwwat). The Qur'an recognizes prophets akin to Judaism and Christianity, such as Abraham, Noah, Moses and Jesus. The prophets are believed to be the most perfect human who are chosen by God, but they are never part of divinity. God speaks to his messengers through angels or makes them hear a voice or inspires them. According to the Qur'an and Islamic tradition, Muhammad belongs to a long line of prophets and messengers going back to Adam. In the Qur'an, Prophet Muhammad is referred as *Khatam al-Nabiyyin*, the Seal of the Prophets. The Quran emphasizes that Muhammad's message confirms or verifies the messages that were revealed before it. The Qur'an was brought down to Muhammad's heart by the archangel Gabriel. In the Qur'an, Gabriel is represented as a spirit whom Muhammad could see and hear. According to historical sources, Muhammad received the first revelation in a state of trance accompanied by heavy sweating. As Qur'an share so much with Jews and Christians, they are referred to as *Ahl al Kitab* (People of the Book) and are set apart from the pagans. However, the book here does not mean the Bible, rather it refers to a heavenly text, written by God. According to the Muslims, the Qur'an is the only perfect manifestation among the heavenly texts, such as the Christian Bible (both the Old and New Testament) and the Torah. Allah has provided humans with the ability to distinguish between good and evil therefore, and they will be held accountable for their deeds on the Day of Judgement.

Islam also teaches about the day of judgement in which all humanity will be judged on their actions in this life and the reality of the afterlife. Muhammad reminded people that they are responsible for their actions. He taught that there will be a Day of Judgement when good will be rewarded and evil punished. There are many verses in the Qur'an that talk about the Day of Resurrection. Like Christianity, Islam teaches about the afterlife which is the permanent adobe of the soul. There are references to the garden, *'Iliyyln*, the fire, *Jahim*, and *Jehenna* (a term related to the Biblical term *Gehenna* used for a pit of the dead and later as a term for punishment in the afterlife). Islam teaches about the existence of angels, who are helpers of God. According to Islamic doctrine, angels were created from light. It is also believed that angels are immortal beings, who do not commit any sin, who serve as guardians and record deeds.

Contrary to Christianity, in both Judaism and Islam, it is believed that humans are not born sinful but they are on path of wrongdoing only through sinful activity. Muslims believe that the human problem is pride. Human beings have the tendency to become proud and there are different types of pride. The pride can be unnoticeable or it can be at a level at which Muslims pray not to be among the proud and arrogant people. The issue of pride goes back to the time when Adam was created. When Allah commanded all the angels to bow down and prostrate before Adam, *Ibliss* (Satan) refused to prostrate out of arrogance and pride. Satan defied the command of Allah because he thought he was superior to Adam as he was created from fire and Adam out of clay. In this way, Satan was expelled from Paradise and made one of the dwellers of Hellfire. This is why Muslims prostrate while performing *Salat* because prostration shows the humbleness of Muslims before Allah, enacts humility and helps in the remembrance of more ultimate concerns. It is during the salat where all Muslims become equal whether they are kings or poor and old or young, they all stand in a single line.

Social services and guidelines for moral behavior constitute an integral part of Islamic teaching and is the pillar of zakat and teaching of 'adl. The Qur'an stresses on helping the needy and alleviating suffering in the world. It also contains many guidelines for moral behavior. Islam discourages the hoarding of wealth without recognizing the rights of the poor and threatens with the direst punishment in the hereafter. Muhammad reformed the Arab society and protected the weaker segments such as the women, orphans, poor and slaves. The Qur'an gave slaves their legitimate rights which included their right of freedom in return for a payment agreed by the slave and his master. In Islam, slavery was not abolished but freeing slaves was encouraged as an act of great virtue. Moreover, if a female slave gave birth to the child of her master she was automatically freed after her master's death. In pre-Islamic Arabia certain tribes used to bury their daughters alive which was the Quran highly discouraged and it was forbidden with the rise of Islam.

Apart from Qur'an, the *Sunnah* (the study of Muhammad's life) is believed to be another important source of authority. The *Sunnah* became an important source in the development of Islamic faith, law and theology. The Sunnah is deemed a sacred text because the Muslims believe that Muhammad was a perfect man. Although he was not considered to be divine, his life eventually became an important source of inspiration and guide for the Muslims. All practicing Muslims hope that they will be able to acquire Muhammad's interior attitude of perfect surrender to God by imitating the smallest details of his life like eating, washing, loving, speaking and praying. Muslim know about how Muhammad lived through literature, which contains reports collected by his close friends and family, who are also known as his companions. *Hadith* became the third most important source that complements the Qur'an and provides the most extensive source for Islamic law. There are thousands of references to the sayings and teachings of Muhammad which are part of the *hadith* literature. These *hadiths* were collected and documented through a meticulously reconstructed and uninterrupted chain of people (*isnad*), which traced back to the immediate family and entourage of Muhammad.

The understanding of the Qur'an is dependent in the context of Muhammad's life and the ways in which he applied its message. After the death of Muhammad, his companions invoked his sayings and practice to answers different questions raised about Islam. In the early period of Islam, these hadith were orally transmitted and no attempt was made to codify it into law until the beginning of the second century of Islam. Since the hadith were collected and compiled years later after the death of Muhammad, many scholars questioned the authenticity of these reports. They argued that many of the hadiths were deliberately used by different political and sectarian groups to support their claims. To establish the authority of the hadith on a firmer ground, many Muslim scholars begin to verify these reports attributed to

Muhammad by establishing several disciplines. These scholars carefully scrutinized the content of the saying as well as the reliability of the transmitter. The hadith were then categorized into various groups based on the varying degree of authenticity which ranged from to fabricated and rejected. In the 9th century several collections of sound (*sahih*) hadith were compiled. Muslims consider two collections of these six compilations highly reliable; these are compilation of Sahih Muslim and Sahih Bukhari (the sound books of Muslim and Bukhari).

The teaching of Muhammad met with severe and hostile opposition by the powerful people of Quraysh in Mecca who did not find Muhammad's message appealing. Therefore, the people who accepted Islam in the beginning were mostly the weak segment of the society such as the poor, orphan, women and slaves. It can be argued that the powerful people were uninterested in Muhammad's message because the Arabs had supported the idea of egalitarianism. They did not acknowledge the idea of monarchy because it was against their old tribal values. They rejected the idea of groveling on the ground like slaves while praying. The act of prostration countered the arrogance and self-sufficiency of the Meccan elites as the postures of praying in Islam teaches Muslims to lay aside their pride and selfishness and recall that they are nothing before Allah, which was unacceptable for the Meccans. That is why most of the Meccan elites rejected the message of Islam.

The History of Islam

Muhammad began preaching in Mecca after receiving the first revelations of the Qur'an. His preaching was controversial which challenged the polytheistic practices in Mecca, and Meccan elites made trouble for the new Muslims. Eventually, Muhammad encouraged his followers to migrate to Medina in 622. This was a turning point in the history of Islam which came to be known as *hijra*. This event marked the new beginning of Islam and the Muslim calendar starts with the day of this migration.

In Medina, Muhammad took on many new roles and oversaw political, social, and religious matters. Islam expanded rapidly across the Arabian Peninsula through both nonviolent political alliances and military conquests. Later, with well-organized finances and a vast army, Muhammad conquered and converted Mecca as well. He did not stop here but sent numerous emissaries to different parts of Arabia. By 632, Muhammad was the leader of much of Arabia.

After the death of Muhammad in 632, in less than a century, Muslim had disagreement over the authority of leadership. A minority believed that Muhammad had designated his young cousin 'Ali to succeed him. Islam did not sustain a centralized organization like the Christianity. Those who led the young Muslim community after the death of Muhammad came to be known as caliphs. They claimed to be the representatives of God and Muhammad and ruled as religious and political leaders. After the death of Muhammad, majority of Muslims choose Abu Bakr therefore, he became the first caliph of Islam.

The Caliphate

The first period in the construction of the Caliphate is known as the period of the *Khulfa Rashidun* (the rightly guided caliphs). This title was given to the first four caliphs by the Sunni Muslims. The first four caliphs were Abu Bakr (632-34), Umar (634-44), Uthman (644-56) and Ali (656-61). All these caliphs had personal connection to Muhammad. The caliphs conquered new lands and became the military and administrative chiefs of these lands, and therefore, some caliphs claimed to be the deputies of God on earth. The appointments and reigns of the caliphs described in historical sources reflect an institution in turmoil. Abu Bakr's appointment was a 'last minute sleight-of-hand', while Umar and Uthman were both assassinated. Ali's reign was also controversial as he was appointed by the rebels responsible for Uthman's assassination. Ali had to fight several civil wars against Uthman's cousin Muawiya ibn Abu Sufyan, and was lastly murdered by an opponent.

In 661, when Ali was killed, Mu'awiya claimed the caliphate and founded the controversial Umayyad Dynasty and made Damascus his center of power. This dynasty was the first Islamic empire which was built explicitly on the claims of the one family to the right of leadership. Muslims who accepted Mu'awiya as the caliph after Ali came to be known as Sunni, followers of Sunnah. Those Muslims who believed that Ali was the rightful leader after Muhammad and that his descendants had the right to rule came to known as the Shia derived from *Shi'at Ali* meaning the party of Ali. The Shia's focused more on the religious aspect of the Caliphate while the Sunnis limited its religious role and were more tolerant towards its political involvement.

When Mu'awiya came to power in 661, he contributed towards the reconstruction of both the authority and power of the caliphate. He dealt with factionalism within the ruling elites and transformed the coalition of the Arab tribes into a centralized monarchy. Mu'awiya expanded the military and administrative powers and developed new moral and political bases for loyalty to the caliphate. During this time, there were important developments in language, literature, religion, architecture, and government. Some of the Umayyad caliphs made enormous contributions to the Islamic art and architecture. Coins, papyri, and inscriptions had clear and consistent reference to Allah and Muhammad. The Umayyad Mosque in Damascus is one of their magnificent architecture.

Nonetheless, Mu'awiya's rule had to face several challenges including the civil wars. When Mu'awiya appointed his son Yazid as the next caliph, people outside Syria revolted against him. Yazid fought against the Meccan rivals led by Abdallah bin Zubayr. Ali's son Hussain attempted to move from Mecca to Kufa on the invitation of his followers to lead them, but he along with his supporters was intercepted at Karbala. Hussain was killed with his small party at the plains of Karbala by the army of Yazid. The event of Karbala is considered another turning point in the history of Islam. This event impelled a movement of penitence among Muslims who felt shame at failing to support Hussain. This small group of Shia came to be known as Tawwabun, who lamented that they had not helped Hussain. Over the centuries, anger at the tragic event at Karbala had taken on a political cast who demanded revenge for the murdered family of Muhammad. Today, Hussain's shrine at Karbala has become an important site of pilgrimage for the Shia pilgrims who come there to pray and pay their respect. This event further divided the Muslims over law and theology.

Umayyad Dynasty

The Umayyads ruled from 661 to 750. This period is often divided into two phases. The first phase (661-684) is called the Sufyanid rule named after Muawiya ibn Abu Sufyan. The second phase (684-750) is known as the Marwanid rule, after the caliph Marwan ibn al Hakim. The final years of the Umayyad dynasty faced several criticisms and discontentment by several groups for various reasons. An increasing number of Muslims, representing different groups, came to oppose the Umayyad caliphs because of the way in which they ruled. They believed that the Umayyads were not ruling according to the teachings of Muhammad. One opposition group, the Abbasids, led by Abu Muslim, agitated for revenge of 'Ali. Their revolt was supported by many other groups including the Shia's, Kharijis, Arab and non-Arab converts (mawalis), who were not happy with the Umayyad rule. These revolts led to the downfall of the Umayyad dynasty.

Abbasid Dynasty

In 750, the Abbasid Revolution succeeded in overthrowing the Umayyads. When the Abbasid troops arrived in Syria, Palestine, and Egypt, they killed many members of the Umayyad family. One of the Umayyad princes who managed to escape was Abd al-Rahman, who later founded a new Umayyad dynasty in Cordoba, Spain. Abu al-Abbas al-Saffah, a member of the Abbasid family, was declared as the first caliph of the Abbasid caliphate. He was a descendant of Muhammad's uncle al-Abbas. The Abbasids built the city of Baghdad near the old Sasanian capital, Ctesiphon. The center of power was shifted from Damascus to Baghdad that opened the door for the Golden Age of Islamic civilization. Baghdad became a great cosmopolitan city for foreign trade where textile, leather, paper was produced immensely. People of different ethnicities, languages and religions settled in Baghdad. People bought almost everything in Baghdad, from Chinese silks, to dates from Basra, and frankincense from Arabia.

During this golden period, there were significant developments in different areas of learning such as science, medicine, philosophy and medicine. The Abbasid caliphs built various learning institutions and study circles. The most popular learning academy and library of the Abbasid time was the Bayt al Hikma (the house of Wisdom) in Baghdad, popular among the Muslim and non-Muslim scholars. The caliphs sponsored the translation movement in which scholars translated all the works in Greeks, Persian and Sanskrit into Arabic. Classic works of the great Greek philosophers were translated into Arabic and studied by Muslim scholars, who engaged with and challenged these earlier ideas. This helped in making fresh discoveries in various subjects and produced many new works.

Abbasids faced several challenges due to the weak and fragmented political power of the central administration. Some of the developments during the Abbasid reign had a significant impact on the evolution of religious identities and practices. Moreover, in the late ninth century, Turkish origin slaves, freedmen and tribesmen were imported for military power. Eventually, these Turks replaced the Arab soldiers and at the time transformed the nature of the military support to the central state. Thus, the caliphal regime remained a symbol of Islamic unity whereas the political power in the provinces outside Iraq passed into the hands of local administrations. In 1055, the Seljuks, Turkish tribesmen, seized Baghdad and became the masters of the Abbasid caliphate. The Seljuks were overthrown but the Abbasid caliphate also declined. In 1258, Baghdad was captured by the Mongols who destroyed the city and killed the caliph, al-Musta'sim. The libraries were also plundered, and inhabitants were killed by the Mongols. The most significant challenge faced by the Abbasids came from the Fatimid Caliphate in Egypt.

Fatimid Caliphate

In 909, Ismailis, a branch of Shia Muslims established a Caliphate-Imamate in Tunisia. Its foundation was laid by the Ismaili *dai's* (missionaries) who prepared for the concealed Ismaili Imam to publicly reveal himself as the rightful leader and establish a Caliphate to rival all others. The Fatimid took their name from Fatima, the daughter of Muhammad and traced their descent and religious authority through the male progeny of Fatima and Ali. In 969, the Fatimid Caliphate captured Egypt and built Cairo as their capital from where they ruled the Mediterranean, North Africa, Syria, Iran, and India.

In 1171, the Fatimids were overthrown by Salah al-Din who was a Kurdish general known as Saladin in the West. Saladin defeated the last Fatimid caliph in Egypt and brought the region's population back into the folds of Sunni Islam. He founded the Ayyubid dynasty and ruled over Egypt, Syria and Yemen. Later, Saladin defeated the Crusaders and recaptured Jerusalem in 1187. The Ayyubid dynasty was overthrown by the Mamluks whose army consisted predominantly of slaves. The Mamluks then established their own dynasty in the Near East.

Two decades after the establishment of Fatimid Caliphate, another caliphate was created in *al-Andalus* (present day Spain and Portugal). Abd al Rahman, who traced his ancestry to the Umayyad Caliphate, proclaimed himself Caliph and assumed the title 'Commander of the Faithful'. The Umayyads asserted independence from Abbasid and Fatimid and ruled as caliphs from Cordoba, Spain until 1031. Later, their central government collapsed due to civil wars against regional leaders which led to the downfall of the Umayyads in *al-Andalus* (Gregorian, 32). In addition to the Caliphates, there were several other regional dynasties that rose and fell and reconstituted themselves again and again over the centuries. These dynasties included the Ottoman Empire in Turkey, the Safavids in Iran, and the Mughal Dynasty in India.

Sunni Islam

In the Sunni tradition, a diversity of schools of fiqh (law) developed. Eventually, four main *madhhabs* (schools of law) survived. These were the Hanafi, Maliki, Shafi'i, and Hanbali *madhhab*. They were named after four well-known scholars who lived during the Abbasid period: Abu Hanifa (d. 765), Malik ibn Anas (d. 795), al-Shafi'i (d. 820), and Ahmad ibn Hanbal (d. 855). Some schools of theology came to be known as the Mu'tazilite. The Mu'tazila were an early group of mutakallimun (people who studied kalam). They rejected viewing God in human terms and insisted that He is unique and unlike anything else. They held that phrases such as 'God's hand' and 'God's face' are not to be understood in a literal sense but metaphorically. Furthermore, the Mu'tazila believed that we can interpret phrases like 'God's hand' through our intellect. For example, they argued that this phrase means God's power over all things. In their view, God is Unique, One, and Eternal. This is how they understood the concept of *tawhid*, God's Oneness. The Mu'tazilite scholars called for a rational theology. They argued that God has a rational nature and that moral laws and free will were part of the unchangeable essence of reason.

Another group was also formed around al-Ash'ari (874–936) known as the Ash'arites. They disagreed with some Mu'tazila arguments. For instance, the Ash'arites argued that the human intellect is incapable to distinguish between good and evil therefore, we can know these things only through the prophets and revelation. Since there was not a centralized religious authority for the Sunni Muslims it led to many different interpretations within the *ulama* at many theological centers in many regions.

Shia Islam

In the Shia tradition, Ali, Muhammad's son-in-law, is recognized to the first Imam in the line of Imamate. Shia's believe that Ali was divinely inspired and sound in his interpretations of the Qur'an (*tawil*) and the teachings of Muhammad. In addition, Ali is believed to be chosen by Muhammad to lead the community after him. According to Shia doctrine, the Imamate is the line of succession passed through Ali and Fatima and their male descendants Hassan and Husayn. In the Shia tradition, two schools of fiqh emerged: the Ja'fari school of law, named after Ja'far al-Sadiq, and the Zaydi school of law, named after Zayd ibn Ali, the brother Muhammad al-Baqir (a.s.). The Shia turn to the guidance of the Imams in matters of fiqh. With the passage of time, succession disputes arose dividing the Shia's into various sects. Three of the major Shia sects are the *Zaydis, Ismailis* and the *Ithna Asharis* (Twelver). There are around 140 million Twelver Shia Muslims living in various parts of the world today, predominantly in Iran, Iraq, Bahrain, Lebanon, but also as a big minority in Pakistan, Saudi Arabia, and so on.

Sufism

Sufism, Islamic mysticism, is not a branch but rather a dimension of Islam. In the 10th century, Sufism emerged as a new dimension that focused on an inner search and contemplation of God. It is argued by many scholars that Sufism was an attempt to reform Islam by emphasizing more on the afterlife rather than the worldly life. They also challenged the literal and legalistic approaches to Islam and the Qur'an. Their goal was to draw closer to and personally experience God through meditation, ritual chanting and dancing. Therefore, Sufism has sometimes been called Islam's 'counterculture'.

Some Muslims comprehend Sufism as controversial because some Sufis worshipped Jesus and others Muhammad which other mainstream Muslims considered as polytheistic and blasphemous. In addition, Sufism was seen as rupturing the ordinary pattern of Muslim religious activities and ignoring obedience to Quranic law in search of a transcending religious self-realization. Some of the Sufis were even persecuted by the rulers, such as Mansur al-Hallaj who claimed perfect unity with God. Religious scholars were shocked at this exclamation 'I am Truth!' (*ana al-haqq*). He claimed that God's spirit had mixed with his 'as amber has mixed with fragrant musk.' People thought he was committing blasphemy by claiming to be God. He was imprisoned for many years in Baghdad and was finally executed (Lapidus, 92). Nevertheless, Sufis contributed to the Muslim literature especially love poetry in Arabic, Turkish, Persian and Urdu. Sufi were believed to the most energetic missionaries of Islam.

Islam in modern times

In the twentieth century, the political organization of the world was dominated by the nation state. Therefore, the leader of Muslim countries had different interpretations of the relationship between religion and the nation state. Some Muslim nationalists proposed a close relationship between Islam and their new states. These leaders wanted a legal system that was based on the principles of Islam and Islamic law. There were leaders who distanced their national policy from Islam and favored European political model. From the eighteenth century to the present, many Muslim reform movements emerged who were concerned about the decline in the Muslim communities and in Muslim power around the world. Some focused on reforming Islamic religious practice and others on resisting colonialism. One of these movements was the most influential Muslim Brotherhood movement in the contemporary times.

There are around 6 million Muslims living in the United States today. Through immigration, this number is growing rapidly. However, the Muslim population also consist of the African American Muslims. The Nation of Islam was playing a vital role in the US Muslim community, but most of the African American Muslims are not part of this organization.

Islam as a Way of Life

The Five Pillars are believed to be the unifying characteristic of Islam. The majority of Muslims consider the five pillars to be the basic fundamentals of Muslim religious practice under the Sharia law which are performed faithfully by the conservative

Muslims. These pillars are the foundation of traditional Muslim life and have been described in this way:

Shahadah

The *Shahada* is central article of faith, in which a Muslims confess that there is no god but God, and Muhammad is the messenger of God. This is a prerequisite to enter the Muslim community. In addition, this is the heart of the faith of Muslims and the expression of their identity.

The first half of the *shahadah* implies justification by works, humility and submission to God, defiance of tyrants and other gods, vicegerency of man on earth, and self-fulfillment. The second part of the *shahadah* asserts the prophethood of Muhammad. This denotes that the confessor accepts the message Muhammad has conveyed from heaven as truly what God's revelation.

Moreover, the *shahadah* means to bear witness to the unity of Allah because His signs are seen and his presence is felt but he is actually not seen. It is also believed that God sees the action and activities of humans. Thus, with the *shahadah* Muslims acknowledge the presence of God and accept Muhammad as the gift of the guidance of God as represented by the prophecy.

Salat

Salat, the daily prayers, is another important pillar of Islam. In Islam prayers can be categorized as formal and informal. Salat or namaz forms the formal prayers which are performed five times a day, at dawn (*fajr*), noon (*zuhr*), mid-afternoon (*asr*), sunset (*maghrib*) and nightfall (*isha*). Salat is usually offered in the prayer-hall called masjid which means a house of prostration or bowing in worship). It is considered necessary to face the *qibla* (direction towards *Kaba* in Mecca) while performing *salat*. These prayers are proceeded by the call for prayers (adhan). Before praying, a person should perform the ablution which is washing the face, hands and feet. The five prayers consist of seventeen raka'at, or prostrations. In addition, there are informal prayers such as *dua* (supplication) and dhikr (remembrance of the names of God). These informal prayers can be offered at any moment and in any place.

Zakat

Zakat means purification of wealth giving alms which is obligatory in Islam. In this pillar Muslims are required to pay a certain percentage of their income in charity. Mostly, Zakat is granted to the trustees of various charitable organizations for distribution.

However, it can also be given to individuals who are needy, sick, poor, widow and orphan. When Zakat exceeds the basic percentage of two and a half percent, it is considered as *sadaqa*. Religious donation from charity money is known as *waqf.*

Sawm

Sawm is called fasting which is an essential pillar in which the Muslims fast in the month of Ramadan every year. It is believed that by abstaining from eating and drinking a person will be able to empathize with those who are less fortunate and remember the bounty of God. During the month of Ramadan, Muslims abstain from eating and drinking from sunrise to sunset. The month of Ramadan rotates over the course of the solar years because the lunar month is less than the solar month by ten or eleven days. Therefore, the month of fasting can occur in every season of the year. There are some exceptions in fasting for example, if a person is travelling or is unwell, they can defer the fast and keep it at another time of the year. Moreover, fasts can be kept out of devotion or by ways of vows and so on. At the end of the month of Ramadan, the fasting is concluded by celebration and thanksgiving on the day of *Eid al-Fitr.*

Hajj

Making the pilgrimage to Mecca, the hajj, once in one's life if possible is another obligation in Islam. Muslims make an annual pilgrimage to the site of *Kaba* on the tenth day of the second lunar month called *Dhul-Hajj*. At the end of the pilgrimage, one or more goats are offered for sacrifice for God commemorating the event when God accepted the goat in place of Ismail. This is done by Muslims all around the world in a festival called *Eid al-Adha*. It is commanded that hajj is the obligation every Muslims should fulfill if they can, once in their lifetime. If they cannot go then they can designate another person on their behalf and contribute towards the cost or they can participate in another good cause.

On the first day of Hajj, before reaching Mecca the pilgrims need to enter a state of ritual purity known as *ihram*. To do this, the pilgrims (both men and women) need to wear two pieces of white seamless cloth. One of the white cloth is worn around the waist and the other is worn over the left shoulder. Women are required to cover their hair but not their face. In this state, it is forbidden to swear, fight, wear perfume, have intercourse, cut their hair and nails, and harm plants or animals. When the pilgrims reach Mecca, they perform a series of rituals in the remembrance of Abraham, his wife Hagar, and their son Ismail. First the pilgrims enter the Holy mosque and perform the *tawaf,* circumambulating the *Kaba*, seven times in anticlockwise direction. Then the ritual of *sai* is performed, in which they run or walk seven times back and forth between the hills of Safa and Marwa reenacting Hagar's desperate search for water when she and Ishmael were forsaken by Abraham. The Pilgrims then drink water from the sacred Well of *Zamzam* which Allah miraculously revealed to Hagar when she was in need. The night is spent at Mina and then the pilgrims travel towards the Plain of Arafat where they gather at the Mountain of Mercury which is believed to the place where Muhammad gave his last sermon. Pilgrims spend some time here standing and reading verses from the Quran and asking God for forgiveness. The night is spent in the desert at *Muzdalifah*, where pilgrims pray and collect pebbles for the next day which will be used to stone the Devil at Jamarat.

The next morning, Pilgrims proceed to Mina where the stoning ritual takes place. The pilgrims throw seven stones at each of the three pillars representing the Devil followed by the reenactment of Abraham's sacrifice with their own sacrifice at Mina. After the sacrifice, men shave their heads, women cut their hair and all pilgrims change back to their normal clothes. This is the point where they leave the sacred state of ihram and are free of all restrictions. They travel back to Mecca to circle the Kaba and again run back and forth between the hills of Safa and Marwa. They then return to spend the night at Mina. For the next two to three days, they will again stone the Devil at the Jamarat. The final ritual of the Hajj is a farewell circumambulation of the Kaba. The Haj is completed here and the pilgrims are believed to be in a blessed state, spiritually renewed and free of sin. These pilgrims are titled as hajji (for men) and hajja (for women), a sign to all that they have performed their obligation of hajj.

More than two million Muslims from all over the world gather in Mecca to perform the *Hajj*. 'Pilgrims mix across the line of ethnicity, nationality, sect, and gender that divide them in everyday life. They affirm a common identity by communally performing identical rituals and dressing in similar garments that emphasize their equality'.

Under the Saudi rule, the management of Hajj transformed the ritual of pilgrimage. The management of Hajj was now a public utility industry. The Saudi government took various steps to regulate the Hajj which included the introduction of tighter passport control in the form of Hajj visa system, establishment of a formal vaccination program, professionalization of the guide system, publication of fee rates for food, rent and transportation, and increased measure of safety and security of all pilgrims. Until World War II and the rapid growth of the oil industry, the Hajj remained the primary source of revenue for the newly established Kingdom of Saudi Arabia. All these arrangements will facilitate pilgrims during the Haj however there are chances that the rituals of Hajj may lose their true essence with these luxuries.

The Islamic Calendar

The Islamic calendar dates from 622, when Muhammad and the first Muslims moved from Mecca to Medina in a migration known as the *hijra*. The dates in Islamic calendar are often followed by the letters AH which stands for Anno Hegirae, the Latin word for 'in the year of the '*hijra*'. Muharram is the first month of the Islamic calendar.

It was during the caliphate of Umar that the new Islamic calendar was introduced which is used by Muslims throughout the world today. The Islamic calendar followed the ancient tradition of marking time by making observations of the moon. The lunar calendar contains 12 months each with 29 to 30 days. The length of the month depends on the time it takes for the moon to orbit around the earth which is 29.5 days. A lunar year has 12 months and has around 354 days.

The Islamic calendar is mostly used for religious purposes. The dates cannot be confirmed in advance because it depends on human sightings of the lunar crescent and various factors can have an impact on the sighting such as the observer's location, atmospheric conditions, and local weather. The Islamic calendar is not used in daily life but is calculated in advance by using astronomical data rather than visual sightings of the moon (Gregorian). Mostly, the calendar is used to calculate the dates of religious events like Hajj and Muharram, Ramadan and so on.

The Shari'ah

After the death of Muhammad, Islam spread from Spain to the boarders of China. Different people started asking various questions related to faith and practices. During the life Muhammad, he was the interpreter of religious doctrine, but now people were looking towards the *ulama* or body of clerics for such interpretations. The hadith of Muhammad, transmitted by his companions, forms an important part of the *Sunnah*. The *ulama* interpreted the Quran and the teachings of Muhammad for guidance on legal matters. The attempt to find solutions to legal issues was called *fiqh*, a word that means 'understanding'. Today fiqh is widely understood to mean the study and formulating of law in Islam.

Shari'ah literally means a way or path. It is mostly translated as Islamic law in English but it encompasses a much broader range of legal activity than it is normally associated with law in the Western sources. Shari'ah is the entirety of God's will regarding human action as represented in the Quran and Sunnah, whereas *fiqh* is the human attempt to interpret it. Devout Muslims seek to follow God's will in accordance with the Sunnah by looking at these interpretations to live their life. These interpretations help Muslims in best understanding the performance of devotional acts, regulate marriages and business deals and to care for the poor and needy. There are few laws that address criminal acts however, the majority of the laws are related to ritual and devotional practices.

Marriage and family life are the foundations of Muslim communities. Devout Muslims, who try to follow the *Sunnah* of the Prophet in their daily lives, consider Muhammad to have set the example of marriage and to have been the perfect husband and father. In Islamic belief, men and women are considered equals in the eyes of God, and when we consider the historical context in which it was revealed, the Qur'an introduced many new legal rights and privileges to women. However, there is much variation in the way in which gender roles are interpreted throughout Muslim cultures. In the nineteenth and twentieth centuries, reformers sought to improve women's status in Muslim countries and cultures. Many reforms focused on marriage and divorce rights, and the status of women in Islamic law.

Till today, Islamic laws have continued to shape the devotional lives of Muslims and regulate marriage, divorce, banking and other social and business contracts. Some countries consider it as a rigid set of religious laws which are challenged. For example, some men and women in Saudi Arabia challenge interpretations of Islamic laws that are codified as laws restraining women from driving cars. Such examples suggest that there should be efforts to revisit *shari'ah* to address new situations.

KEY TERMS AND DEFINITIONS

Abbasids An important Muslim empire that ruled from 750 to 1258 c.e.

adhan (a-than; Arabic) The call to prayer.

Aisha A beloved wife of Muhammad who is known for transmitting many *hadiths*.

Allah (a-lah; Arabic) The Arabic term for God.

Ashura The tenth day of the month of Muharram, recognized by Shi'a Muslims as the anniversary of the martyrdom of Husayn.

caliph (ka-lif; Arabic) Leader of the Muslim community after death of Muhammad.

hadith (ha-deeth; Arabic) Literary tradition recording the sayings and deeds of the Prophet Muhammad.

hajj (hahj; Arabic) The annual pilgrimage to Mecca, one of the Five Pillars of Islam.

hijra (hij-rah; Arabic) The migration of the early Muslim community from Mecca to Medina in 622 c.e.; the Islamic calendar dates from this year.

Husayn Grandson of Muhammad who was killed while challenging the Umayyads.

imam (ee-mam; Arabic) Prayer leader; in the Shi'a tradition, one of the leaders of the Muslim community following the death of the Prophet Muhammad.

Islam (is-lahm; Arabic) Literally "submission"; specifically, the religious tradition based on the revealed Qur'an as Word of God.

jahiliyya (ja-hil-ee-ah; Arabic) The "age of ignorance," which refers to the time before the revelation of the Qur'an.

jihad (jee-had; Arabic) Lit. "striving"; sometimes the greater *jihad* is the struggle with one's self to become a better person; the lesser *jihad* is associated with military conflict in defense of the faith.

Khadija Muhammad's beloved first wife.

Mecca The city in which Muhammad was born; place of pilgrimage for Muslims.

Medina The city to which Muhammad and his early followers migrated to escape persecution in Mecca.

miraj (mir-aj; Arabic) Muhammad's Night Journey from Mecca to Jerusalem and from there to heaven, where he met with God.

mosque (mosk) Place of prayer, from the Arabic term "masjid."

muezzin (mu-ez-in; Arabic) The person who calls the *adhan.*

Muhammad The prophet who received the revelation of the Qur'an from God. The final prophet in a long line of prophets sent by God to humanity.

Qur'an (kur-an; Arabic) The holy text of Muslims; the Word of God as revealed to Muhammad.

Ramadan (rah-mah-dan; Arabic) The month in which Muslims must fast daily from dawn until dusk; the fast is one of the Five Pillars of Islam, the month in which the Qur'an is believed to have been revealed to Muhammad.

salat (sa-laht; Arabic) The daily prayers, which are one of the Five Pillars of Islam.

sawm (som; Arabic) The mandatory fast during the month of Ramadan; one of the Five Pillars of Islam.

shahadah (sha-ha-dah; Arabic) The declaration of faith: "There is no God but God and Muhammad is the Messenger of God"; the first of the Five Pillars of Islam.

shari'a (sha-ree-ah; Arabic) Lit. "the way to the water hole"; specifically, Islamic law.

shaykh (shaykh; Arabic) A title sometimes used for someone with a high degree of religious learning.

Shi'a (shee-ah; Arabic) One of the two major branches of Islam. The Shi'a believed that Ali should have succeeded as leader of the Muslim community after the death of Muhammad.

shirk (sherk; Arabic) The sin of idolatry, of worshipping anything other than God, the one unforgivable sin in Islam.

Sufi (soof-i) A follower of the mystical tradition of Islam, **Sufism,** which focuses on the believer's personal experience of God and goal of union with God.

Sunnah (sun-na; Arabic) Lit. "way of life" or "custom"; specifically refers to example of the life of the prophet Muhammad; important religious source for Muslims.

Sunni (soon-e; Arabic) One of the two main branches of Islam. The Sunnis believed that the Muslim community should decide on a successor to lead after the death of Muhammad.

surah (soor-ah; Arabic) Chapter of the Qur'an; there are 114 *surahs* in the Qur'an.

tafsir (taf-seer; Arabic) Interpretation of or commentary on the Qur'an. There are several types of *tafsir*, which aim to explain the meaning of the Qur'an.

Umayyad Dynasty Controversial Muslim dynasty that ruled from 661 to 750 c.e.

umma (um-mah; Arabic) The worldwide Muslim community.

zakat (za-kaht; Arabic) Regulated almsgiving; one of the Five Pillars of Islam.

ACTIVITIES AND ASSIGNMENTS

1. Look at the rules for attaining the state of *ihram* before going on the hajj. What ceremonies have you attended where everyone is required to dress the same way? What might the purpose be of having Muslims from countries all over the world dress and groom themselves in the same way during this ritual? How might this affect the way Muslims think about themselves after going on the hajj?

2. How has the ritual of the hajj changed over time as Saudi Arabia has become a modern, economically developed country? Do you think these changes are good or bad for the hajj? Explain your answer.

3. Muslims do not believe human beings are born with sin. Where Christians believe the human problem is sin, Muslims believe the human problem is pride. What do you think this distinction means? Can you point to specific beliefs and practices in Islam that suggest human pride is a problem?

4. Christians, Muslims, and many Hindus are all monotheists. But Muslims are described as "strict monotheists." What does this mean? In what ways are Muslim ideas of divine unity stricter than those found in Christianity or Hinduism? How has this idea shaped Muslim culture?

5. Allah is traditionally said to have ninety-nine names. But these names often contradict each other—for example, Allah is first, but also last; merciful, but also just. What is the purpose of talking about God in this way? Why does God need to have "names" listing attributes?

6. The first converts to Islam were primarily "women, slaves, the poor, and working classes." The powerful people of Mecca were mostly uninterested in Muhammad's message. Why do you think this is? Is this pattern similar to or different from the way other new religions have spread?

7. Explain why Sufism is so different from other forms of Islam. Why is it seen as controversial?

References

Al-Faruqi, Isma'il R. *Islam*. International Institute of Islamic Thought, 2005.

Armstrong, Karen. *Muhammad*. Phoenix, 2009.

Berkey, Jonathan. *The Formation of Islam*. Cambridge University Press, 2003.

Clingingsmith, David Lawrence et al. "Estimating The Impact of the Hajj: Religion and Tolerance in Islam's Global Gathering". *SSRN Electronic Journal*, 2008. *Elsevier BV*, doi:10.2139/ssrn.1124213.

Danforth, Loring. *Crossing the Kingdom*. University of California Press, 2016.

Davies, T. Witton. "Islam: A Sketch with Bibliography". *The Biblical World*, Vol 8, no. 5, 1896, pp. 337-346. *University of Chicago Press*, doi:10.1086/471969.

Gregorian, Vartan. *Islam: A Mosaic, Not a Monolith*. Brookings Institute Press, 2004.

Haq, Muhammad Abdul. The Meaning and Significance of Shahadah. *Islamic Studies*, Vol 23, no. 3, 1984, pp. 171-187., Accessed 15 July 2021.

Hazleton, Lesley. *The First Muslim*. Atlantic Books, 2013.

Lapidus, Ira, M. *A history of Islamic Societies*. Cambridge University Press, 2002.

Madigan, Daniel A., "Revelation and Inspiration", in: *Encyclopaedia of the Qur'ān*, General Editor: Jane Dammen McAuliffe, Georgetown University, Washington DC. n.d.

Rubin, Uri. *Muhammad The Prophet and Arabia*. Ashgate Variorum, 2011.

Sells, Michael Anthony. *Approaching the Qur'án*. White Cloud Press, 2007.

CHAPTER 10

Jainism

Jainism, with approximately 5.6 million adherents (all but about 275,000 of whom live in India), is a relatively small religion. Through the centuries, however, Jainism has earned a special reputation for having exemplified the ideal of nonviolence, while it also has many connecting points with other large religions of India, Hinduism and Buddhism, particularly in understanding laws of the world such as karma and reincarnation. Similarities also include a cycle of rebirth and reaching freedom from it (moksha), but unlike Hindus, Jains do not have a concept of god or gods. These similarities among three great Indian religious traditions bear a question how did they develop into three distinctive religions. Some claim that Jainism was, together with Buddhism, a sort of reform of the old Vedic religion of North India. In Jain view, the ever-changing cycles of cosmic time prove that Hinduism is in fact quite new religion, while Jain arguments are rediscovered and thus challenge the Hindu notion of their religion as the oldest in the world. Others say it is a leftover from a pre-Vedic and non-Indo-European tradition that was reinvented and incorporated into Vedic heritage. Lastly, there are those who see in Jainism a local influence of contemporary Indian states such as Uttar Pradesh and Bihar on the larger Vedic faith tradition. It is essentially a non-theistic religion. This chapter sheds light on the main elements of Jainism, with regard to both the ascetics and the laity—and the interplay between the two groups.

The Teachings of Jainism

We begin to explore Jain teachings by looking to the distant past, to the foundational figures whom all Jains revere as the Tirthankaras, "makers of the ford (or river crossing)." Each is considered to be a Jina, "conqueror"—whence comes the name Jainism. It is not a physical conquest, but a spiritual one, a victory over one's ego.

The conqueror uses asceticism as one's spiritual weapon to fight against passion, lust, and bodily sensualities in order to attain enlightenment, knowledge and purity of the soul. Jina is a more novel term; an older one for a person who was successful in attaining enlightenment was Nirgrantha, meaning the Bondless One. It is interesting to point out that both Buddha and Mahavira were from the warrior caste (Kshatriya), who employed military terminology for such spiritual warfare. Similarly, both were acting against the Brahman elite in Indian society.

Through having conquered the realm of samsara, the "cycle" of moving from one birth to another, the Tirthankara has, metaphorically, successfully crossed the river from the worldly realm to the beyond—the realm of the liberated. Jains believe in an eternal succession of Tirthankaras who form tirtha or the Jain community. This word is now almost exclusively used to denote the religious community. The cycles are eternal, as the universe is considered to be without beginning and end. But cosmic cycles (Kalpa) are not eternal, albeit they last for billions of years. In each kalpa, 24 tirthankaras emerge. Jains believe we are now approaching the final time of this Kalpa, as the 24th Tirthankara already lived and died among us. In keeping with the general Indian notion of samsara, Jainism conceives of time as cyclical and envisions the cycles as upward and downward turnings of a wheel. The current age is said to be Kali Yuga, to be followed by a sixth and final stage of degeneration before the cycle starts over again. Spatially, Jains describe the universe as the Loka, a vast and yet a finite space, within which all beings dwell. Beyond the Loka, there is nothing but strong winds. The Loka, together with everything in it, has always existed and will continue to exist eternally. Jainism thus does not believe in a creator god.

The founder of Jainism is Mahavira (the Great Hero), although the tradition remembers him only as a re-discoverer of eternal truths. Mahavira, the twenty-fourth and last Tirthankara of this world cycle, was probably born near Vaishali (located in the northern Indian state of Bihar). The Jain tradition mentions Rishabha as the first Tirthankara; that is why they call him Adinath or the First Lord. However, he is the first in a line of our cosmic time and is responsible for discovering agriculture, law and human civilization as we know it. Scholars tend to date his lifetime to the second half of the fifth century BCE, placing him close to the age of Buddha; in fact, the Buddhist scriptures mention Mahavira and his ascetic disciples. However, it seems Mahavira lived before Buddha, maybe even one century before. In the thirteenth year of ascetic wanderings, Mahavira is believed by Jains to have attained the state of kevala, or omniscience, the complete and perfect knowledge that leads at the time of death to liberation from the realm of samsara. They also think Mahavira chose deliberately to fast until his death, after the Salekhana ascetic practice. Now perfectly enlightened, Mahavira set about preaching the tenets of Jainism. Mahavira preached for some thirty years until, at the age of seventy-two, he died in the town of Pava (like Vaishali, located in the northern Indian state of Bihar). Mahavira also established four tirthas: Jain monks, nuns, laymen and laywomen. They are four parts of the Jain community or four limbs, often depicted in the svastika. This symbol is very much used in Jain ritual practice. Apart from the male and female monks and laypeople, svastika is also used to represent the four possible incarnations of the Jiva – they may be incarnated as heavenly beings, hell-beings, human beings, and animals. Thus, svastika also depicts the community of all life forms.

Mahavira was vehemently against the adoration of gods, as is seen in Hinduism. Jainism was, from the very start, a very non-theistic religion. There is no creator of physical reality; the universe simply exists. However, the presence of Tirthankaras questions the Jain refusal of deities. The Tirthankaras are regularly venerated (if not adored) and soon after Mahavira's death legends started to be made about him. Some of them regard Mahavira as a being that came from the heavens, was sinless, and through meditation, he showed how to free oneself from earthly desires. The Jains do not consider this veneration as deification, as they do not accept a principle of higher being. A higher level of reality is not deified because it is part of every soul. The freed souls are here to be venerated as a goal for one's soul and they exist in an egalitarian perfection.

In any event, all Jains agree on its most important ideals: ahimsa (nonviolence) and asceticism. While prevalent throughout the traditional religions of India, Jainism emphasizes the central place of ahimsa, the "pure, unchangeable, eternal law," to cite a well-known passage from the Acarangasutra. Jains are strict vegetarians and go to great lengths to try to avoid harming life forms. Some are strict vegans because they think that all usage of any animal product, such as milk, egg, cheese, is essentially violent. This radical veganism is seen in the small amount of food Jains eat, barely surviving and with many fasting periods.

Jain scriptures spell out the categories of existing things in meticulous detail. The categories of existence can be said to begin with a simple distinction: that between the living, which is termed jiva, and the nonliving, ajiva. Jiva, or simplistically soul, has a durable and fixed nature, consisting of never-ending blessedness, energy, and consciousness, but its aspects are always changing because of a multitude of karmic experiences. The nonliving is further divided into four: motion, rest, atoms, and space. Ajiva controls and manages the universe and the world we inhabit. Jainism holds that the universe has an infinite number of atoms, forever distinct from one another, along with an infinite number of jivas, or souls. All jivas are essentially equal, regardless of the bodies they inhabit. They are locked in this material world and destined for long samsara cycles until the self-sacrifice makes them transfer to the state of moksha. Jainism contains a very sophisticated epistemology about reality. Everything deemed real is, in fact, relative and this relativism is further accentuated in the concept of Anekantavada. it is a doctrine of reality's complexness and not, as it might sometimes seem, an understanding of relativism as if there is no absolute truth or if there is an absolute truth, people would not be able to know it. According to this doctrine, the reality is complex and multileveled. All things have eternal aspects and none can be just one term, as it may be conceived, for instance, in Western philosophy. Relativism is rooted in the idea that no one person can be all-knowing or understand an absolute truth in its totality. One must always stay open to another person's view and incorporate it into one's own worldview. It is often illustrated with a famous Indian fable about blind men and an elephant. Each blind man touches a different part of the elephant and creates a different idea and "truth" about the elephant's appearance. There are only Tirthankaras who can know the absolute truth and they should teach about it to other people. Not only the Western system but also the Indian religions tend to believe in the illusion of change and difference (like in Hinduism) or the idea of durability (in Buddhism). Jainism is even more abstract and more radical in that matter. All aspects of experience are seen as equally real and nothing can be an illusion. As a primary example, Jains point to the person of Mahavira. He is eternal because his Jina or soul is fixed and does not change, but he is also not eternal as physical Mahavira.

Based on Anekantavada, the doctrine of perspectives (nayavada) suggests there are several ways to question an entity through its aspects. The general notion is that there exists an eternal aspect that may be defined in a single way – this would be the soul. There are changing aspects too where every other thing must be defined in accordance with these aspects. Various possibilities are explained in the Syadvada rule. It says that every factual saying may be true and false at the same time, based on the perspective from which it is said. Thus, the truth of any argument is relative and depends on the perspective from where it came from. Jains usually consider seven values of truth (saptabhanginayaili). Based on perspective, an argument may be: (1) true; (2) false; (3) true and false in the same time; (4) neither true nor false, basically without an answer; (5) true but unutterable; (6) false but unutterable; (7) true, false and unutterable. This complex epistemology is sometimes used by Jain masters to call for a way to understand different world religions and philosophies that are sometimes in conflict.

The basic aim of life is to attain the internal perfection of one's soul. This perfection already exists within the soul itself, but it is darkened because of the karma effect during a long period of time. Liberation or release of the soul (Jains, like Hindus, use the term "moksha") require that one attains the state of kevala, or omniscience. The religious life strives to clean away the dirt that, through the process of karma, has tarnished the jiva. Karma in Jainism is more than a principle of moral causation as seen in other Indian religious traditions. It is also seen as a substance through which this principle acts. Karma is almost like any other ajiva thing. Some karma produces unhappy experiences, some lead to happy ones. It is good karma or Punya karma. This depends on an act of soul and passion one experiences in one's life. The positive and good activities return the soul to its original state of pristine purity and release it from samsara. Kevala frees the jiva completely from the tarnishing effects of karma. Moksha and kevala are distinguishable in that one who has attained kevala normally goes on living in the physical body, confined to the realm of samsara, while one who achieves moksha is liberated from the body. Just as the universe is eternal, without beginning and end, so is the soul. Jains believe that souls are equally present in humans and animals. It is a life force that is eternally present in the world. However, if one's soul is acting badly, it will cause regression. Passion (Raga) is the central reason why regression occurs. The worst passion produces anger, bad thoughts, bad words and activities, and it leads to the most vulnerable kinds of karma. This is the bad karma or papa karma. If one acts as a compassionate soul by helping others, one may receive good karma. But the goal is to get rid of karma in its entirety, which means that one should be indifferent and without anxiety in all situations. This would cause the absence of karma and would lead to perfect freedom.

Somewhat like Buddhism, Jainism incorporates an ability to accept other religious traditions. Due to the concepts of relativism (anekantavada), Jainism can accommodate differences and develop respect for many other religions and systems of belief. This may not be an acceptance of another faith, but it may push Jains to think about perceptions of others and find elements of truth in it. In contemporary interfaith movements, Jainism has often been neglected, but with reassessing the role of Jainism in the Mahatma Gandhi's non-violent movement, the concept of Ahimsa became a very prominent topic in the interreligious peace initiatives. Not only non-violence towards humans and animals but also compassion for others fit well into the Golden Rule found in many religions (Do unto others as you would have them do unto you). Anekantavada also helps in such an interreligious dialogue, as different perceptions and experiences produce various "truths" about the others. If Jains can accommodate every man's understanding in a mosaic of absolute truth, then it means that Jainism cannot be fundamentalist in its approach. Another good aspect for interfaith and peace initiatives is aparigraha as desires for material things are not part of the Jain lifestyle. In an essence, Jainism offers non-violence, tolerance and non-possession to every religion without any discrimination and, thus, may suffice as a common ground for many religions.

The History of Jainism

Perhaps because Jainism believes in a never-ending succession of world cycles, Jains have not kept a detailed historical record of their tradition. Historians tend to agree with the traditional view that Mahavira himself followed an already established form of Jainism—possibly that of Parshva or Parshavanatha, the twenty-third Tirthankara of this world cycle. Parshva is very important for Jainism as he envisioned a path of asceticism and taught about four basic moral rules: nonviolence (ahimsa), truthfulness (Satya), non-stealing (Asteya), and non-accumulation of possessions (Aparigraha). Scholars situate Parshva's lifetime in the eighth century BCE. He is imaged as an ascetic sitting in a yoga position (asana), with a seven-headed cobra behind him who protect Parshva from outer elements while he meditates.

Tradition puts also the earliest Jain scripts in the age of Parshva. These are the Purvas or Old Texts, regarded as extinct, but their content is transmitted and recorded in later Jain texts. Customarily, Jains add to Purvas also 12 Angas (where Bhagavati Sutra is especially dedicated to the Mahavira's life), 12 Upangas, six Chedasutras (rules for ascetics), four Mulasutras, ten Prakirnasutras and two Culikasutras; together they constitute a canon that comprises almost whole knowledge about Jain beliefs, cosmology, ethics, and history. While some are focused on the life of Mahavira and his disciples, other texts are oriented more to the right understanding and practice of asceticism, rules of monastic life, and the principle of nonviolence. Just like Buddhist scripts were written in vernacular Pali language, so the Jain texts were written in the local Prakrits language, and not in Sanskrit. This shows a will of Jain (and Buddhist) masters to distinguish themselves from Brahman caste and Hinduism, which used Sanskrit as their official religious language. It also shows an understanding that Jainism is a specific religious teaching, not connected to Hinduism.

Jain scriptures constitute the main source of the religion's teachings. The Digambara and Shvetambara sects differ with regard to the recognized sets of scripture. These two schools differ in some questions. For instance, the Digambara believes that Mahavira, after attaining the enlightenment, no longer acted as a human being: a kevalin, as an enlightened being, spontaneously emits a sacred sound (divyadhvani) which may be interpreted only through a sacred knowledge of his disciples (ganadharas). The Shvetambara school, on the contrary, illustrates

Mahavira's life after his enlightenment as very conventional, but with engagements in battles against enemies such as Makkhali Gosala, who formed another school that went extinct in the Middle Ages.

When Mahavira passed away, he left eleven of his disciples (ganadharas, lit. supporters of the gana or Indian martial traditions; later this term would be used for monks) behind him, chief of them being Indrabhuti Gautama, who will become a leading figure in the Shvetambara canon. Another one was Sudharman and both of them are considered as the founding fathers of the Jain monasticism. The third disciple, Jambu, is considered to be the last person of the present time to attain enlightenment. The Jain knowledge has been transferred from teacher to student in a teaching lineage (guru parampara). Jain monks formed distinct monastic lineages but without any effort to make separate teachings. Because of their utter reliance on laypersons, who even have to cook for the monks and nuns as they cannot accidentally kill any creature, wherever there was a presence of Jain monasticism, there was also Jain settlement. The biggest presence was in the area where Mahavira came from, the northeastern Indian region of Greater Magadha. They had royal support from King Chandragupta, a cousin of King Ashoka who will become a royal patron of Buddhism. Kings of that time were the most secure bet for new religious communities. Due to the political instability, Jains moved from Magadha to the south, effectively causing a split between two communities. Even today, Magadha has a small community of Jains. Most of them live in the northwestern states of Gujarat and Rajasthan, as well as in the southern states of Karnataka and Maharashtra.

With time, different monastic lineages caused a schism into two sects: Digambara and Shvetambara. While the emigration of Digambaras to the south did cause the two communities to grow apart, the primary reason for a split happened before and in Magadha itself. In second century CE this split was already visible in the creation of the Six-Part Scripture (Satkhandagama), kept by the monk Dharasena for safekeeping of a particular Digambara knowledge. Most of the early Jain knowledge was memorized in its entirety by some monks. In the 4th century CE, Jains gathered in the capital of Magadha, Pataliputra (today Patna), to write down all the Purvas and Angas. However, there is a disagreement between two sects which texts are valid and which are not. Most of the Jain canon is same for both sects, but there are some important differences regarding the ascetic nudity, the nature of liberated being, and the nudity of ascetic women. Namely, the Shvetambara sect called for wearing of white robes by monks and nuns (thus, its name means White Robe). On the other hand, the Digambara sect is known for their nudity (thus, their name means "dressed in heaven", i.e. naked). However, this nakedness is reserved only for monks but not for nuns. In other matters, they are virtually identical, as codified in the Tattvarthasutra, which may be considered as universally accepted Jain text. All Jain religious teachings are now based on Tatthvarthasutra, which is interestingly written and kept in Sanskrit language.

In fifth and sixth century CE, Jainism reached its intellectual and theological zenith. Individuals such as Umasvati, Samantabhadra, Siddhasena Divakara and Kundakunda, albeit controversial in some of their teachings and thoughts, contributed not only to Jainism, but to other Indian religions too and to the Indian civilization in its entirety. From 2nd to 12th century Jainism thrived and this may be considered a golden age of this religion. In the ninth century CE about the time that the influence of Buddhists was severely diminishing in India, the country's religious landscape was undergoing a rather sudden shift with the influx of Islam, beginning in 1192. This caused a final fall for presence of Buddhism in India, but not of Jainism. Although many temples were destroyed, Jains were a very close community and this helped them survive. Some Jains even had cordial relationships with the Muslim rulers. Always a minority, Jain influence waned and was minimized to a mercantile class living with both Hindus and Muslims. They did spread all over the Indian subcontinent, but not outside of it. The threat of violence kept Jains home. They were also very critical of new forms of spiritual and ascetic growth and particularly of tantric activities.

In the 17th century, both Digambara and Shvetambara experienced further divisions among themselves. Digambaras have split into the Bisapanthis and Terapanthis, largely due to different authorities of the administrative monks in charge of monastic institutions (bhattarakas). They wore orange robes to be able to communicate dressed with the public. Because of this, Terapanthis did not regard them as true monks, as the monks are nude. Among the Shvetambara community, a split occurred between the Sthanakavasis and Shvetambara Terapanthis where the reason was an objection to the worship of images (murtipuja). The 17th century was thus a period of great rethinking and it is no wonder that the last Jain philosopher Yasovijaya lived exactly in that century.

For centuries, Jains have been very successful in business, perhaps due to their religiously motivated focus on trade as opposed to agriculture. Also, the Jain community is highly respected for its charitable giving. In keeping with their profound emphasis on ahimsa, Jains commonly take in and care for animals that are maltreated or are targeted for slaughter. Although they generally do not actively seek converts to their religion, Jains tend to be outspoken advocates of universal vegetarianism and so have exercised wide influence in this regard.

Among the recent remarkable Jain figures, Shrimad Rajacandra (1867–1901) is especially known outside India due to his connection to Mohandas (Mahatma) Gandhi. Jain influence has also reached well beyond India through the Indian diaspora population. They are today more ready to accept some novelties and to borrow from Hindu tradition. A stronger accent is given to mysticism, even the tantric experiences, which would have been radically refuted in earlier centuries. Jains are also very active in the environmentalism, fighting against climate changes and its consequences worldwide. One should not overestimate a desire for such a fight, though: care for the environment is not because of the world itself, but out of compassion for all living beings. However, in the Jain worldview, it would be better to leave such a world, i.e. to attain freedom from samsara and detach oneself from this physical reality. The laypersons are becoming more visible in spreading the Jain messages. Also the schism between two sects and their subgroups are now less visible and there is a tendency to promote Jainism as a united whole. Jainism is presented to the world in its efforts for a better world, with more good karma, albeit with constant reminder that it is not, in fact, important. A largely individualist movement is present in diaspora, particularly in the United States. This diaspora forms a novel approach to Jainism and challenges some traditional preconditions and divisions.

Jainism as a Way of Life

Jainism is often visualized through monks, although they make a very small percentage of this religious community. However, their followers are very attached to the ideas and rituals of nonviolent asceticism. This includes some extreme measures such as sweeping the floor in front of them just not to unintentionally kill some small being. While laypeople do admire and cherish such radical nonviolent asceticism, they mostly feel it is an extraordinary and very difficult activity for them. Jains believe that asceticism is necessary to free one's soul and reach enlightenment, in other words, to free oneself from continual transmigration of the soul into the mortal bodies. Radical asceticism asks for complete withdrawal from the world, without ties to family or society, and devoting oneself to pure ascetic practices full time. With the help of three jewels – true faith, knowledge and behavior – asceticism may free the soul or move it to the higher form of being in the next generation. Sinful life, on the other hand, leads to the lower form of life.

The two main sects of Jainism, the Digambaras and the Shvetambaras have many things in common, yet there are interesting and instructive differences. Digambara (or "sky-clad") monks, as their name infers, go about naked; Digambara nuns do not, donning simple white garments like their counterparts in other Jain sects. A sizable majority of Jains are Shvetambaras. Unlike the Digambaras, they use alms bowls when begging for food; they accept the possibility of a woman attaining kevala; and, of course, they wear clothing. Within Shvetambara Jainism, there are two distinctive sects, the Sthanakvasi and the Terapanthi. There is no central authority of Jainism.

Jains believe that the ascetic life offers the spiritual path that best replicates the lives and follows the teachings of the jinas. Most Jains, however, do not choose this arduous life, taking up instead the lifestyle and duties of the Jain laity. Ascetics depend on the almsgiving of the Jain laity, and sometimes of Hindus, to eat. Usually wandering in groups, they spend eight months of the year traversing the land, and then four months, during the rainy season, with lay communities. Ascetics commit to five "Great Vows," the vow of ahimsa being the centerpiece. Others include commands not to kill a single living being, not to lie, not to be greedy, not to indulge in sexual experiences, and not to attach to any worldly matter. The main institutional difference among Jains is that a minority are monks and nuns, while the majority are laypersons and they have different obligations and vows. The great vow of ahimsa is radically followed. Many monks and nuns wear mouth protection (muhpatti) which helps them not to swallow by accident some flies or other smaller beings. An ascetic is responsible for the wellbeing of another life form whenever he or she is aware of it. Such awareness is an important aspect of Jain life, as negligence causes bad karma. This led, indirectly, to a large ecological awareness within the Jain community. The vows are divided between monks/nuns and laypersons. The Great Vows are more radical, while the Lesser Vows are adjusted to the everyday living in the world. While ahimsa seems to be a very focused activity in the Great Vow, in the Lesser Vow it means a Jain cannot intentionally kill no one and should be a vegetarian. In the case of sexual purity, the Great Vow calls for complete celibacy, while the Lesser Vow commands marital faithfulness. Ascetics do not owe anything in the Great Vow (at least technically, as they use ceremonial pots and robes in the case of Shvetambaras), and layperson should live simply and without extravagant style or greed, according to the Lesser Vow.

Jainism is quite misogynistic religion. Although professing total equality of all souls, present in all living beings, it also states important differences in this-worldly reality. Women nuns (sadhvis) cannot be nude in most of the Jain sects, mostly on the pretext they might be vulnerable to sexual assault. But women are also often considered the source of many evils. Digambaras see male nudity as a precondition for liberation from samsara. The women cannot follow this path, so they have to wait to be reborn as males. Shvetambaras do not agree with such understanding. Based on their scripts, they believe that both mother of Mahavira and the 19th Tirthankara Mallinatha, considered to be a woman, reached liberation. They also point to the fact that even a naked monk may have feelings of possession and in that way would not follow his vows. That is why a cloth can be used for both men and women as it is the inner feeling of non-attachment that counts. After Mahavira left this world, there were far more women than men within the ascetics. This continued for a long period of time. Such an understanding is yet another point of disagreement between two great Jain schools.

The Jain laity, along with providing for the ascetics, engages in a wide variety of worship activities, including worship of the Tirthankaras and pilgrimages to Jain holy sites. Jains are very focused on meditation directed to cleanse the karma from within (from the soul) and to train oneself to be indifferent and thus avoid karma in its totality. That is why meditation is an important part of the path to liberation (moksha marga). Many Jains, however, orient their meditation to the goodness in the world, for healthy, wealthy and long life for oneself and one's family, although these desires are part of passions that might create bad karma.

Jain rituals are very similar to Hindu rituals. Just like Hindus, Jains also embrace image worshipping (murtipuja). It is accepted by all Jain sects except by Shvethambara Terapanthis and Sthanakavasis who consider it neither permissible nor impermissible but unknown and thus better avoided. They stress that murtipuja was never recommended nor written about in the holy scripts. Murti puja is done in a very similar way to the Hindu traditions. First, the top of an image is anointed with "clean matter" such as milk, yoghurt, sandalwood paste and water in an act called abhisheka. Candles or lamps are flown in front of the images, usually followed by singing, chanting and bells (this act is called arati), and in the end, the food is offered. This may indeed be seen in Hinduism as well, but the veneration of images has a different cause, based on profound distinction how two religious traditions imagine the deities and what is the link between human and divine world. For a Jain, there is no "god" but an eternal and freed soul, personified in Tirthankara. These souls are not creators of the world and do not intervene in one's life. They are venerated because they gave us path, knowledge and practice to use to attain soul liberation by ourselves. In other words, by venerating Tirthankaras, Jains venerate the soul within, what is divine within themselves. When Jains give food, they do not eat it afterwards, as it is common in the Hindu tradition. Quite contrary, it is a symbolic refusal of food, an act of separation from this world. As the food has to leave the Jain area, it is commonly given as a donation to the poor from neighboring communities. As it may be seen, Jainism does not sacralize their clergy (although a strong distinction between the clerics and laypeople exists) like in Hinduism. The rituals are sometimes identical in Jainism and Hinduism, but their soteriology is sometimes completely different and the right understanding of the final aim of these rituals are necessary to grasp to see how differentiated the two traditions are.

The images are used also for other and more explicit rituals. Prostrating in front of the images and chanting various hymns and mantras from the Jain sacred scripts is chief among them. After that, a person meditates in a specific kayotsarga position, considered to be a pose of liberated beings, i.e. the meditative position in which Tirthankaras attained enlightenment. A person then recites Namokara Mantra, one of the most commonly used mantras in Jainism. This mantra is in the ancient Prakrit language. The original mantra is Namo arihantanam, Namo siddhanam, Namo ayariyanam, Namo uvajjhayanam, Namo loe savvasahunam, and it means: I bow to the Jinas/Tirthankaras, I bow to the perfect ones (those who gained liberation), I bow to the leaders of the Jain order, I bow to the teachers of the Jain order, I bow to all the ascetics in the world. It is a mantra used every day and is similar to many other main and short prayers in other world religions. Jainism suggests also practising 48-minutes long meditation, which is a traditional Indian measurement of time (muhurta).

SUGGESTED READINGS, WEBLINKS, AND OTHER MEDIA

Readings

- Babb, Lawrence. *Absent Lord. Ascetics and Kings in a Jain Ritual Culture*. Berkley, CA: University of California Press, 1996.

- Bronkhorst, Johannes. *Greater Magadha. Studies in the Culture of Early India*. Leiden: Brill, 2007.

- Chapple, Christopher Key. *Nonviolence to Animals, Earth, and Self in Asian Traditions*. Albany, NY: State University of New York, 1993.

- Dundas, Paul. *The Jains*. 2nd ed. London: Routledge, 2002.

- Jain, Shri Satish Kumar, and Kamal Chand Sogani, eds. *Perspectives in Jaina Philosophy and Culture*. New Delhi: Ahimsa International, 1985.

- Jaini, Padmanabh S. *The Jaini Path of Purification*. 2nd ed. Columbia, MO: South Asia Books, 2001.

- Long, Jeffrey D. *Jainism: An Introduction*. London: IB Tauris, 2009.

- Lopez, Donald S. Jr., ed. *Religions of India in Practice.* Princeton, NJ: Princeton University Press, 1995.
- Radhakrishnan, Sarvepalli, and Charles A. Moore, eds. *A Sourcebook in Indian Philosophy.* Princeton, NJ: Princeton University Press, 1957.
- Tobias, Michael. *Life Force: The World of Jainism.* Freemont, CA: jain Publishing Company

Weblinks

- The Forum on Religion and Ecology at Yale (Jainism Introduction)—www.fore.yale.edu/publications/books/cswr/Jainism-introduction/
- The Jaina (Federation of Jain Associations in North America)—www.jaina.orgWabash   Center—www.wabashcenter.wabash.edu/resources/result_browse.aspx?topic=575&pid=361—The Wabash Center, a trusted resource for all aspects of the academic study of religion, offers links to a wide variety of dependable Internet resources on Jainism.

SACRED TEXTS

www.sacred-texts.com/jai/sbe22/sbe2281.htm
The first of five sections of the *Kalpa Sutra* on the life of Mahavira

www.sacred-texts.com/jai/sbe22/sbe2220.htm
Acarangasutra 1.4.1.1–2, including the well-known passage on ahimsa

www.sacred-texts.com/jai/sbe22/sbe2240.htm
Acaranga Sutra, 1.7, 6, on *sallekhana*

KEY TERMS AND DEFINITIONS

ahimsa (ah-him'suh; Sanskrit, "nonviolence," "not desiring to harm") Both the avoidance of violence toward other life forms and an active sense of compassion toward them; a basic principle of Jainism, Hinduism, and Buddhism.

ajiva (uh-jee'vuh; Sanskrit, "nonsoul") Nonliving components of the Jain universe: space, time, motion, rest, and all forms of matter.

dana (dah'nuh; Sanskrit, Pali, "giving") Ritual of giving.

Digambara (dig-ahm'buh-ruh; Sanskrit, "those whose garment is the sky") The second largest Jain sect, whose monks go about naked so as to help abolish any ties to society; generally more conservative than the Shvetambara sect.

jina (ji'nuh; Sanskrit, "conqueror") Jain title for one who has "conquered" samsara; synonymous with tirthankara.

jiva (jee'vuh; Sanskrit, "soul") The finite and eternal soul; also the category of living, as opposed to nonliving, entities of the universe.

karma (Sanskrit, "activity") "Action" and the consequences of action; determines the nature of one's reincarnation; in Jainism, all activity is believed to involve various forms of matter that weigh down the soul (jiva) and thus hinder the quest for liberation.

kevala (kay'vuh-luh; shortened form of Sanskrit *kevalajnana*, "isolated knowledge" or "absolute knowledge") The perfect and complete knowledge or omniscience that is Jain enlightenment; marks the point at which one is free from the damaging effects of karma and is liberated from samsara.

loka (loh'kah; Sanskrit, "world") The Jain universe, often depicted as having the shape of a giant man.

Shvetambara (shvayt-ahm'buh-ruh; Sanskrit, "those whose garment is white") The largest Jain sect, whose monks and nuns wear white robes; generally more liberal than the Digambara sect.

tirthankaras (teert-hahn'kuhr-uhs; Sanskrit, "makers of the river crossing") The Jain spiritual heroes, such as Parshva and Mahavira, who have shown the way to salvation; synonymous with jinas.

CHAPTER 11

Native African Religions

R eligion in a broader sense is a tendency of a human being to be connected to God or higher forces. It contains a feeling of dependency upon these deities, in order to find an explanation for one's own being, the world and existence. Religion also includes beliefs transformed into rituals, cults, customs and various practices. This broad definition of religion is necessary to open the doors to a huge diversity of African religions. Indigenous religions are understudied in the field of religious studies and textbooks barely mention them. The common understanding of native religions is also full of stereotypes. While generalizations of these religions are difficult, due to the diversity of African cultures, they do have some characteristics in common. Generally, they are oral rather than scriptural, include belief in a supreme being, belief in spirits and other divinities, veneration of ancestors, use of magic, and traditional medicine. The role of humanity is generally seen as one of harmonizing nature with the supernatural.

Categorization of African religions

While adherence to traditional religion in Africa is hard to estimate, due to syncretism with Christianity and Islam, practitioners are estimated to number over 100 million, or at least 10 percent of the population of the African continent. African diasporic religions are also practiced by descendants of Africans in the diaspora in the Americas such as Candomble, Umbanda, Quimbanda in Brazil, Santeria in Cuba and the United States, Lucumi in the Caribbean and Vodun/Voodoo in Haiti and the United States. The largest native African religion is Yoruba, which was the religion of the vast Yoruba state which existed before European colonialism. Its practitioners today – certainly those in the Caribbean, South America and the U.S. are integrated into a technological and industrial society, yet they still proclaim affiliation to this African-based religious system. Cohesive rituals, beliefs, and organization were spread throughout the world of Yoruba, to an extent characteristic of nations and many organized religions, not simply small ethnic communities or tribes. Practitioners of native religions in Sub-Saharan Africa are distributed among 43 countries, and are estimated to number over 100 million, although the largest religions in Africa are Christianity and Islam. West African religious practices generally manifest themselves in communal ceremonies and/or divinatory rites in which members of the community, overcome by force, are excited to the point of going into meditative trance in response to rhythmic or mantric drumming and singing. In its totality, the word African within the African native religions, means it is about the religion of the African people, wherever they may be – in Africa or beyond. That is why Voodoo is presented here. One should seek to find something specific African, as the belief in God, gods, spirits, ancestors, magic, sorcery and witchcraft are universal, and present in various countries and continents. it is the way how these practices apply to Africa is what constitutes African native religions.

This field is so vast that there should be some terminology employed right at the beginning. In the past, the African religions were termed as fetishism. This word comes from the Portuguese feitico, meaning witchcraft or talisman. Such an understanding focused on African religious feelings towards various material items (clams, teeth, etc). The Portuguese invaders understood these amulets as some sort of fetishism and the name stayed. However, as the religion studies advanced, it became clear that Africans do not adore the item itself, but as a symbol of divinized ancestors or tribe. At various times, African religions were termed "primitive" and "naturalistic" which is now considered as pejorative. The latter term is additionally incorrect as there are no naturalistic religion anywhere in the world. Many religious traditions in Africa are known as animism. It is a belief that all natural objects, and universe itself, contain a soul. Animism is one of important but not exclusive characteristic of the African religions. Thus, it is not right to call religious identity of the African continent as animistic in its entirety. These religions are also often called traditional. It is ideologically neutral but also very broad term for whole African religiosity.

Thus, we opt here for the Native African Religions. This term has its logic behind it because the African religions are not universal but ethnocentric or tribal, although central structure of rituals and beliefs run the entirety of the African continent. Apostasy or taking another religion virtually never existed, although all tribes included some beliefs of other peoples. There are huge differences between particular religious understandings as well as a huge similarity. It is, therefore, possible to talk collectively about their main characteristics, by comparing tenets of faith of particular people with universal problems of life, death, afterlife, deities, etc. Such similarity exists not only among the African faith systems but among different races and cultures as well. Possibly the main concept of division between various beliefs is based on occupation. Agricultural societies would have different religious aspects than hunters' or herders' communities. The religious concepts differ also due to an ambient where a tribe or a people lives. There is a remarkable difference between faith of those wo dwell in forest areas and those in the steppes.

Are African religions animist?

The native African religions very probably stem from animism. The word is based on the Latin anima which means soul or spirit. Animism is the attribution of a soul to plants, inanimate objects, and natural phenomena and the belief in a supernatural power that organizes and animates the material universe. It is also connected to shamanism and the cult of ancestry. The religious studies differ in naming the indigenous religions of Africa and the Americas as animism, however, some scholars argue that animism is the primordial religion from which all other religions stem. The classic sociologists of religion thought of the evolutionary development of religions from animism through polytheism and monotheism, only to reach a pinnacle of civilization in scientific rationalism. This was particularly a scientific standard developed by Edward B. Taylor. Modern scholars have mainly rejected such a version of animism because of too much ethnocentrism and evolutionism. These theories are not testable in arguments such as the one that primitive cultures in the dawn of civilization did not know the difference between dream and reality, as the spirits usually talk through dreams to humans. Additionally, these theories were done by colonial researchers with a huge Christian bias. The traditional societies of Africa responded to European colonialism, adapting their beliefs to Christianity, sometimes struggling against them. However, animism in its right understanding of the role of spirits in the world is a predominant worldview in Africa. And while many colonial researchers thought animism is void of the revelation of God, the native African religions include the God of creation.

Are African religions totemism?

This theory goes back to William Robertson Smith (1846 1894), linguist and Old Testament scholar. With his conception of the origin of religion, he stayed within the evolutionist scheme of Tylor but emphasized the precedence of ritual over myth (the explanation of the world). According to him, religion did not emerge from animistic explanations of the world, but from ritual action, which he viewed as an activity that strengthened the community. An essential function of religion was therefore the worship of divine representations of the social order: Religion consisted of a series of actions and regulations, its purpose was not to save souls but to give existence and prosperity to society. Robertson Smith's totemistic sacrifice theory borrows its main term from an Indian language, namely "totem", which we all know from the totem pole. Totemism is either a universal evolutionist theory of the explanation of the origin of the religion or the name for a, with certain differences, widespread cultural phenomenon, namely the systematic symbolization of social realities through images of concrete phenomena, mostly animals, but also plants or (less often) general natural phenomena such as rain etc. That means totems serve, for example, to establish group membership by means of one of the clan members sacred animals so that hunting and eating of these animals are taboo for the members of the clan. At the same time, this clan is strictly exogamous. This theory has also rooted in visible rituals and totemism in the African native religions.

The Teachings of African religions

African religions are tightly connected with all forms of social life. The political, economic or social activity contains religious significance too. The vision of the world is unique, as there is no separation between sacral and profane. It is primarily spiritualistic and determines everything transcendentally. All aspects of life are controlled by spiritual beings and forces. It may be very visible, as the sky, sun, moon, earth, forest, water may have religious experiences. An African human being lives in harmony with nature, i.e., stresses its connection to the cosmos. It does not mean the Africans do not transform nature. They do, often negatively and detrimentally of managing the natural resources, but in a religious sense, they should respect the natural environment. This harmony may take various forms.

First, there is the harmony with the human. A human being is seen in a historical sense as the one who lived in the same place before, he/she is an ancestor. In present, human is the one who continues the gift of life. In the future, human is the father or the mother of their descendants. African religions pay big respect to humans in all three temporal stages, but harmony with the ancestors seems to be very profound. If a person angers the ancestors, it is necessary to make peace immediately, as the consequences may be dire for the person or his/her family. Second, there is harmony with the animals. The African myths explain the origin of families or tribes through some animals which played a crucial role in the dawn of existence. These animals are venerated and members of the tribe cannot kill them. Some eat the venerated animals as part of the sacral ritual. Third, there is harmony with the plants. Trees are of particular importance for the livelihood of the African population. As in other religions, here too the mythology finds a place for the tree of life, potency and protection. Holy woods are important for initiations when the groups of youth go to the sacred forest and away from their home to receive the wisdom of their teachers and to become adults. Fourth, there is harmony with the earth and natural elements. Agricultural societies understand the earth as a living deity and connect it with fertility. Certain communities also have special connections to particular elements. Smiths venerate fire, herders rain and water, etc.

Human is a dynamic being. Human contains an element contained on a border between consciousness and unconsciousness that gives the possibility of transformation and transmigration. In fact, everything that exists contains such a life force. The Bantu people call this concept of a being ntu. Ntu is an intuition of reality and the basis for a more or less determined life structure. The scale of determination is various: mu ntu is the intelligent being while ki ntu is an item or a being without intelligence. Ku ntu denotes the kind of existence (quality and quantity) while ha ntu position in time and space. Such an understanding of the comprehensive life force is very important. Its laws are mastered by specialists who can manipulate that force through magic. The human person itself is fluid. He grows step-by-step and reaches its maturity in old age. In the past, the Venda people of South Africa, considered someone a human only if one has teeth. Children were not seen as human until they grew teeth and it was not a sin or a crime to leave a baby if it had a handicap. Another such group of unfortunate children are twins. Relation to twins is not unique in Africa, as some tribes almost venerate and certainly welcome the twins, while some think it is a curse. In Cote d'Ivoire, in the Bona tribe, twins have been nicely accepted if they were of the same sex. Otherwise, they would be a sign of misfortune for the family. Accepted twins would have a special altar dedicated to the twin spirits and people would pray to them and make offerings.

Images and words are given tremendous power. An image asks its realization, i.e., it realizes whatever it represents. If it is an image of potential danger, one has to flee from it as it is a real danger. There is a widespread custom of pregnant women to run away from a rope as they have a fear that the child which is going to be born might strangle to death through magic on distance. Words are commonly important. They contain the dynamism of realization and give life to any concept imagined. Moreover, the African concept of the world is full of symbols as they are the visible things that signify the invisible ones. This gave way to the wearing of masks that embody invisible spirits or ancestors. The logic of symbolism is based on rules of similarities, continuity, and contrast. What is similar produces similarity almost automatically, says the law of similarities. The law of continuity is based on a continuity of a being and the content it emanates, whether it is a shadow, an image, a name. This is the founding principle of African magic. By manipulating an image of a person, one may influence that person itself. The law of contrast is based on knowledge from nature. For instance, a dangerous snake may also have an antidote and may be used further as a medicine.

The central topic of African religions is humans with all the dimensions of social and cultural life. Human is the center of the universe. All African cosmogonies give humans such a position and they are all anthropological. Descriptions of the making of a human put the human being in a special position in contrast to the floral, animal and spiritual world. There are numerous accounts of how humans are made. For example, Fon people from Benin and Dugon people from Mali believe God made humans directly. The Bambara people from Mali believe that humans came out from a tree, while the Zulu tribe from South Africa argue it was the cane. However, cosmogony is not so developed as in other world religions, as the African faiths are mainly concerned with human existence. The African conception of the world is highly egocentric. It may be explained in a way how a traditional house is built. A person envisions oneself in the center of a future house and builds everything around oneself. The same may be applied to a village that is organized in the East-West direction. East is identified with life, happiness, health, while West is death, evil, sickness. Such a conception is clearly seen in rural architecture.

Human is a unique being that has body and soul. Many tribes tend to believe there are several kinds of souls. The heavy soul animates the body, the light soul appears in dreams, and it may also be the soul that reincarnates in another person after the human dies. The light soul may exit the body in times of dreaming and be in another place, including within an animal. Dogon people from Mali and Fang people from Gabon know eight kinds of human souls, four male and four female, and they are situated within the vital organs such as heart, blood, liver, etc. The soul is not tightly connected to the body. During one's lifetime, the soul gradually separates from the body, as one nears the time of death. Dying persons may double themselves and possibly hurt others by provoking various illnesses or accidents. Death is not considered necessarily a natural event. It may be only in the case of old people who died in quite an old age. In all other cases, death is caused by evil spirits, sorcerers, the entities that eat the soul, etc. Special rituals have been developed to engage various entities. The guilty party should be determined and he or she has to substitute the loss in goods or money, per discussion with the family of the deceased. While the immediate cause of death may be a sorcerer or some of the lesser spirits, there is a belief that God lets people die. Death is a consequence of the enemy's activity but is under God's omnipotence. God is the master of life and death. If God does not kill, then a human cannot kill as well. When a person dies, a funeral must be held in accordance with a community's customs. Otherwise, the soul wanders around the village and represents a danger for the community and particularly for the family of a dead person. Such a belief explains the huge importance of funeral rituals which usually take a long time.

Those souls that are calmed with ritualistic goodbyes go to the world of shadows, situated in the west. A soul exists there but does not live. Souls often come into the contact with own family if the members of the family make offerings. In the world of shadows, the soul is closer to the ancestors and may help the living members of the family by taking care of their material progress, ensuring their descendants, protecting them from the influence of the evil spirits. The living receives the messages from deceased ones through dreams or with help of a seer.

A human needs to ensure one's progeny. The descendants will remember the ancestors' names, will make the offerings and sustain their existence in the afterlife. Such an understanding explains a moral obligation to marry and procreate. The deceased ones know the needs of their family members and they are the best intermediaries between God and people. People may talk to them about all kinds of needs. However, the living ones are not too happy if the dead ones appear too often. They offer them food as a sign of hospitality but also as a request to be left at peace. The dead ones are mightier than the living ones and may revenge if they feel insulted before the death. The same may happen if the living ones do not listen to the advice of the dead ones or if they do not make offerings.

Not every dead person becomes automatically an intermediary between the community and higher spirits. Worthy ancestors may only be those dead people that met certain preconditions. These are having authority in time of their life, having a progeny, being healthy, being socially accepted and cherished, being wealthy so they could be also hospitable. Even if a deceased person became rich in a dishonest manner, he or she may become a cult object. In such a case, this person's soul sheds fear. Children, sterile men and women, mutilated sick people and those who died far away from their home, those whom the community condemned and those with whom peace was not made cannot become worthy ancestors. When no one of the living knows the deceased one anymore, that person experiences second death. The person goes to a resting place, in a village settled deep into the earth. The messages stemming from these dead people cannot be understood by the living. These persons cross from the intermediate stage of the dead-live principle to a collective afterlife. A special place among the dead hold heroes, founders of a clan, etc. They remain in memories of a particular tribe forever and the most important ones will reach the spirit level and will embody a real cult.

One cannot know much about the afterlife. While death is always thought of as evil, a deceased one should have peace after death strikes. He or she must feel good in the grave so that this person does not roam around making evil. In Senoufomi-nkyanka tribe, dead people are laid to rest in a grave on the right hand, while the left hand is free. Namely, the tribesmen shake the left hand on definitive goodbye as a sign of breaking the relationship. The afterlife depends on the morality of earthly life. After death, humans participate in spiritual powers, but African religions never convey much content about proximity between God and men. In general, the African religions did not find a solid answer to the problem of death.

Spirit world

There are two kinds of spirits, based on their origin. One kind is made by God, while the other was once human that came to the spiritual world through the death experience. However, there is another substantial difference between spirits: ones are higher (deities), and others are lower. The deities personify activities and godly manifestations, phenomena and natural objects (the nature spirits), divined heroes and mythological figures. These higher spirits were made by God and they are tightly connected to God and may even replace God in everyday activities. They are often understood as personifications of Supreme Being or as spiritual beings whom God entrusted forms and functions of nature. Sun, moon, sea, lakes, mountains have godly shapes or embody deities. Humans often meet them and consider them closer than God. These deities become intermediaries between men and God, as they are both physical and spiritual beings. A spiritual being, thus, can act physically. In the spiritual world of the Yoruba people in Nigeria, there are 1700 deities in a strict hierarchical structure. Furthermore, mythological spiritual figures are used to explain the origin of customs, institutions, and traditions. For instance, the Ashanti people of Western Africa consider earth as a female deity that is positioned hierarchically immediately after God and Thursday are celebrated as her day.

Spirits, unlike deities, are spiritual beings whose position is higher than that of people. Some of them are made as a special race but most of them are souls of people who died. Spirits are not dead-live souls in special relation to their families.

They lose their personality and became almost a simple matter. Together, they are mightier than people, but some specialists can manipulate them as well. Spirits are present everywhere, but there are places where they especially like to dwell, such as in the underground. Some African peoples also find spirits in the air, in the sun or in light. They may dwell near the people, in trees, forests, rivers, mountains, around the villages. Many spirits simply remain in the same ambient where they previously lived. Spirits are closer to the Supreme Being than people and may become their intermediaries but they do not appear so often to the people as their dead-live family members. Many African legends described their activities: they sleep in the day and act in the night, they may transform into people, plants and animals. Traditional medicine men and sorcerers may make a contact with them. If spirits appear often, they may even settle down in a person. Such a condition is not bad. This stage is desired and it may be realized through dancing or trance. However, total possession is bad because it tortures a person and depersonalizes it. They are liberated through exorcism. These terms, however, are under a different understanding from Christianity which usually refers to demonic possession, where a demon attacks the human body. In African religions, it is believed that during a ceremony with drumming and dancing, the spirit can be invited into one's body. It is not a negative bodily invasion but an honor. The African priests and priestesses call it the riding of a horse or ritual mounting where the practitioner temporarily becomes a horse that carries a spirit.

Vodou and Voodoo – an African religion in the Americas

Although Haiti is in the Americas, it is not a native American religion but an African one. That is why Vodou is explained here as a major African religion with ties to many beliefs and practices in the African continent as well. The word "voodoo" conjures all sorts of horrific ideas and images of malevolent magic like voodoo dolls or the villain doctors and priests who indulge in brutality and even human sacrifice. These are inaccurate stereotypes of the African diaspora religions, sometimes also called the African derived religions. These are faith systems largely concentrated in the Americas, including the Caribbean, that originate in part from communities of enslaved Africans who were abducted from their homeland and forced to work in the European colonies in times of the transatlantic slave trade. The Haitian religion known as vodu is not primarily based on magic or witchcraft. The vast majority of Vodou practitioners, called vodawizan, have never seen a voodoo doll, let alone used one. This Haitian religion primarily involves serving spirits called Lua and a lot of

Haitian Vodou practice is blended with Roman Catholicism. Haitian Vodou differs from the New Orleans Voodoo. The latter sometimes manifests as a cultural theme, but it may also mean the beliefs and practices of people who trace their origins back to the Atlantic slave trade when the enslaved Africans were brought to Louisiana in the 17th and 18th centuries. Thus, Haitian belief is termed Vodou, while the beliefs in ex-French colonies in what is today the United States is called Voodoo. The name itself derives from the designation for spirit in the West African languages, particularly those spoken in Benin and its surroundings. Vodun refers to beliefs and practices in West Africa today.

Haitian Vodou emerged in the 1600s within communities of enslaved Africans who were forced to the island of Hispaniola, which is today a two-state island: one half is French-speaking Haiti, another is the Spanish-speaking Dominican Republic. They stem mostly from Benin and Western Nigeria, from the Fon and Ewe peoples and various Yoruba-speaking ethnic groups. Congo communities from Central Africa also played a significant role in Haiti's demography. The Vodou practitioners speak of their ancestral homelands in Africa as Guinea and this is a major part of their mythology and practice. Vodou played an important role in throwing off colonial rule during the Haitian Revolution. On August 14th, 1791, a group of enslaved Africans met at Bois Kayaman (The Crocodile Forest) which was described as both a political rally and a religious ceremony led by the Vodou priest Dutty Boukman and the priestess Cecile Fatiman. They made a wild boar offering to the spirits and made a blood pact to win their freedom. It was the start of the Haitian Revolution and a decade later, on January 1st, 1804, they won their independence. Since then, the position of this religion in Haiti was controversial. The second president of Haiti, Alexandre Petion, outlawed many Vodou practices, but in 2003 the newly elected Haitian president and former priest Jean-Bertrand Aristide controversially decreed Vodou as the official religion in Haiti, together with Roman Catholicism.

In the Haitian religion, there is one supreme god called Bon Dieu (or BonDye in Haitian Creole language). Since there are a lot of contact points between Vodou and Catholicism, many Haitians equate the "Good God" with the God the Father in Christianity. However, the primary way of believers interact with the divine is through a pantheon of spirits called Lwa. They are the divine energies, the principles or entities that guide the world forward. They may be both energies of nature and the human realm and work both with and under the Bon Dieu. People do not typically pray to the Bon Dieu, except in times of great desperation. The believers more often interact with the Lwa, whom they refer differently: sometimes as Seyu (the saints), mysteieou (mysteries), invisible (invisible ones). They are also categorized by their "nations", the primary ones being the Rada, the Petwo, and the Gede. The Rada are the ancestral spirits associated with Vodoun spirits stemming from Benin. Some prominent Rada spirits include Papa Legba (the Gate Opener), Danbala (a spirit represented by a serpent who is considered a kind and loving spirit and often called upon for help), and Ezili Freda (a Lwa of femininity, womanhood, sexuality, prosperity, and fortune). The Rada nation of spirits are generally considered to be serene spirits and are often associated with water. This is in contrast with hot and volatile spirits of the Petwo nation that includes some Congo spirits such as Simbi (meaning spirit in the ancient Congo language). The Petwa spirits also include some of the Haitian-born heroes, including those from the Haitian revolution that have achieved status as Lwa. There is also the Gede nation, the spirits of death and fertility. The Baron Samedi is probably the best known Lwa in this nation, often depicted as a fancy skeleton man dressed in a top hat and a coat with tails. The Baron is the lord of the cemetery and the lord of the dead. There are supposedly 21 different spirit nations and it is very difficult to name all of them. Most of these nations are based on which part of Africa belief to these spirits comes from. One serves all 21 nations, meaning all 21 places of African origin are kept as equal.

Serving the Lwa (sevi lwa) is the major practice of the Haitian Vodou. It is not about servitude to the spirit but reciprocity as a basic understanding of African religions, both on the African continent and in the diaspora. When one enters into a relationship with a spirit formally, in initiation, one devotes oneself to providing offerings, to reciting the spirits' names, to singing songs that honor their legacies, to maintaining the heritage that one has been instilled with. In turn, one will be protected, cared and led by the spirits. Lwa have favorite foods, favorite colors, favorite dances and music that one can offer typically on annual saints days. In that way, believers summon the spirits and ask for their protection and help. Generally, practitioners wear white for such rituals, but this can change based on the Lwa being honored. Rhythms are associated with every nation, some are militaristic, others more transcendental, depending on the spirit.

One may also consult the spirits through the help of a priest or priestess in a special kind of temple called the Ounfo, where a perestil is erected in the center. It is a central pole or a tree called the Potomitan. There are also eclectic altars holding all sorts of offerings for the Lwa such as images, candles, flowers, food and drink. In traditional Haitian customs, there is a mention of animal sacrifice but this terminology is somewhat misleading. A party for the spirits would include specific foods, meat included, and it stems from rural areas where people would butcher their own animal. Preparation of food feeds the entire community, in a very similar way to how Kosher and Halal are done in Judaism and Islam.

African religions as a way of life

The African religions do not have big temples as in other world religions. The traditional African belief is tightly connected to the cosmos, so the holy places in Africa are regularly found in places tied to one of the cosmic elements: water, earth, fire, and air. Water is necessary for life, it is the source of living and fertility, and a symbol of renewal and resurrection. Rivers and springs are places where the water spirits dwell. Freshwater places, and in particular the big lakes, are tied to the concept of creation. The big lakes of central parts of Africa are good examples. They are the sites where various rituals are being made, such as summoning rain. The sea is equally important to the communities living next to it, particularly for the fishermen who join various rituals that would guarantee better fishing.

The sanctity of the earth is based on contrasts. The earth gives and takes away life, it feeds and destroys, it is important for every aspect of life and yet one buries the dead in the earth. Africans sanctify rocks, cliffs, crossroads. The rocks are hard, eternal and stable, and if they have a phallic outlook they may also contain a fertility significance. Hills and caves represent a solid character and potency. Caves are even more than that. With entering a cave, a human return to the core of the earth dies only to regain a new life. The crossroads, moreover, are important and food for the spirits is often left there. Air is a symbol of holy places connected to the forest and holy woods. Trees have a direct relation to time and seasons. They represent power, richness, truthfulness and durability. Africans see trees in a very narrow link with deities and holy wood is a very important place of worship. It is primarily a place of initiation, where youth comes in only to come out as adults. In the middle of the forest, true holy trees may be found. Such an initiation is a slow process of individual transformation, a progressive crossing in one's humanity. A young man incorporates himself into the clan by learning about the traditional wisdom, laws, and customs. The one who is not initiated remains blind and ignorant. Initiation is a rebirth, a process where a young man becomes a mature man, on his way to death and resurrection. According to many myths, fire is stolen and its use is secret. The fireplace is the central point in a household, but in the same category of holy places are also the volcanoes and smitheries. A smith is a very respected person as he makes tools to cultivate the earth and weapons to use in battles. Although this categorization of places according to elements is a good way to understand the way of worship, it is necessary to accentuate that any place in Africa may become a holy site.

Magic is an often term in Africa, but one should be aware of what it really means. One should differ between a medicine man, mage or shaman, and the wizard or sorcerer. The sorcerer is always connected to evil and with destruction, as his actions are always oriented against society. He/she works at night and rests during the day. A sorcerer has a desire to increase the power of his/her lifeforce by eating the souls of the living. On the other hand, a medicine man has a positive social role. He is usually the seer. Clairvoyance is based on the principle that every single thing is connected to a cosmic element. In that way, the seers may announce the arrival of the rain, predict future events of interest for the local community, or hint at peace and war. The seers may also discover the sorcerers and protect people from their evil influence. He or she may also foretell the future, mainly in two ways. A person is often connected with a spirit that helps in finding future events. Another technique involves observing, intuition, telepathy, etc. The seer is also the traditional medicine man. He or she knows well local medical herbs but the basic approach in treatment is through psychosomatic aspects of life. Every disease influences the spirit. If the spirit is recovered, the material illness will vanish as well.

Further readings

Barnes, Sandra (1989) *Africa's Ogun: Old World and New*. Bloomington: Indiana University Press

Chidester, David; Kwenda, Chirevo; Petty, Robert; Tobler, Judy; and Wratten, Darrel (1997) *African Traditional Religion in South Africa: An Annotated Bibliography*. Westport, CT: Greenwood

Gbadagesin, Segun (1999) *African Philosophy: Traditional Yoruba Philosophy and Contemporary African Realities*. New York: Peter Lang

Idowu, Bolaji (1995) *God in Yoruba Belief*. Plainview: Original Publications, rev. and enlarged ed.

Lugira, Aloysius Muzzanganda (2009) *African Traditional Religion*. New York: Chelsea House Publications

CHAPTER 12

New Religious Movements

In many Western countries, new religious movements sprung up after the Second World War. It is a time of modernity crisis, a time when many conservative ideas were questioned and redefined. In the 1960ies in particular, the exponential rise of various movements gave way to new kinds of worldviews. This included movements for human rights, university reforms, women emancipation, against war and racial discrimination, the LGBT rights. It was not a coherent movement. Rather, a more political wing acted as the New Left, inspired by the ideas of Herbert Marcuse, and oriented against capitalism and imperialism. The other was the hippy movement, which criticized the lifestyle of the middle classes and accentuated counterculture. Both were keen to go against Western values such as materialism, utilitarianism, consumerism, rationality, individualism, bureaucracy. In the domain of spirituality, this countercultural movement also called for new religious movements.

And while the countercultural movement was disappearing, the new religious movements (NRM) did not. They are still very popular, although the sociologists of religion do not know exactly why. Some argue that traditional churches and religious communities have too little spiritual content and too much ritual. The traditional religious system is depersonalized, while the NRM are not. They seem to offer personal safety amid quick changes in our societies, as well as a feeling of belonging. This may also explain why many younger people seek to join a NRM, as they are more prone to isolation and abandonment from the regular or traditional religious system. Instead of that, they feel confident and safe in the NRM which may be classified in many ways such as new faith movements, a new religion, alternative religion, unconventional religion, new sects and cults, mystical communities, marginal religiosity. Some scholars consider them simply sects and cults, but it may not be so simple.

Sects cannot be understood in a coherent way. The sects are the product of an earlier period when some Protestant communities withdrew from a larger Christian group to form a smaller one. It is, thus, a quintessential Western term that seeks a motif of exclusion of a smaller religious community because it sees itself more rightly guided in terms of theology. The NRM, on the other hand, are completely new religious expressions, made in times of increasing secularization and a kind of spiritual void in modern societies. Thus, one must find what is "new" in the NRM.

Typical characteristics of NRM, which may stand for something new, is (1) their exotic origin and new culture and lifestyle; (2) engagement level which is increasingly different than in traditional religions; (3) charismatic leaders; (4) mostly younger faithful, recruited from the middle class and better educated; (5) social visibility; (6) international activities, with roots in 1960ies and 1970ies. The exotic origin here does not mean only in a geographical or cultural sense. While some NRMs are indeed based on Eastern religions, others are more Christianity-rooted such as neo-charismatic and fundamentalist groups. They are mutually very different and we may not generalize about them. A good way to distinguish between them is to determine do they accept or refuse the world around them and do they live within it.

Movements that refuse the world are very critical of their surroundings which they see as unsatisfactory, non-spiritual and sinful. These NRMs ask their followers to withdraw completely from the world and to change their lifestyle, primarily through their dietary and dressing habits. They often form the new community based on a communal life without much contact with the outer world. Here, the members can be effective, very engaged, loyal to a deity or a spiritual master, hold tightly to their ethical rules, and are often void of their personality. The Hare Krishna movement and God's Children are the two best examples. The movements that accept the world and life in it are not conventional religious movements as their rituals, temples, and theologies are loose or non-existent. Everything that is not acceptable in the outer world an individual may choose to correct oneself, not through society. That is why such movements are mostly focused on spiritual health and spiritual development, liberating hidden human potentials. Among such movements, one may find Scientology, transcendental meditation, New Age. There is also the movement that adjusts itself to the world, and it is the closest to the traditional religions (a good example may be Neo-Pentecostalism). They accentuate the importance of the inner and spiritual life in relation to the world. The members seek a spiritual purity they consider lost in the traditional religions that have become too much worldly. The members in these NRMs do not change their lifestyles and sometimes do not show any visible changes in their everyday activities.

At the same time, all of the NRMs were a subject of great controversies and research done by many scholars of social sciences and humanities, as well as psychologists, criminalists, law scholars. One of the issues is the way how new members are recruited. Some of the NRMs have been accused of brainwashing, kidnapping, use of hypnosis and other techniques to control the mind, drug abuse. They destroyed careers, the future and life of new members, manipulated the youth, made profits and promoted immorality. This is, of course, overgeneralization, although such things did occur. However, it is nothing new to accuse the new movements. When something is new, different, unusual, and especially if it contains a threat to the established and mainstream institutions, it becomes a subject of accusations. In essence, the sociological and statistical research showed there is no more abuse within the NRMs than in mainstream religious organizations. This is valid also for various criminal activities. One may, still, warn that NRMs are regularly smaller than the major religious institutions and that such illegalities are therefore more prevalent in NRMs.

Following the classification of NRMs, we will present here several of these movements that fall into various categories.

Jediism

Star Wars material describes the Jedi as following a religion. The Jedis are basically monks, they live a celibate life in a Jedi Temple, they dress in brown Jedi robes, and they have the sacred Jedi texts. The Jedi religion seems to have jumped from fantasy to reality as a real-world movement called Jediism. There is the Temple of the Jedi Order, the legally recognized Jedi Church and the ministry of Jediism. According to their website, Jediism is a religion based on the observance of the Force. Jedis or Jediists live by three tenets of focus, knowledge, and wisdom. They hold to the Jedi Code, a mantra that developed out of Star Wars movies. The Code is as follows: "Emotion, yet Peace; Ignorance, yet Knowledge; Passion, yet Serenity; Chaos, yet Harmony; Death, yet the Force". There is little or no evidence the Jediists are ironic in their online presence and it seems they are deeply committed to the Jedi Code and Jedaiism as religion. On the online forums of Jediists, one may find help in meditation techniques and debates over the existence of Force powers such as telekinesis. While most forum members regard force powers as scientifically baseless, some are very open to their existence. Jediism does not exist only online. There is another group, the Church of Jediism, which hosts meetups and real-life conventions and even offers Jedi wedding services.

Jedi or Jedaiist is someone who follows the philosophical and ideological concepts of the Jedi Knights of Star Wars in their everyday life. It entails the world-betterment through self-betterment, wrapped up in Star Wars terminology and inspiration. The followers want to live as a Jedi in everyday life in the most applicable, practical, beneficial and positive way positive. The Jedi lifestyle entails five practices: meditation, physical wellness, awareness, diplomacy, and self-discipline. It also has five tenets of peace, knowledge, serenity, harmony, and force. Five traits are patience, decorum, empathy, equity, and accountability. There are also five values of self-honesty, erudition, guidance, gratitude, and commitment. Five goals are proficiency, service, defense, create and discover. All together makes a Jedi Circle.

The whole Jedaiism religion is about the Force. It is an ineffable term and may be defined by the practitioners of Jedaiism as a product of spiritual exploration and spiritual wellness that speaks to an individual. It is an open way to explore the universe and human place within it. Some consider it more in the Eastern religions' terminology and equate the Force with the Dao or the Chi or the Prana. On the other hand, some see in the Force the working of the Holy Spirit or just an intuitive human experience.

Many people do not regard Jedaiism as a real religion and its emergence in the wider public came to be a joke answer on the census in the United Kingdom, Australia, and New Zealand. Some enlisted as Jedi as a joke, others for political reasons and protest against the government, while some did it because they are really religious in that way. The media latched on and the term Jedaiism became world-known. Before that, the Jedi community did exist, but the term Jedaiism did not. In the 2001 UK census, 0,7% of the population of Wales and England claimed that their religion was Jedi. In 2011, over 170,000 claimed to be Jedi. Without a doubt, many of these people wrote it down as a joke, but even with that standpoint, they did run against government bureaucracies refusing to acknowledge their status as a religion. In 2016, the UK government rejected an application for Jedaiism to be registered as a religious charity, saying it "lacks the necessary spiritual or non-secular element". No one really knows what the UK government meant by this statement, as Jediism is a religion, at least as it manifests itself on the internet forums. Religious communities that draw from pop culture like Jedaiism are simply engaging in the same sort of cultural production that humans have been doing for thousands of years, endlessly adapting and reworking culture as the raw materials for their religions. For centuries, people have been adapting beliefs, myths and rituals into new forms. What does make Jedaiism different though is that the raw material comes from copyrighted property. This fact diminishes people's ability to participate in the creation and interpretation of that culture. And while spiritual characters such as Buddha and Christ belong to every-one, the exemplars such as Yoda and Obi-Wan Kenobi belong to a corporation.

The fact that people tend to become religious based on pop culture is a sub-group of the NRM that sociologists call hyper-real religions, which are defined as "innovative religions and spiritualities that mix elements of religious tradition with popular culture". Hyper-real refers to the attempt to make experiences more intense and fantastic than daily life. This may include Virtual Reality simulations or amuse-ment parks, but obviously, also some religious beliefs are part of this category of life experiences.

Jediism is also syncretistic in its appearance. While the ritual narratives and symbols stem from pop culture, other doctrines come from some other religions. For instance, the Jedi Creed is adopted from the Prayers of St Francis of Assisi, and Franciscan robes is definitely visible in the way how Jedi knights dress in the popular movie series. Jediism is but one of many similar "participatory cultures", which includes also followers of Matrix, Harry Potter or Lord of the Rings. Those people who dwell deep into the participatory cultures are not only consumers of these popular movie hits, but also coproducers of media, as they create fan edits and sequences based on the primary blueprint. Almost all of these hyper-reality religions exist entirely online, which the UK charity commission used to strike against Jedai-ism, which it does not regard as a real religious organization. But a cyber-religion is no less religious than any other, as the religion as a system is endlessly adaptable and religious communities have been adapting to the Internet for decades.

UFO religion

Since no aliens or extraterrestrials are not discovered yet, they are all in our imagi-nation. They are often portrayed as almost God-like deities, super-advanced scien-tifically and morally, and successful in overcoming war and poverty. This is very similar to the religious impulse where we are not alone. Even agnostics know "there is something out there", something far more powerful than us, who knows about us and cares about us. That something or someone also loves us. It is the same impulse many people get when they think about extraterrestrials. According to some research, people who have such longing, but are not religious, are more likely to believe extra-terrestrials are out there. On the other hand, practitioners of traditional religions might be less in favor of glorifying extraterrestrials because they already got their reli-gious impulses. Both ways are valid in reasoning and arguments, although without any real empirical evidence.

The concept of aliens in popular culture is largely limited to the Little Greens or Little Greys, as seen in Sci-Fi movies. The UFO religion is completely different from the UFO researchers who rely on what might be described as scientific and empirical pieces of evidence for the UFOs. Those who religiously believe in UFOs more readily look for the spiritual connection to the extraterrestrials, whether they regard the aliens as gods or as superior in terms of cosmic spirituality. There are many UFO religious groups and we will mention just a few of them here.

The Aetherius Society was founded in 1955 in London and now has over 35 religious centers across the world. For them, aliens are gods. This group came to be after the London cab driver George King after he claimed he came to contact with aliens. The Venus-based alien master called Aetherius would communicate his wisdom and guidance through King's voice. Their members focus on prayer which is then "stored" in a battery that is used to hold off disasters and helping humanitarian crisis situations. They used it in the past to move hurricanes and to aid peace talks that prevent nuclear war and the destruction of our planet. The members believe the human species is destroying our habitat, but other beings can help us. Lord Buddha is seen as a cosmic master from planet Venus, as was the Master Jesus. Sri Krishna was a cosmic master from Saturn. According to their belief, Master Jesus gave his life to earth, so that she might be saved from imminent catastrophe. In return, he asks his followers to give all that they can give. The members gather annually for the Operation Prayer Power in Holdstone Down in North Devon, UK. This is where Jesus first came down with a spaceship from Venus. The members believe the Aetherius Society is playing a huge role behind the scenes by cooperating with the masters and through their spiritual energy radiation equipment. Among the recent masters are Gandhi and George King himself. They send thousands of prayer hours to uplift everybody's consciousness. They focus on the selflessness of the Sun, which is great and powerful and gives energy to the whole solar system.

How dangerous some UFO cults may be is best shown by the Heaven's Gate group, whose mass suicide of 18 men and 21 women shocked the world. Their bodies were found in their bunks and cots in a beautiful mansion outside San Diego. All were dressed in identical black clothing and sneakers, covered by purple shrouds. Their leader was Marshall Applewhite, knowns by his fellow elders as Doe. He was able to talk to his followers about consuming a toxic mix of vodka and chocolate pudding or applesauce laced with barbiturates, which was the cause of death. Doe claimed that upon death they would all board an extraterrestrial alien spacecraft, following the Hale-Bopp comet. Heaven's Gate still has its supporters and its website is up and running just as it did in 1997. They share quite bizarre beliefs. The followers wore drab loose clothing to minimize men being attracted to women and vice versa. Nine of the men were actually castrated by their own desire.

In 1974, sports-car journalist and test driver Claude Vorilhon started a religion. From his account, laid out in two books he wrote in the mid-1970s, Volilhon claims aliens abducted him and explained to him how the world works. These aliens, called the Elohim, were the true creators of humanity. Using advanced cloning technology, they created us in their image. When they intervened with our early species they called themselves angels, cherubim, or gods. In different eras of human history, Claude claims the aliens enlightened Jesus, the Buddha, and a few others to be messengers of their time, preparing humans for when we can join them in space. The religion he founded was to be the last messenger from these Elohim. Their goal is to make humanity more peaceful, more democratic, and aware as they prepare to be welcomed into the interstellar community. He changed his name to Rael and founded Raelianism. Raelians are well-meaning people. To become one, they ask that a person formally disavow any other religion. One has to upload one's genes to a space computer, allowing for digital reincarnation and immortality. They perform these "baptisms" on one of the four major holidays in the Raelian calendar. One marks the anniversary of the bombing of Hiroshima, one marks Rael's first encounter with the Elohim, one is for the day he first saw Elohim starship where he had a meal with Jesus, Buddha, and some other religious figures, and one for when aliens cloned up Adam and Eve. The symbol the Raelians use is a Star of David with a swastika in the middle. They suggest swastika is the symbol of peace and prosperity, but that did not stop the Israeli government from banning the Raelians from building a big alien embassy in Jerusalem. They decided to replace the swastika with a swirl, but the embassy was not opened. The Raelians are also devout believers in free love. Sex and sexuality is a big part of the Raelian doctrine and has attracted some clergy from other faiths. They believe in free sexual liberation, as well as full equality for LGBT people. They practice "sensual meditation", have been vocal advocates for self-love and the distribution of condoms. Sexual pleasure is a gift from the aliens. The Raelians are big supports of science. They believe that GMO crops and nanotechnology can eliminate the need to work and create a world that embraces science. The most exciting technology for them is cloning. Rael founded an organization called Clonaid in 1997, that advocates for the advancement of human cloning. They claimed in 2002 to have cloned a little girl named Eve, but have not provided her with any sort of authenticity. They think that with cloning they could help with immortality, as well as retroactively punish war criminals and terrorists. One of their biggest projects is to build a large alien embassy in neutral territory. The Raelians have some 90,000

members in 90 countries, most popular being in Europe, Canada, and Japan. They
have a tiered system of membership: 0: trainee; 1: assistant organizer; 2: organizer; 3:
assistant priest; 4: priest; 5: bishop; 6: planetary guide. While the Raelian religion is
2/3 male, there is a special women-only Order of Angels. The women preach openly
about sex-positive feminism. They even have a special sect of women who work in or
support women in the sex industry.

Scientology

Scientology was developed by an author named L. Ron Hubbard. This is important
as it is controversial already, as L. Ron Hubbard was an established author, known
for works of fiction, mostly science fiction. Over his lifetime, he published over 600
fiction pieces, including both short stories and novels and he holds the Guinness
World Record for the author with the most published works. When the religion of
Scientology came to be, many people did not believe the religious texts he wrote
to be anything more than a work of science fiction. Hubbard was a United States
veteran, serving as a Navy officer during World War II and commanding two ships
but was removed from his post because his superiors found him incapable of command. In of these instances, he fired upon a Japanese submarine that no one else saw
and could later find no proof of, and the other instance involved him firing upon
an island that turned out to belong to Mexico, an ally of the US. The Church of
Scientology gives a lot of weight to his military career, as his injuries and near-death
experiences were partially responsible for his ability to see the truth of things and create the foundation for their belief set. The Church of Scientology also disputes a lot
of records about Hubbard, including medical records and even says that sections are
falsified, to protect his possibly secret activities as an intelligence officer. These Navy
records also dispute many of the injuries he claims to have suffered.

Throughout the 1930s and 1940s, Hubbard continued to write but also began
to experiment more with the occult, including practicing as a hypnotist and diving
into other religious acts, some pretty unconventional. In 1950, the world saw the
arrival of his book "Dianetics: The Modern Science of Mental Health". This year is
crucial for Scientologists as it is the beginning of everything. Dianetics is focused on
a technique still used today in Scientology called "auditing". Either through con-
versation or through a machine called an "e-meter", these professionals would help
the patient recall past traumas and get through them or over them, removing the
emotional trauma of memories in a process called "clearing". The e-meter picks up
on signals from the body, in the same way, a polygraph lie detector might, and it

tells the auditor what phrases or memories trigger negative feelings and when they can conclude certain conversations. Initially, Scientologists hoped to get this process approved in the larger world of medicine but these proposals were rejected. At this time, Hubbard also coined a term called "thetan", which is essentially our soul which is immortal and allows us to tap into past lives and potentially past traumas from those lives that still might affect us. Dianetics is part of Scientology but not a religion in itself, rather one way to enhance the religious experience.

Hubbard claimed that Scientology may answer all the questions an individual might have about oneself. He pivoted to Scientology and made the argument that this whole process is a religion and not a science. With this came his idea to monetize, charging at the time 500 USD for an entire 24 hours of auditing. This created a wave of churches being formed across the world, including the central headquarters in Washington DC, which now stands as a museum. The headquarters now exists in California, in Riverside County. About 1000 people live on the property and it is well protected with high fences and constant security. There is a public road that drives through it, though it is constantly recorded and monitored. There are many rumors about this place that are hotly debated, including lousy working wages, pursuit teams that bring people back and do not allow them to leave, and required confessions if they hear of other people in the compound talking or gossiping about the Church or its members. This is debated because no one inside the base will complain or make a statement to the police about their experience there. Only a few made complaints after they left the Church and those cases have all been tossed out or not taken seriously due to lack of information or evidence.

The Scientologists believe that their soul, the Thetan, is immortal and our lives are not confined to this single lifetime. They also believe we are capable of anything, even if we have not been able to realize it yet. They do believe in a God-like figure called the Supreme Being, that its members learn about and discover on their own unique journeys. Eight dynamics drive us forward, including the urge towards infinity, which includes discovering God. Other dynamics include the urge to protect animal life, the urge to exist as a peaceful community, and the urge to exists as one mankind across all races. When speaking about Scientology, words like faith and belief are often avoided and supplemented with concrete terms based on science and technology. Once one is "clear", meaning one has been cleansed of traumatic memories and feelings, one can climb the ladder to more meaningful and powerful positions. After that comes a state called Operating Thetan or OT for short. This allows one to control the world around self, including life, energy, and matter. Persons can also leave their bodies, as the Thetan itself is not confined to it. There are many levels of Operating the Thetan and it costs money through the auditing process to progress. The cheapest level is 2,750 USD and that is assuming one is free of those memories and feelings, otherwise one will have much more auditing to do before this. The third level of OT involves a major discovery that Hubbard discovered after Scientology had been founded. While people reaching this level have signed confidentiality agreements, some of these documents have been released to the public and tells a story that again causes a pretty major controversy.

According to this belief, 75 million years ago, an ancient being called Xenu was a dictator of the Galactic Confederacy. He brought humans to Earth, dropped them into volcanoes, and killed them, releasing their Thetans into the environment. These Thetans are angry and upset, causing us now to be infected and affected by these negative emotions. To overcome these negative emotions from this traumatic event is done by reaching an OT level III but it is dangerous. L. Ron Hubbard claims that it is a tough thing to do and many illnesses might plague people attempting to conquer it. The Church itself does not enjoy telling this story and will block its telling. The total to get to the point of knowledge about this event through auditing is around 100,000 USD. If one does not become enlightened and does not solve these life mysteries, one must pay to try it again.

Another controversy arrives in the form of taxes and if Scientology should actually be considered a religion by the IRS. The IRS tried to claim back taxes in the 1960s but the Church responded with thousands of lawsuits against the IRS, resulting in about 25 years of back and forth litigation, eventually resulting in the decision that Scientology was indeed a church and exempt from taxes. By the time this landmark decision was made, L. Ron Hubbard had passed away. The Church's official statement was that he no longer needed his physical body and that he continued to write and research without it. This was in 1986 and a man named David Miscavige took over the Church. A lot of claims have come out against Miscavige, including violence and abuse towards church members, but nothing has been substantiated. Something notable that happened around the time of the leadership change was the rise in celebrity Scientologists, prime examples to help recruit others. First came John Travolta, then Tom Cruise, and they are the two most well-known, but many other Hollywood types came to Scientology, able to play for the auditing sessions that could relieve them of their past traumas. These auditing sessions, essentially counseling, covering their deepest and darkest secrets, are all kept in records, so each member of the church has a file that can be used at any time to either discredit them or blackmail them. This might be the reason why people stay in this community and do not tell the truth when asked.

New Age

New Age Movements are sometimes identified with the NRMs, but this is not the same thing. The New Age Movements emerged in the 1980s and they are defined as very loosely organized spiritual movements that require very little commitment and they could include things like yoga, crystal healing, meditation, tarot cards, etc. There is a massive overlap between the New Age and therapy, so a lot of them will be providing a service and may be regarded as client cults where people are paying for a service or for knowledge about some sort of technique which they use to improve their life. There are a large variety of beliefs and some aspects will be world rejection, where practitioners focus on the spiritual life, alternative lifestyles and reject mainstream society (Paganism is such a type) or they may affirm the world but teach techniques and ideas to help people be more successful in the world (the best example would be alternative medicines).

New Age is a syncretic idea of postmodernity, where the world is going beyond the traditional religions, particularly Christianity, Judaism, and Islam, and tends to offer a unique world religion awaiting the "Aquarius era". The creation of a new era, new world order, a new religion, with peace and welfare of all people is a vision of such Aquarius era, although many New Age movements are practically mutually exclusive and contradictory. It is a synthesis of various postmodernist philosophies, pseudo-religious tendencies, wake culture, parapsychology, occultism, and Eastern religious ideas.

Some scholars call the New Age Movements "watered down eastern religions", with some elements of Hinduism, Buddhism, Sikhism, Jainism, etc. The practitioners, however, water down these Eastern religions and strip themselves of commitments. Their growth reflects the consumerist, "pick and mix" strategy of picking just one part of a religion and mix it with another appealing part, leaving everything else behind. This pick and mix practice is basically a religious supermarket. As the Western world fell into naturalism, nihilism, hedonism, relativism, subjectivism, with the legacies of two world wars and scientific discoveries, many people felt the emptiness and weakness of all philosophical and religious systems. A way out was found in the East. New Age practitioners want to search for the new world and new consciousness by taking the Eastern path of mysticism and pantheistic monism. Already in the 1960' Europe, students started to learn about Eastern wisdom. It created New Age as a worldview that is very syncretic and eclectic. It takes bits from various worldviews and mixes Eastern mysticism with Western naturalism. More than that, New Age is the Western version of Eastern mysticism and ancient animism of esoteric kind. In that way, New Age is a temporal sensibility, almost a Zeitgeist, born in the ruins of modernity for the post-modern world.

The New Age Movements are characterized by self-spirituality, where the authority of traditional religions is rejected and where people look inside themselves for answers. It means finding one's message and one's own path through ideas The second feature is detraditionalization through dismissing traditional ways of worshipping (e.g. sacred texts, priests, sacred building) in favor of people finding their own "truth". At the same time, New Age leaders optimistically warn about the need to collectively awake the new consciousness, which will change everything from the economy and social system to science and religion.

Some sociologists argue the growth of the New Age is linked to a postmodern society, where people reject meta-narratives, i.e. big stories which claim to have the answer to everything. For example, science, communism and fascism all promised a better world but instead created disasters such as wars, atrocities, famine and global warming. These big stories came to be in the early 20th century and claimed they were going to lead to constant progress and life is going to improve significantly and continuously. By the late 1970s, people lost faith in meta-narratives that claimed to be able to answer everything. People feel the Christian church was also part of a failed Western (European and American) culture or worldview which created the aforementioned problems. The Church is seen by many Westerners as part of the problem and they do not feel that mainstream Christianity has an answer anymore. The New Agre, moreover, attracts people because it is based on Eastern religions and not Western ideas (particularly so on Buddhism); it reconnects with nature; it is based on non-scientific belief systems which Western culture viewed previously as "primitive", like the Native American's worldview.

Other sociologists disagree with the post-modern idea and connect the New Age Movements with modernity. They suggest that rapid social change in modern society disrupts established norms and values. People experience anomie, a state when society is not limiting or guiding their behavior. Another aspect of the rise of the New Age is secularization, a process linked to modern societies. Perceived secularization has created a gap in the religious market. Put quite simply, Christianity's decline means New Age Movements may flourish. There is also an impact of the consumer culture which is characterized by buying things or experiences for pleasure. Consumerism promises a "perfect" life but in reality, leaves people dissatisfied. New Age usually offers services or ways of life that allow people to live their perfect life.

A major feature of the New Age in the postmodern perspective is its regressive tendency towards rationalism. The ratio is abandoned for irrational, subconscious, romantic tendencies, akin to the various shamanic practices. However, many are not even sure if New Age may be called a religion or one of the new religious movements, or is it a philosophy, sect, philosophical system, or everything mixed. Some argue New Age includes many religious phenomena but without dogmatic structuring or doctrinal accommodation. There is no single New Age lifestyle.

God is accepted in New Age but without transcendence and embodiment. God is a completely non-personal cosmic power where everything is one (monism) and where God is part of the universe (pantheism). Here, one can see the influence of Daoism and Hinduism. A problem of creation does not exist because everything is one and differences are nowhere to be found. Human has a special value. New Age accentuates the huge importance of an individual, quite contrary to the Eastern, pantheist and pessimistic way of the understanding human. Every person is part of God, but human is also free of any obligation to any deity. This human is the center of the universe who understands the connection to the eternal force. The universe and world is one living organism. The cosmos is seen as an ocean of energy, where the material and spiritual worlds are not very different. The universe is based on cycles 2160 years long. In the year 2000, the Aquarius era came to be. United in itself, the universe manifests two dimensions: the visible universe, accessible to usual consciousness, and the invisible universe (all-comprehensive mind) accessible only to the altered consciousness. In essence, everything is one big energetic vibration where all things are connected. Evil exists and to be saved from it one needs a new consciousness. With it, there is no suffering and no death. Most New Age practitioners also believe in reincarnation.

Concluding remarks

New Age is a radical break from the past. That break caused a big crisis in all aspects of human life, as most things are relativized and subjectivized. In times when traditional society is dead and new society is not yet built, postmodern time offers fear and uncertainty. It is a time very suitable for new movements, philosophies, ideas, and religions. If one looks at the New Religious Movements in general, we may see it is an umbrella of movements, ideologies, philosophies, cultures, all focused on building a new society in a new world. At the same time, it is not one worldview, not one religion, nor a unified movement. As it is characterized from within, the NRMs are full of subjectivism and relativism. Despite the differences, they all share the tendency to awaken the new consciousness which would affect all areas of human life.

Literature:

Barker, Eileen (1989) *New Religious Movements: A Practical Introduction*. London: Her Majesty's Stationery Office

Clarke, Peter B. (2006) *New Religions in Global Perspective: A Study of Religious Change in the Modern World*. London and New York: Routledge

Colavito, Jason (2005) *The cult of alien gods: H.P. Lovecraft and extraterrestrial pop culture*. Buffalo (NY): Prometheus

Hume, Lynne and McPhillips, Kathleen (2006) *Popular spiritualities: the politics of contemporary enchantment*. Burlington (VA) and London: Ashgate Publishing

Hunt, Stephen J. (2003) *Alternative Religions: A Sociological Introduction*. Burlington (VA) and London: Ashgate Publishing

Lewis, James R. (1995) *The Gods have landed: new religions from other worlds*. Albany (NY): SUNY Press

Partridge, Christopher Hugh (2003) *UFO religions*. London and New York: Routledge

Rael (2004) *Geniocracy*. The Raelian Foundation

Websites

International Church of Jediism https://www.templeofthejediorder.org/

The Aetherius Society https://www.aetherius.org/

Raelism https://rael.org/

Church of Scientology https://www.scientology.org/

About the Author

R. L. Cohen is a University Lecturer residing in Redlands, California. His research focuses on political science, ethics, and religious studies. Cohen has a passion for social justice to create a better world. When he is not lecturing, he often can be found at the beach, at a unique coffee bar, or traveling back to his home in New Zealand.

CPSIA information can be obtained
at www.ICGtesting.com
Printed in the USA
BVHW011135191221
624455BV00013B/733